DICTIONARY OF PROVERBS OF THE SINHALESE

DICTIONARY OF PROVERBS OF THE SINHALESE

Including also their

Adages, Aphorisms, Apologues, Apothegms, Bywords, Dictums, Maxims, Mottoes, Precepts, Saws and Sayings, together with the connected Myths, Legends and Folk-Tales

By

John M. Senaveratna, F.R.H.S.,

Author of
"The Story of the Sinhalese," "Vidiya Bandara," "Dona Catherina, the Catholic Queen of Kandy," "Edirille Bandara (Domingos Corea)," "Stories from Ceylon History," Etc., Etc.
Editor of the
"Ceylon Antiquary" and "Historical Gazetteer of Ceylon."

GYAN

Published by

Gyan Publishing House
5, Ansari Road
Daryaganj, New Delhi-110002
Phone: 011-47034999, 9811692060
E-mail: books@gyanbooks.com

Distribution Network
gyanbooks.com
India, USA, Canada, UK, Australia, France

ISBN : 978-81-212-3327-9 (PB)
First Published, 1936

2nd Impression 2020

Printed at: Gyan Press, Delhi.

The book at your disposal is the edition of an old book originally published long back. The Text quality of this book may not be at par as compared to our other books but many readers approached us to reprint this important book so that it could satiate their hunger. We request all the readers of this book to help us to improve its quality by providing the necessary text of those pages which are not properly visible. Your valuable support in this case will be highly appreciated and acknowledged and our future readers will be benefitted immensely.

DICTIONARY of PROVERBS

OF THE

SINHALESE

including also their

Adages, Aphorisms, Apologues, Apothegms, Bywords, Dictums, Maxims, Mottoes, Precepts, Saws and Sayings,

together with the connected

MYTHS, LEGENDS AND FOLK-TALES

BY

JOHN M. SENAVERATNA, F.R.H.S.,

Author of

"The Story of the Sinhalese," "Vidiya Bandara," "Dona Catherina, the Catholic Queen of Kandy," "Édirille Bandara (Domingos Corea)," "Stories from Ceylon History," Etc., Etc.

Editor of the

"Ceylon Antiquary" and "Historical Gazetteer of Ceylon."

1936

PRINTED BY

THE TIMES OF CEYLON COMPANY, LIMITED,

COLOMBO.

HIS EXCELLENCY SIR REGINALD EDWARD STUBBS, G.C.M.G.
Governor of Ceylon

FOREWORD

A YEAR or two ago Mr. Senaveratna was kind enough to give me an opportunity of reading the manuscript on which this book is based, and I have advised him to publish it in order that other people may share the pleasure and profit which I have derived from its perusal.

The proverbs, popular anecdotes and familiar sayings of a people are a most interesting index to its modes of thought and its philosophy of life; and I feel that such a collection as Mr. Senaveratna has put together in this little book will be of real value to students of human nature.

If the book meets with the success that I wish it, I hope that Mr. Senaveratna will, in a later edition, amplify it by including a greater number of parallel proverbs from other countries. I have always found the comparison of the proverbs of different nations a fascinating study.

It is most interesting to see the varying shapes in which the same idea presents itself to different peoples. For instance, the English proverb, "Any port in a storm" has, as its counterpart in Jamaica, "Trouble come, puss run up prickly pear." The Chinese version of "Penny wise and pound foolish" is "Go to bed to save candles and beget twins."

Similar examples will readily occur to all readers of this book. I hope, for their own sakes, that they will be numerous.

PREFACE

"The People's Voice, the voice of God we call;
And what are Proverbs but the People's Voice?"
(James Howell.)

THIS work—a labour of years—represents the largest collection yet published, in a single volume, of the Adages, Aphorisms, Apologues, Apothegms, Bywords, Dictums, Maxims, Mottoes, Precepts, Proverbs, Saws and Sayings of the Sinhalese. The collection, if not exhaustive, may at least be said to be fairly complete in regard to those which are current among the people to-day.

Many of these proverbs derive their point, pungency, pithiness and beauty either from "apt alliteration's artful aid," or from puns and idiomatic phrases which cannot effectively be reproduced in English dress. I have done the best I can, but I am still not satisfied with the English rendering in a number of cases. Any suggestions for improvement in this, or any other, direction will be gratefully welcomed and embodied in the next edition, if the work runs to it.

A large number of Tamil proverbs and sayings has been included under the corresponding Sínhalese ones, and wherever possible, English and Latin equivalents have been noted. The cross-references under each head are intended mainly to help the reader to get what he wants almost at a glance, as it were.

What I conceive to be a valuable feature of this book is the large space devoted to the Myths, Legends, and Folk-tales which gave rise to a good many of these "Sayings" of the Sinhalese. I have, moreover, not only added numerous Notes intended to elucidate obscure terms and references to customs which are either obsolete or little known, but also made them full and copious enough for the benefit of readers who may be totally unacquainted with the Sinhalese, their country, and their ways and modes of life.

PREFACE

Of the multitudinous works, periodicals and other publications which I have laid under contribution during a collection spread over some twenty years—I began the work when editing the "Ceylon Antiquary" in 1915—I desire to make particular acknowledgment of indebtedness to the "Atíta Vákya Dípaníya," a rare little book, which came into my hands but recently, when my own work had made considerable progress. I have derived some assistance, too, from Denham's "Ceylon at the Census of 1911," and from Arthur A. Perera's "Sinhalese Folklore Notes."

I have also to make acknowledgments to the late Meedeniya Adigar (in regard to the "Sayings" of the Kandyan Sinhalese), as well as to Mudaliyar E. A Abayasekara and Messrs. W. M. Fernando and C. Batuwatta, of the Department of Education. These gentlemen not only added materially to my collection, but also helped in the elucidation of many knotty points. I am greatly beholden to them for their scholarly assistance.

I am particularly indebted to His Excellency the Governor, Sir Reginald Edward Stubbs, whose gracious kindness to me and good-will made the early publication of this book possible. I am also deeply grateful to His Excellency for placing at my disposal a collection of Jamaican Proverbs (compiled by Mr. Frank Cundall, O.B.E., Secretary of the Institute of Jamaica), most of which I have incorporated in this work.

JOHN M. SENAVERATNA.

Colombo,
April 13th, 1936.

"*Acquaint thyself with proverbs, for of them thou shalt learn instruction.*"
(Ecclesiasticus, VIII-8).

INTRODUCTION

By

THE HON'BLE THE MINISTER OF EDUCATION.

THE sayings of the wise offer food for thought for all time. Every language has a stock of them and they are an index of the culture, genius and peculiar characteristics of the people who use the language. The languages of the Sinhalese and the Tamils are rich in such sayings.

Although a few earlier collections of Sinhalese sayings have been made, hardly any author has taken the trouble to make a comprehensive collection and to present them in a form in which they can be used and are ready for reference.

The Author of this Dictionary of Proverbs of the Sinhalese has earned the gratitude of the people by producing a fairly wide and representative collection. These stray and subtle sayings cannot easily be acquired by the people unless they are carefully collected and preserved in book form.

Many of the valuable Folk-songs of the past are being lost and have become unknown to the people of the present. The Oriental people have not been assiduous in preserving some of the most valuable things in their ancient literature.

Mr. Senaveratna must be congratulated for showing the true spirit of the scholar in making this attempt to preserve for the future generations a collection of the wise sayings of the past.

It must be admitted that it is no easy task to translate into one language short, pithy sayings of another. Very often the pointedness of a remark, the beauty of the sound and rhythm in a couplet or the subtlety and naivete of meaning cannot be translated so as to produce the same effect as in the original.

The Author's attempt is courageous, but naturally the English translation sometimes fails to create the peculiar pleasure one expects to find. Though explanatory notes are given in cases where allusions are made to stories and where names unknown to the public occur, there are still a few short sayings which need some explanation or illustration to make them clearly known to the reader who is not a Sinhalese: It is also to be noted that some of the sayings admit of more than one meaning. It is hoped that these will find a place in the next edition.

The Author is really doing a national service in broadcasting some of the best treasures found in the Sinhalese language to the knowledge of the English reading public. These are days when the races are drawn closer to one another ; and nothing can help more to cement the unity towards which we are moving, except an intelligent and sympathetic understanding of the best thought of each race. The Author's book will achieve something in this direction.

I have much pleasure in writing these few words to introduce the book to the reading public of Ceylon.

C. W. W. KANNANGARA.

COLOMBO, *28th April, 1936.*

DICTIONARY of PROVERBS

OF THE

SINHALESE

ABODE

The bat visiting another bat's abode—see "*BAT.*"

ABUSE

Paddy and money are a preventive remedy against abuse.

කුලු මල නැති වෙන්ට බෙහෙතකි වී කාසි.

ACHIEVEMENTS

Blacksmith's boast of his achievements—see "*BLACKSMITH.*"

ACT

Better to act well than to speak sweetly.

රස ලෙස කීමට වඩා යස ලෙස කිරීම හොඳලු.

ADD

Adding straw to a raging fire—see "*FIRE.*"

ADORNING

The chameleon adorned with gold—see "*CHAMELEON.*"

ADVERSITY (See also "*POOR*" *and* "*POVERTY.*")

Sweet cakes are bitter, but sweet are misfortunes.

අති රස තිත්ත රසයි, පැමිණි දුක් පැණි රසයි.

[In other words, adversity is more enjoyable than prosperity. The Tamils have a proverb: "In adversity, a fan is a luxury ; in time of prosperity, furniture made of *acha* (ebony) and teak becomes a necessity."]

When Prosperity and Adversity come—see "*PROSPERITY.*"

ADVICE

Advice by the unlearned is like "Bana" preaching by Veddas.

දුසිරිත දනන් දෙන ඔවා වැද්දන් කියන බණ වැනි.

[*Bana* is Buddhist scripture. The Veddas, as a community, are illiterate and profess no religion.]

A fool and woman's advice—see "*WOMAN.*"
Grandfather Lavanchi's last advice—see "*LAVANCHI.*"

ADZE

The adze which straightens timber is itself not quite straight.

ලීයේ ඇදේ සකින වෑයත් ඇද සකිනලු.

Bad to remain behind adzes and wives—see "*WOMAN.*"

AFFECTION

Overmuch affection means a quarrel, a strong wind means rain.

වැඩිසෙනේ දබරෙමයි, තද සුළං වැස්සමයි.

The tail-less dog's affection—see " *DOG.*"

AGE (*See also* " *ERA.*")

The devil a hermit in old age—see " *HERMIT.*"
The monkey in old age—see " *MONKEY.*"
When youth is an old man— see " *EDUCATION.*"

" AGGALĀVA "

An image is like an " aggalāva " to the devil—see " *DEVIL.*"

" AHIKUNTAKAYAS "

The gypsy tribe of Ahikuntakayás—see " *KORAVA.*"

ALIVE

A thousand though alive—see " *THOUSAND.*"

ALLIGATOR

Teaching the alligator's young to swim—see " *TEACHING.*"

" AMANGALLA "

Amangalla, the servant of God Saman—see " *ESCAPE.*"

" AMBALAMA "

His throat is a needle, but his stomach an " ambalama."

උගුර ඉඳිකටුව, බඩ අම්බලම

The " gavva " does not become short because the " ambalama " is broken down.

අම්බලම කැඩුණාට ගවුව කොට වෙන්නේ නැහැ.

[The *gavva* is a measure of distance of the Sinhalese mile, 5,600 yards, or about three and a half English miles. The *ambalama* is a kind of shed built on the road-side for travellers to rest in.]

AMBITION

Ambition begets vexation.

තණ්හාවෙන් ඇන්නෑ හැපෙනවාලු.

" AMU "

He who sows " amu " will reap " amu," he who sows paddy will reap paddy.

අමු කළ කෙනෙක් අමු ගෙනියත්, වී කළ කෙනෙක් වී ගෙනියත්.

[*Amu* is a kind of inferior paddy. It is also the name of a plant—Lat. *Paspalum scrobiculatum*, Sansk. *Kodrava*, Tam. *Varagu* — of which there are five or six species in Ceylon. Cf. the English "Whatsoever a man sows, that shall he reap."]

" Kávalu " blossom before " amu. "

අමුවට ඉස්සරවෙලා කාවලු පූදිනවාලු.

[*Kávalu*—a species of Tares or Panic grass, *Panicum glaucum*. It is of spontaneous growth and "is in the ear" sooner than *amu*, on which much labour is bestowed.]

Rooting out " amu" plants—see " *PADDY.*"

" AMUDE "

Like tying the " amude " when the Valavé-ganga is still seven " gavvas " away.

වලවේ ගඟ හත්ගවුවක් තියා අමුඩේ ගැහුවා වගෙයි.

[The *amude* is the handkerchief, truss, or, according to Clough, " the piece of cloth used to pass between the legs, from the front to behind, for the purpose of tucking up the lower garments." The Sinhalese villager usually ties his *amude* preparatory to fording a river. One man did it when the river he had to cross (the Valave-ganga) was still some 25 miles distant—thus giving rise to the saying, which is used to describe anything that represents a too premature preparation.]

The Gamarála and his " amude "—see " *FOOL.*"

" ANAM "

Does one go a deer-hunting only to eat " ánam " ?

මුව දඩයමට යන්නේ ආනම් කන්ටම යැයි ?

[*Ánam* is a peculiar kind of Sinhalese curry, generally consisting of coconut-milk, jak and pumpkin.]

ANCIENT

The fowl of the ancient capitals—see " *FOWL.*"

" ANDA "

Eating " Ándá " flesh—see " *EEL.*"

" ANDARE "

I hear a voice, (the first) since Andaré's death—see " *VOICE.*"
The way Andaré ate sugar—see " *SUGAR.*"

" ANDIYAS "

As the " Ándiyás " cooked congee.

ආඬි කැඳ ඉව්වා වගෙයි.

[This phrase about the Ándiyás—a tribe of fakirs or religious mendicants—had its origin in the following story:—Seven Ándiyás, who happened to be in the same lodging, agreed to cook a pot of congee for their common use as breakfast for the day. Each one undertook to contribute a handful of rice. Accordingly, a pot of water was placed over the fire, and each of the Ándiyás, thinking that the others would put in their quota of rice, went near the pot and pretended to put in his handful. When, however, finally, the contents of the pot were poured out, it was found to contain nothing but water.]

Though Ándiyás belong to the same " iname," their " kokkanam payiya " they keep separate.

ආඬි ගොල්ල එක ඉනමේ, කොක්ක නම් පසිය වෙන වෙන මේ

[That is, they fraternise in all things except money, which they keep separately, each in his own purse. *Inama* is a general name for any low caste. The *kokkanam payiya* is a sort of wallet or bag used by pilgrims or Sanyásis, which they hang upon their arm.]

The Ándiyás' permission to rub ash—see " *ASH.*"

" ANDRISA "

Andrisá and a hair-cut—see " *HAIR.*"

" ANDU "

" Andu " leaves and the snake—see " *SNAKE*."

ANGER

Anger evaporates against a thousand men.

දහට උදහස් නැතිලු.

[In other words, numbers have an overawing effect.]

If you jump into a well on one provocation—see " *WELL*."
The anger of the clinging " Dimiya "—see " *ANT*."
The God and the Kapurála's son—see " *KAPURÁLA*

ANIMAL

An animal's pain no consideration to the crow—see " *CROW*."
Any animal in the " Korava's " trap—see " *KORAVA*."
Catching an animal's tail after letting it run away—see " *TAIL*.'
Killing animals behind cover of decoy buffalo—see " *BUFFALO*."

ANOTHER

Hospitality at another's wedding—see " *HOSPITALITY*."
One's tooth gum and another's axe—see " *GUM*."
The headache of another—see " *HEADACHE*."

ANT

Like the ant which fell into a pot of honey.

පැණි හැලියේ වැටිච්ච ඇඹලයා වගෙයි.

The red-ant clings to you, not through bravado, but, however helpless, through the impulse of anger.

දිමියා එල්ලෙන්නේ හපන්කමටයැ, බැරි නමුත් වේගෙට වද.

Ants abound where there is honey—see " *HONEY*."

ANT-EATER

The ant-cater's life is in its head.

කබල්ලෑවාගේ පණ තියෙන්නේ ඔළුවෙයි.

The ant-eater, who forcibly occupied the porcupine's hole, swore by his forbears that he would never leave it.

ඉත්තෑවාගේ ගුලේ කබල්ලෑවා වැදී " මුත්තාපා කීවත් යන්නේ නැත " කීවාලු.

[Eng. " Possession is nine-tenths of the law."]

ANT-HILL

Don't go near a low ant-hill—see " *SHORTNESS*."

ANURADHAPURA

The fowl of the ancient capitals—see " *FOWL*."

ARECANUT

Like the arecanut caught in the cutter.

ගිරේට අසුවුණ පුවක්ගෙඩිය වගෙයි.

ARGUMENT

Arguments and umbrella handles—see " *UMBRELLA*."

ARRACK

Like the man who said : " My own arrack is beating me."

" මගේ අරක්කු මටම ගහනවයි " කීවා වගෙයි.

[The man was thrashed by the guest who had got drunk on the arrack he had been served with. The Tamils have a saying, " The number drowned in alcohol (arrack) exceeds those drowned in water."]

ARRANT-FOOL

The man who was called Arrant Fool—see " *MAN*."

ARROGANCE

The arrogance of a barber—see " *BARBER*."

ARROW

The arrows at Kitalagamuva—see " *TALK*."

ART

Healing Art next to Kingship—see " *KING*."

ASCETIC

Ascetic's life on needle point—see " *NEEDLE*."

ASH

Do you need an Ándiyá's permission to rub yourself with ash from your own fireplace ?

ලිපේ අළු ගාගන්ට ආඬියාගේ අවසර මොටද ?

[The Ándiyás daub themselves with ash on face, breast and hands.

Where camphor is burnt—see " *CAMPHOR*."

ASH-PLANTAINS—See " *PLANTAINS*."

ASH-PUMPKINS—See " *HAND* " *and* " *THIEF*."

ASSOCIATE

Ruin for the Goldsmith's associate—see " *BADÁLÁ*."

ASTROLOGER

Astrologer stays even after death—see " *VEDARÁLA*."

" ATTIKKA "

Flowers on an " attikká " tree—see " *FLOWERS*."

" ATURA "

Like the snapping of the " at-vela " when midway on the " atura. "

අතුර මැදදී අත්වැල කැඩුණු වගෙයි.

[To enable toddy-drawers, when extracting toddy, to walk from one tree to the other without descending to the ground, coconut trees are tiea to each other from the top with two strong ropes, parallel-wise—the one above being the *at-vela* or hand-rope, the other the *atura* or foot-rope. The snapping of the *atura* would not be so dangerous since the climber would still be able to remain suspended from the *at-vela* or hand-rope, till relief came. The snapping of the *at-vela*, however, would mean his instantaneous fall, with serious injury, if not death, as the result.]

AUNT

Smaller " kevum " despite even Auntie's arrival.

කුඩම්මත් ඇවිත් කැවුම් පුංචි කළා වගෙයි.

[This was said by some children when their Aunt (mother's younger sister), whilst assisting their mother in making *kevum*, made smaller ones than usual. They naturally expected that, with the arrival of so near and dear a relation, they would have a better time, at least in the matter of eatables. The *kevuma* is a sort of cake made of rice flour, honey or jaggery and coconut oil.]

AUSPICIOUS

The nine planets auspicious—see " *PLANETS*."

AXE

When the axe-heads were coming by ship, the forest cried out : " One of ourselves is required to bring about our own destruction."

පොරව කප්පර එද්දි "අපව නසන්ට අපෙන් එකෙක් ඕනැයි" කියා බැද්ද කෑගැසුවාලු.

[" One of ourselves " is, of course, a forest tree which would serve as the timber needed for making handles for the axe-heads.]

The tree that defied the axe—see " *TREE*."

The tooth-gum that was better than an axe—see " *GUM*."

" AYAMUDAIYAN "

How a Kallan may become an Ayamudaiyan—see " *RANK*."

" BADALA "

Like the " Badálá's " father thrashing his son for taking up urgent work.

ඉක්මන් වැඩ බාර ගත්තායි කියා බඩාලාට පියා ගැහුවා වගෙයි.

[A *Badálá* is a gold or silver-smith or a man of that caste. The story which originated the above saying is as follows : A certain woman ordered, for the use of her little daughter, a pair of ear-rings to be worn on the day of the latter's weaning. As the silver-smith failed to give it on the appointed day, she made him promise that he would give it on the day that her grand-daughter (i.e. that daughter's daughter) would be weaned. The silver-smith's father, on hearing of the promise his son had made, gave him a thrashing for taking up such urgent work !

The *Badálá* is in bad repute among the Tamils also, who have the following sayings ; (*a*) " A goldsmith will pilfer the gold dust even of his mother," and (*b*) " He who associates with a goldsmith is a ruined man." (See also under " Dhoby.")]

BAG

Like rats being put in the " malla " even after paying for it.

ගෙවලාත් මල්ලේ මීයෝ දැම්මා වගෙයි.

[A man asked a neighbour for, but was refused the loan of, a *malla* (a bag made of anything but cloth) to take to the market. He then paid for it and, on taking it away, discovered some rats inside.]

Coconuts in my bag—see " *COCONUTS*."

Mad woman's bag of herbs—see " *MAD*."

Men who had eaten salt out of one bag—see " *SALT*."

" BAKMASURAYA "

Bakmasuraya and the fire-charm—see " *FIRE-CHARM.*"

" BALIYA "

One's inborn perversity cannot be cured even by a " Bali " ceremony.

උපන් ගෙසි ගතිය බලි ඇරියත් අරින්ට බැරිලු.

[A *Bali* ceremony is the performance of incantatory services before clay images to avert the evil influences of the planets.]

Such a mouth is good enough for such a " Baliya."

ඔය බලියට ඔය කට ඇති.

Like tightening screws on a " pol-piti baliya."

පොල්පිති බලියට ඉස්කුරුප්පු තද කළා වගෙයි.

[*Pol-pitta* is the stem of a coconut branch.]

There came sixty men to lift up the " mal-baliya" of a tavern-keeper.

තබෑරුම් කාරයාගේ මල් බලිය උස්සන්ට මිනිස්සු හැටදෙනෙක් ආවා.

[The point of the saying is that it is the tavern-keeper who has most friends in the village. The *mal-baliya*, which is a flower offering to the Planets, as a sacrifice, can be raised by one or two men. In the incident which gave rise to the saying, when the sixty people were assembled to raise the *mal-baliya*, another man came running up to the tavern-keeper and said : " Ah, Renter, you did wrong not to inform me about this in time."]

Eating " bali " will not cure illness—see " *ILLNESS.*"

BAMBOO

Bamboo jungle afire—see " *FIRE.*"
Dog's tail in a bamboo—see " *DOG.*"

" BANA "

" Bana " and birth at Totagamuva—see " *TOTAGAMUVA.*"
" Bana " preaching by Veddas—see " *ADVICE.*"
Even the grandfather talks " bana "—see " *GRANDFATHER.*"
Sleep and interrupted " bana "—see " *BUDDHISM.*"
The learned (in " Bana ") and the proud—see " *EDUCATION.*"

BANANA

Ash-plantain and black-plantain—see " *PLANTAIN.*"

BANE

The bane of the village is the vagabond, and that of the tree is the parasite.

ගමට අවලමින් ගසට ඇහැවුවත් විනාශයලු.

BANNER

Patient man and banner of victory—see " *PATIENCE.*"

BARBER

To the lowly barber, even the goat offers its chin to shave.

නිවට ඇම්බැට්ටයාට එළුවත් නිකට පානවාලු.

[" The arrogance of a barber and the affection of a dhoby " is a Tamil proverb used when inferiors give themselves airs. " Employ a new dhoby but an old barber " is another Tamil saying in regard to the men who pursue these avocations.]

New dhoby and old barber—see " *DHOBY*."
The Gama-Máyiyá's shave—see " *GAMA-MÁYIYÁ*."

BARBET—See " *KOTTÓRUVÁ*."

BARK

Peel the bark from a rock—see " *ROCK*."

BARKING

Barking dogs do not bite—see " *DOGS*."
Barking of dogs and smell of meat—see " *DOGS*."
Barking of dogs will not frighten elephants—see " *DOGS*."
Barking of familiar dogs—see " *DOGS*."
Dogs bark even at the moon—see " *DOGS*."
Moon unruffled by dog's barking—see " *DOGS*."
The teeth of the dog which barks at fortunate people—see " *DOGS*."

BARREN

Barren women getting children—see " *WOMAN*."
Barren women and sorrows of children—see " *CHILDREN*."
The remark of the barren woman—see " *WOMAN*."

BASKET

Drawing water in a basket full of holes—see " *WATER*."

BASTARD

The son who does not do what his father did—see " *SON*."

BAT

The bat visiting another bat's abode must also remain suspended.

වවුලාගේ ගෙට ආ වවුලත් එල්ලී සිටින්ට ඕනෑලු.

" BAT " (Rice)

Marriage and " nembiliya " of " bat "—see " *MARRIAGE*."

BATHING

Elephant bathing in " koraha "—see " *ELEPHANT*."

BATTLE

The sword not available for battle—see " *SWORD*."

BATTLE-FIELD

Banner of victory in battle-field—see " *PATIENCE*."

BEARS

Like the tiger jumping before the bear.

වලහට ඉස්සරවෙලා කොටියා පැන්නා වගෙයි.

Bear's death and lamb's salvation—see " *DEATH*."
Making bears dance at a " Pinkama "—see " *TIGER*."

BEARD

Lighting a cigar from a flaming beard—see "*CIGAR.*"
The beard and the congee—see "*CONGEE.*"

BEATING

It is the same whether you tie and beat him or beat and tie him.

ඇණලා බැන්දත් බැඳලා ඇන්නත් දෙකම එකයි.

Beat the drum you have tied on—see "*DRUM.*"
Beating the elk-skin at home—see "*DEER.*"
Beating the silversmith's son—see "*BADÁLÁ*"
Blacksmith beating a malleable iron—see "*BLACKSMITH.*"
He who beats the more another cries for mercy—see "*FOOLS.*"
The man whose arrack was drunk—see "*ARRACK.*"

BEAUTY

Beauty without chastity—see "*EDUCATION.*"
A daughter with beauty—see "*CHILDREN.*"
Beauty and fortune of owl and yellow-bird—see "*OWL.*"

BED

The old man and the unavailable bed—see "*OLD.*"

BEEF-EATING

If you must eat beef, need you keep it dangling round your neck (while eating) ?

ගෙරි මස් කනත් කරේ එල්ලාගෙන කන්ට ඕනෑද ?

[" Must one wear a necklace of bones because one eats flesh ? " say the Tamils who, as is natural amongst a Hindu people, express themselves in still stronger disapproval as follows : " Is a beef-eater accustomed to decent words ? "]

BEE-HIVE

He who breaks a bee-hive will lick his hand.

මීයක් කැඩූ කෙනෙක් අත ලෙවකත් ලූ.

Is it to lick your hand that you break a bee-hive ?

මීයක් කඩන්නේ අත ලෙවකන්ටද ?

Like blowing on a bee-hive.

මීයට පිම්බා වගෙයි.

Like a bee-hive built (by the bees) on a dog's fundament.

බල්ලාගේ පිටි පස්සේ බැන්ද මීය වගෙයි.

[A good thing in a bad place.]

BEFOULING

The God and the Kapurála's son—see "*KAPURÁLA.*"

BEGGAR

Like Saturn falling into the bowl of the beggar.

සිඟන්නාගේ පාත්‍රෙ සෙනසුරා වැටුණා වගෙයි.

[As, for instance, when a guest turns up at the house of a man who finds it difficult to feed even his own family.]

What hot rice for beggars ?

සිඟන්නන්ට මොන උණු බත්ද ?

[Rice that is hot is, of course, more tasty than the cold. Cf. the English " Beggars cannot be choosers."]

BELLY —See "*STOMACH*".

" **BERAVAYA** " —See "*KORAVA.*"

BERUVALA

Whatever rubbish floats goes into the Béruvala " bokka."

පාවෙන පාවෙන කුණු බේරුවල් බොක්කටලු.

[Béruvala is a sea-coast town of Ceylon, not far from Colombo. *Bokka* means, literally, " stomach."]

BETEL

In every one's betel-pouch there is some little chunam.

කාගෙ පසියෙත් හුණුපොඩි තිබෙනවාලු.

[Cf. the English " Skeletons in every house or cupboard."]

BIG

Going to get the " láha " made bigger—see " *LÂHA.*"
The Pidi-bat Hámy bigger than Geyi-Hámy—see " *HÁMY.*"

BILE

No heart without bile—see " *HEART.*"

BINTENNA

The man who went to Maha-Bintenna—see " *KURAKKAN.*"

BIRD

Every kind of bird will resort to a fruitful tree.

පල ඇති ගසේ කොයි සතත් වහනවාලු.

Like letting off the bird in your clutch and trying to catch the one on the tree.

මිටේ උන් කුරුල්ලා ඇරලා ගසේ උන් කුරුල්ලා ඇල්ලීමට ගියා වගෙයි.

[Eng. " A bird in the hand is worth two in the bush."]

BIRTH

Are all that are born in Ceylon Rávanás ?

ලංකාවේ උපන් හැමෝම රාවණලාද ?

[This is really a Tamil saying, the reference being to the *Rámáyana* and to the wars between Rámá and Rávaná, the mythical King of Ceylon who abducted Sitá. The people of Ceylon obtained a reputation for fierceness and courage in South India as *Rákshasas* or demons ; and, as Mr. Denham has it, " this saying as used to-day would mean that, though a person was born in Ceylon, he need not necessarily be possessed of supernatural strength."]

A daughter with beauty—see "*CHILDREN.*"
A fourth girl is born—see "*CHILDREN.*"
Better be slave than youngest in family—see "*SLAVE.*"
Birth of a female child on a Friday—see "*CHILDREN.*"
Born unto a quarter measure—see "*FATE.*"
Slave woman's female child—see "*CHILDREN.*"
The learned of low birth—see "*EDUCATION.*"
Those to whom no sons are born—see "*CHILDREN.*"
To be born at Kalutara—see "*FATE.*"
Twins of opposite sex—see "*TWINS.*"

BITE

Snake that bites without discrimination—see "*SNAKE.*"
The cobra and his bite—see "*COBRA.*"
The dog, though King, bites sandals—see "*DOG.*"
When a dog bites your leg—see "*DOG.*"

BITTERNESS

"Labu-gediya" in Buddha-less era—see "*BUDDHA.*"
Sweet cakes and misfortunes—see "*ADVERSITY.*"
Bitterness of "kohomba" seed—see "*KOHOMBA.*"

BLACK

A black Brahman must not be trusted—see "*BRAHMAN.*"

BLACK-PLANTAIN —See "*PLANTAIN.*"

BLACKSMITH

When the blacksmith finds a malleable iron, leaping he brings his hammer down.

තැලෙන යකඩේ දුටුවාම ආචාරියා උඩ පැන පැන තළනවාලු.

[That is, he is so pleased he leaps to the stroke. The point of the proverb is that the more one yields, the harder one is beaten. According to the Tamils, "Even the blacksmith (a smiter) boasts of his achievements."]

Blacksmith and the Gamarála's axe—see "*GAMARÁLA.*"
The dog reared in a blacksmith's forge—see "*DOG.*"

BLAME

Crown put on the feet—see "*CROWN.*"

BLINDNESS

Like the stone flung by a blind man.

කණ්ණා ගහන ගල වගෙයි.

What is the use of lamp-light to the blind man ?

අන්ධයාට මොන පහන් එළියද ?

Blind man and the dog-flea—see "*DOG-FLEA.*"
Blind man and the gem he kicks—see "*GEM.*"
Blind men's description of elephant—see "*ELEPHANT.*"
Description of curd to a blind man—see "*CURD.*"
Eye blinded by an eagle bow—see "*EYE.*"
Eye blinded by golden needle—see "*NEEDLE.*"

BLOW

Blow with a pestle—see "*WINK.*"
Blowing a chank to a deaf man—see "*DEAF.*"
Blowing on a bee-hive—see "*BEE-HIVE.*"
Blows move grinding-stone—see "*GRINDING-STONE.*"
Blows set rocks in motion—see "*ROCK.*"
Potter's labour and a single blow—see "*POTTER.*"

BOAR

When wild-boars start smashing "Kekuna" fruits, it is feast time for "haban-kukulo."

වල් ඌරෝ කැකුන තලන විට හබන් කුකුලන්ට මඟුල්ලු.

[The *Kekuna* (Lat. *Canarium Zeylanicum*, Tam. *Pakkilipal*) is a tree peculiar to Ceylon. The *haban* (*saban*)-*kukula* is the Ceylon spur fowl (*Galloperdix biculcarata*), which relishes the *kekuna* fruit more than perhaps any other. An oil extracted from the kernel of this tree is used by poorer classes of the Sinhalese as lamp oil, and is occasionally used in the preparation of medicinal oils.]

The servant and fear of the wild-boar—see "*FEAR.*"

BOASTING

Blacksmith's boast of his achievements—see "*BLACKSMITH.*"

BOAT

It's all the same whether the prow goes foremost or the stern.

ඇණියෙන් ගියත් අවරෙන් ගියත් දෙකම එකලු.

Like saying, when the boat is upset, that the wrong side is better than the other.

ඔරුව පෙරළුණම ඒ පිටට වඩා මේ පිට හොඳයි කීවා වගෙයි.

Like the outrigger that is bigger than the boat.

ඔරුවට ලොකු කොල්ලෑව වගෙයි.

What's the use of a baling-vessel for a boat that does not leak ?

වතුර නේන ඔරුවට දියාලුව මොවද?

Great dhoneys sunk by one small leak—see "*DHONEYS.*"
Maldive fish of padda-boatman—see "*UMBALAKADE.*"
Small boats, too, venture out like big ships—see "*SEA.*"

BODY

Enduring medicine for unenduring body—see "*MEDICINE.*"

BOILING

Quarrel till rice-pot is boiled—see "*MARRIAGE.*"
The man who said . "Now, boil !"—see "*SORROWS.*"

BONE

Like a bone going out of one's body.

ඇඟෙන් ඇටයක් ගියා වගෙයි.

The capacity of the bone-less tongue—see "*TONGUE.*"

BOOK

You have a big book at home, but you cannot recollect anything.

ගෙදර මහ පොතක් ඇත, එකක්වත් මතක නැත කීවා වගෙයි.

[In other words, "More words and phrases are taught than ideas communicated."]

Sinner who will not take up a book—see "*SINNER.*"

BOXING

Can boxing cure a dislocated hip-bone ?

උකුල් ඇරෙව් කොරේට බුකුල් ඇන්නාට සුවවේද?

BOUTIQUE

The Tamby of the adjoining boutique—see "*MOORMAN.*"

BOW

The bow at Dunugamuva—see "*TALK.*"
The eye and the eacle bow—see "*EYE.*"

BOWL

Breaking Buddha's bowl—see "*BUDDHA.*"
Saturn's fall into the beggar's bowl—see "*BEGGAR.*"

BRAHMAN

Never trust a black Brahman or a white Pariah.

කළු බමුණත් සුදු පරයත් විශ්වාසකරන්න එපා.

[A Brahman—one belonging to the highest caste—is, as a rule, fair complexioned. A black Brahman would, therefore, be something in the nature of a prodigy—to be avoided. Similarly, the Pariah, a man of the lowest caste—is usually black in colour. When you find a white specimen of that caste, he is one to be shunned.]

BRANCH

Lost both the branch he had caught hold of and that on which his feet had rested.

අල්ලපු අත්තත් නැ, පය ගහපු අත්තත් නැ.

[This was said of a man who, selling off his land—his sole property—gave the money as dowry to his daughter. Shortly after this money had all been squandered, the son-in-law died. The son-in-law, of course, was the "branch he had caught hold of" and his lost land "that on which his feet had rested."]

Clinging to a thorny branch when about to fall—see "*FALL.*".

BRAVADO

When the "dimiya" clings to you—see "*ANT.*"

BREACH

A breach in a tank and the widow—see "*WOMAN.*"

BREAD

"Masuran" in bread for the sinner—see "*SINNER.*"

BREAKING

Breaking a bee-hive and licking your hand—see " *BEE-HIVE.*"
Breaking Buddha's bowl—see " *BUDDHA.*"
Breaking open a hollow fruit—*see* " *FRUIT.*"
Fish breaking iron chains—*see* " *FISH.*"
He who breaks a bee-hive—see " *BEE-HIVE.*"
The departing devil and the " Koraha "—*see* " *DEVIL.*"
The rat's threat to break a cat in two—see " *RAT.*"
When prosperity goes—*see* " *PROSPERITY.*"

BREATH

When an elephant tramples—see " *ELEPHANT.*"

BREED

When a tusker is stuck in the mud—see " *ELEPHANT.*"

BRIDE

Like the remark of the morrow's bride.

හෙට බඳින්ට ඉන්න මනමාළිගේ කථාව වගෙයි.

[A Sinhalese maid was watching the busy building operations by the side of her house, and a passer-by asked her :—
" Why are these sheds and pavilions being put up ? "
" I don't know," she replied, " they say it's for a wedding."
" Whose wedding ? " the man again enquired.
" I don't know," she coyly replied, " they say it's mine."]

BRIDGE

Although the bridge be washed away, will the ferry go, too ?

පාලම ගහගෙන ගියාට තොටුපොළත් ගහගෙන යාද?

[Eng. " Hope springs eternal in the human breast."]

BRING FORTH

When bulls bring forth—see " *BULLS.*"
The cat in a hurry to bring forth—see " *CAT.*"
The destitute brings forth a female child—see " *CHILDREN.*"

BRINJALS

Eight brinjals, but nine taxes.

අට වම්බොටු නව ශුංගං දුන්නා වගෙයි.

[A certain man took eight brinjals for sale to a village, where there were nine Headmen. He returned home empty-handed and in utter disappointment, as he had to give eight of the Headmen a brinjal apiece, and to the ninth his basket, in order to obtain permission to enter the village.]

BROOM —See " *EAGLE.*"

BUDDHA —(See also " *BUDDHISM,*" " *RELIGION* " and " *DAMBUL VIHÁRA.*")

Even the " labu-gediya " becomes bitter in a Buddha-less era.

අබුද්දස්ස කාලෙට ලබුත් තිත්තයි.

[For fuller reference to *labu-gediya*, see under " *HAND.*"]

Like breaking Buddha's bowl.

බුදුන්ගේ පාත්‍රය බින්දා වගෙයි.

[A very heinous offence, almost a sacrilege.]

Like examining the "Kemana" when returning after worshipping Buddha.

බුදුන් වැඳගෙන එන ගමන් කෙමනත් බලාගත්තා වගෙයි.

[In other words, doing an irreligious act when upon a pious journey. The *Kemana* is a peculiar kind of basket placed in streams for catching fish. Buddhism forbids the destruction of life, and fishing is a form of it.]

Like the "Mára-Yuddhaya" synchronising with the attainment of Buddhahood.

බුදු වෙනකොටම මාර යුධයත් පටන්ගත්තා වගෙයි.

[*Mára-Yuddhaya* is the "war with Márayá," the chief of demons, the enemy and opposer of the Buddha. On the day of Gautama's attainment to Buddhahood, Márayá attacked him with an innumerable host of the fiercest demons, all of whom excited the most infernal rage against him and the most determined opposition to his assuming the sacred character. The Buddha, however, speedily vanquished the whole.]

Toddy drinking cup as Buddha's target—see "*TODDY.*"
The unpluckable flower offered to Buddha—see "*FLOWER.*"

BUDDHISM

Disclosure will ruin the priest, and reticence will ruin the Vihára.

කීවොත් සඟ නසී, නොකීවොත් වෙහෙර නසී

[*Vihára* is a Buddhist temple. The reference is to some scandal about the incumbent priest.]

Even Priests who reside in the same Temple come to loggerheads.

එක පන්සලේ ඉන්න මහණුන්නාන්සේලාත් කුඩ මිටි හරවා ගන්නවාලු.

[Lit. "Turn their umbrella-handles against each other."]

The ex-priest atoned, as it were, for his previous celibacy by taking two wives.

සිරළුවෙක්, මහණව සිටි කාලේ හිබේටත් එක්ක, හිර දෙකක් ගෙනාවලු.

[Celibacy is enjoined upon the Buddhist priesthood.]

The language used by the "Sangha" is easily understood by ex-priests.

සඟුන්ගේ බස් සිරළුවන්ට දැනෙයි.

[*Sangha* means Buddhist priesthood.]

Uninterrupted sleep is better than interrupted "Bana" hearing.

වරද්ද වරද්දා අහන බණට වඩා නොවරද්දා නින්ද හොඳලු.

[*Bana* is the Buddhist scripture, a discourse on which should be listened to attentively and with devotion.]

A "Pánmaduva " mid " Ginimaduva"—see "*PÁNMADUVA.*"
Chief High Priest from Tumpane—see " *TUMPANE.*"
The dance and somersault for the Kapurála—see " *RICE.*"
The devil who swallowed a Buddhist priest—see " *DEVIL.*"
The snake on God Saman's neck—see " *SNAKE.*"
To be born at Totagamuva —see " *TOTAGAMUVA.*"
Worship at Dambulla Viháre—see " *DAMBULLA.*"

BUFFALO

Like killing animals behind the cover of a decoy buffalo.

දඩ මීමාගේ මුවාවෙන් සතුන් මරන්නාක් මෙනි,

The ghee from (the milk of) a blind she-buffalo is insufficient for even her own eye disorder.

කණ මීදෙනගේ තෙල් ඇගේ ඇස් රෝගෙටත් මදිලු.

Yoking a bullock and a buffalo—see " *BULL.*"

BUILDING

Building a house in a cemetery—see " *HOUSE.*"
The bee-hive built on a dog's back—see " *BEE-HIVE.*"
Veddas speaking of building houses—see " *VEDDAS.*"

BULLS

A good bull yoked with a bad one will also become bad.

හොර හරකාගේ කරේ ඇඳූ හොඳ හරකත් හොරා වෙනවාලු.

A wild bull should be beaten only in the mud.

කුළුාට අණිතොත් මඩේදිලු.

[Because it cannot attack you when stuck in the mud.]

[To describe the aggressive bull, the Jamaicans say: " When bull begin fe dig grung (*i.e.*, the ground), you betta look fe tree."]

Like a bull butting a man who lies fallen from a tree.

ගහෙන් වැටුණ මිනිහාට ගොනා ඇන්නා වගෙයි.

[Eng: " Misfortunes never come singly."]

Like loading a bull with jaggery.

ගොනා පිට හකුරු පටවන්නා වගෙයි.

Like the cart running before the bull.

ගොනාට ඉස්සරවෙලා කරත්තෙ දුවනවා වගෙයි.

Like yoking a bullock with a buffalo.

මී හරකාගේ කරේ එළු හරකා ඇඳුවා වගෙයි.

[Mating an ill-assorted pair.]

On a lucky day even bulls are said to bring forth.

පින් ඇති දට ගොනත් වදනවාලු.

The bull's pain is that of his wound, the crow's that of flesh-hunger.

ගොනා වණ ගින්නේ, කවුඩා මස් ගින්නේ.

[This was said at sight of a crow pecking at a wound on a bull's back.]

Why worry about the right and left of a bull that ploughs only half a day ?

වරුවක් හාන ගොනාගේ වම දකුණ මොටද ?

[The laggard deserves no special consideration.]

Bullocks in addition to elephants—see "*ELEPHANTS.*"
Crows round the carcase of a bull—see "*CROWS.*"
The ploughing done by young bulls—see "*PLOUGHING.*"

BUNCH

A black crow on a "ran-tembili" bunch—see "*CROW.*"

BURDEN

Its fruit no burden to the creeper—see "*FRUIT.*"

BURIAL

A mountain road to bury an elephant—see "*ROAD.*"

BURNING

Scalding with cold water—see "*WATER.*"

BUSH

'Tis meet I should approach the bush, you see.
What nonsense that the bush should come to me.

පඳුර ළඟට මා එනවා විනා ඉවි
පඳුර මා ළඟට එනවා ගිනා වේ.

Shot at the hare but hit the bush—see "*SHOOTING.*"
Shot at the bush but struck the hare—see "*SHOOTING.*"

BUTTER—See "*GHEE.*"

BUYING

Buying for a 1,000 *and selling for* 500—see "*TRADE.*"
To buy a horse for two pice—see "*HORSE.*"

CAGE

The parrot's golden cage in the King's palace—see "*PARROT.*"

CAKE

Even a small piece of "kevum" (cake) is acceptable which has not cost you anything in oil or jaggery.

තෙල් පැණි නොනස කන කැවුම් කෑල්ලත් හොඳලු.

[For *kevuma*, see under "*AUNT.*"]

Like returning from the wedding-house without eating "kevum."

මඟුල් ගෙදරත් ගොසින් කැවුම් නොකා ආවා වගෙයි.

[This saying lacks force to-day when the plum-cake has taken the place of the *kevuma*, which was almost a *sine qua non* at Sinhalese weddings of other days.]

Smaller cakes even after Auntie's arrival—see "*AUNT.*"
Sweet cakes and misfortunes—see "*ADVERSITY.*"

CALF

The man who promised to send a she-calf—see "*LEAVEN.*"
The "kattadiyá" and the calf-post—see "*KATTADIYÁ.*"

CAMPHOR

Where camphor is burnt, no ashes will be left.

කපුරු දැවූ තැන අළු නැතිලු.

Gain by selling camphor—see "*TODDY.*"

CANDY

Like a certain man's description of the taste of sugar-candy.

එක මිනිහෙක් සූකිරිවල රස කීවා වගෙයි.

[A certain man, who said that sugar-candy was sweet, was asked if he had ever tasted it. "No," he replied, "my brother told me so." On being questioned as to whether his brother had tasted it, he said: "No, my brother saw some Colombo people eating it."]

CANNIBAL

The man who threatened to eat his own child's flesh—will he not eat up even the bones of another's child ?

තමන්ගේ දරුවාගේ මස් කනෑයි කීවොත් අනුන්ගේ දරුවාගේ ඇටත් නොකාද ?

Rearing chicks in a cannibal country—see "*COUNTRY.*"

CAPITALS

The fowl of the ancient capitals—see "*FOWL.*"

CARCASE

Crows round the carcase of a bull—see "*CROWS.*"

CARPEL

Onion carpel and the stomach—see "*ONION.*"

CARPENTER

Like there being nothing to sit upon in the carpenter's house.

වඩුරාළගෙ ගෙදර වාඩිවෙන්න එකක් නැතුවා වගෙයි.

CART

Cart running before bull—see "*BULL.*"
Good and evil are like the cart wheel—see "*WHEEL.*"

CASSIA-PLANTS

Cassia-plants when elephants fight—see "*ELEPHANT.*"

CASTE

Inquiries about caste for marriage—see "*MARRIAGE.*"
The learned rank with highest caste—see "*EDUCATION.*"
The dignity of caste and the power of wealth—see "*MONEY.*"

CATS

Even "upásaka" cats catch mice.

උපාසක බළල්ලුත් මීයො අල්ලනවා.

[*Upásaka* means "devoted to religious exercises."]

Like getting cats to take (roasted) "jak" seeds out of the fire.

බළලුන් ලවා කොස් ඇට බැව්වා වගෙයි.

[Cf. Eng. "To make a cat's paw of" anybody. The phrase is taken from the story of the cat and the monkey. The latter wished to reach some chestnuts that were roasting on the fire and used the paw of his friend, the cat, to get at them.]

Like the cat on the doorstep.

එළිපත්තේ ඉන්න බළලා වගෙයි.

[You never know which way it will jump.]

Like the cat which has eaten chameleons.

කටුස්සන් කාපු බැළලි වගෙයි

[Sickly within and forbidding-looking without.]

Like the cat which has evacuated on a rock.

ගලේ රිපු බළලා වගෙයි.

[That is, unable to cover up his dirt.]

Like the path taken by the civet-cat.

උරුලෑවා ගිය පාර වගෙයි.

[Trailed by an offensive smell.]

The cat was in such a hurry to bring forth that she forgot to bring forth young ones with eyes.

බැළලි වදන්ට ඉක්මන්වූ තරම කියතොත් ඇස් ඇති පැටව් වදන්ට මතක නැතිවුණලු.

The civet-cat can never become a cat.

උරුලෑවා බළලා නොවෙනවා වගෙයි.

Though a cat be taken to Europe, it will still cry "Mi-aou," "Mi-aou."

ඒරෝපෙට ගෙනිච්චත් බළලා ඤාව් ඤාව් කියාවි.

[Cf. Lat. *Coelum, non animum, mutant trans mare currunt.* See also under "*HAND*"—"Your hands and feet are the same even if you go to Tuticorin."]

You find civet-cats even in a sandal-wood forest.

හඳුන් වනෙත් උරුලෑවෝ ඇතිලු.

[A malodorous animal in a fragrant spot.]

Even cats testify to the value of curd—see "*CURD.*"
Death to the rat and play to the cat—see "*RAT.*"
Give a cat to a Korava—see "*KORAVA.*"
The cat and the rat of clay—see "*RAT.*"
The wild-cat who eats jungle-plantains—see "*PLANTAIN*"

CATTLE

Is it any wonder that cattle come into a garden that has no fence ?

වැට නැති වත්තට හරක් එන එක අරුමයක්ද ?

Like the way in which Tokká tended cattle.

ටොක්කා හරක් මේච්චල් කළා වගෙයි.

[In order to answer the Gamarála's invariable questions at the close of day—" Did you give grass to the ox to eat? Did you give him water to drink ? "—Tokká led the animal near the river bank one day, showed it the water flowing merrily on, and then, sticking a long blade of grass in its fundament, took the animal home. And in reply to the Gamarála's inevitable questions, he said : " See how the ox has fed. It has eaten so much grass that it is evacuating some of it, in the raw, in the excremental way. Look, you can see it for yourself."]

Where there is grass, cattle do not graze.

තණ ඇති තැන හරකා කන්නේ නැතිලු.

Herd of cattle entrusted to care of tiger—see " *TIGER.*"
The hair of cattle and tigers roaring—see " *TIGER.*"
When there's no cattle in the fold—see " *TIGER.*"
White cattle for Paduvás—see " *PADUVÁ.*"

CAUSE

No death without a cause—see " *CAUSE.*"

CAVERN—See " *LADDER.*"

CELESTIAL

Water from the celestial river—see " *CHANDÁLA.*"
Woman who dances like a celestial—see " *WOMAN.*"

CELIBACY

The ex-priest and his two wives—see " *BUDDHISM.*"

CEMETERY

Building a house in a cemetery—see " *HOUSE.*"

CENTS

Quarter cents among the rupees—see " *RUPEES.*"

CEREMONY

Curing by a " Bali " ceremony—see " *BALIYA.*"

CHAINS

Fish breaking iron chains—see " *FISH.*"

CHAIR

Must not the grand-son rise up to place a chair for the grandfather ?

සීයාට පුටුව තියන්නේ මුනුපුරා නැඟිටලාවද ?

Pulling down the loft to make a chair—see " *LOFT.*"

[Of the chair the Jamaicans say : " Chair fall down, bench get up," i.e., when the great fall, there is a chance for the humble."]

CHAMELEON

Like adorning the chameleon with a gold ornament.

කටුස්සාට රත්රන් පැළඳුවා වගෙයි.

[A King, who had observed that a chameleon was in the habit of getting down a tree and saluting him whenever he was seen, ordered a gold ear-ring to be put on the chameleon's ear. On the following day, however, the chameleon, instead of behaving towards the King as before, on seeing him went up the tree and took no notice of him.]

Like the chameleon jumping on a heap of straw.

කටුස්සා පිදුරු ගොඩට පැන්නා වගෙයි.

[Made no impression on the straw which did not feel the weight.]

The cat which has eaten chameleons—see "*CAT.*"

CHANDALA

How can you find water of the "celestial river" in the "labu-gediya" of a Chandála ?

චණ්ඩාලයාගේ ලබු ගෙඩියේ ආකාශ ගංගාවේ වතුර කොයින්ද ?

[By "*celestial river*" is meant the Ganges, whose "*sacred*" waters are taboo to the *Chandála* as being "an outcaste or pariah,"—one of the lowest of the mixed tribes descended from a Sudra mother and a Brahman father. For the use of the *labu-gediya* as a water vessel, see under "*HAND*"—"It is the same hand that plucks the *labba* as well as the *puhula*."]

CHANGING

Changing pillow to ease headache—see "*HEADACHE.*"

CHANK

Blowing a chank to a deaf man—see "*DEAF.*"

CHARCOAL

Can charcoal ever be made white by friction with a stone ?

අඟුරු ගලගා සුදු දකිනැකිනැයි ?

[Cf. Eng. "Can the leopard change his spots, or the Ethiopian his skin?"]

Washed even in milk, charcoal can never become white.

කිරිදියෙනි දෙව්යත්, අඟුරු සුදුවෙන කාලෙක් නම් නැත්.

Offering charcoal to a devil—see "*DEVIL.*"

CHARMS

Charms and the rat-snake—see "*SNAKE.*"

The Ahikuntaka snake-charmers—see "*KORAVA.*"

The fire-charm of Isvarayá—see "*FIRE-CHARM.*"

CHASTITY

Like the chastity of an ugly woman.

අරූප ස්ත්‍රියගෙ පතිව්‍රතාව වගෙයි.

[A virtue of necessity, as it were.]

Beauty without chastity—see "*EDUCATION.*"

CHATTY

The departing devil and the chatty—see "*DEVIL.*"

You'll get no chatties from a friendly potter—see "*POTTER.*"

CHETTIES

Even Chetties run short of spices—see "*SPICE.*"

CHICKEN

Chicken-rearing where children are eaten—see "*COUNTRY.*"

CHILDREN

Depraved children are unlike depraved parents.

යක් දරුවෝ වාති, යක් මවු පියෝ නොවාති.

[Even the most depraved parents bear affection for their children, but the case is different with depraved children, who generally show no regard for their parents.]

[The Jamaicans say: "Children suck dem mudda when dem young, dem fada when dem ole."]

Give birth to a daughter with beauty, and a son with a mouth.

රුව ඇති දුවත් කට ඇති පුතත් වදන්ට කීවලු.

[That is, a son "with the gift of the gab." The preference for a son and the disposition to regard a daughter as being a burden upon the family are most marked among the Tamils, who have the following significant sayings:—

(*a*) "Those who have no capital have no gain; those who have no sons to lean on have no support."

(*b*) "In times of prosperity even a slave woman may bring forth a female child."

(*c*) "A fourth girl is born and there are no means in the house even to procure a staple for a bolt."

(*d*) The Tamils also say, as denoting the depths of misfortune, "The destitute brings forth a female child, and that on a Friday, under the star Puradam."

(*e*) Yet another Tamil saying is, "If my elder brother has a daughter, her paternal aunt becomes an alien," the meaning (acc. to Denham) being that the person who would naturally be the most affectionately disposed—and who, if a son had been born, would most probably become his mother-in-law as well as his aunt—would be the most disappointed at the birth of a daughter.]

Like the fatherless child crying to sit and eat with his father.

අප්පා නැති එකා අප්පා එක්ක ඉඳගන කන්ට ඇඬුවා වගෙයි.

The unthrashed child, like the unstirred congee, is useless.

නොතළා හදන දරුවත් හැඳි නොගා උයන කැඳත් වැදගැම්ම කට නෑ.

The sorrows of children are a sealed book to barren women.

වඳියන්ට දරුදුක් නොදනේලු.

[Among the Sinhalese a barren woman, *i.e.*, a married woman without children, is an ill-omened sight to anybody starting upon a journey, particularly to a bride when leaving her house for her wedding. And a house without children is almost similarly regarded. The Tamils say:

"A house without an infant is not a house, nor is a curry without cummin a curry."

"A shrine without fame and wealth without a child are useless."]

What can the Doctor do to a child born to misery ?

කරුමෙන් උපන් දරුවාට වෙදා කරන්නේ මොකද?

[This is the *kálakanniyá*, the unfortunate victim of the Law of *Karma* or Fate.]

Barren women getting children—see " *WOMAN*."
Chick-rearing where children are eaten—see " *COUNTRY*."
Child's dead body not to be thrown away—*see* " *DEATH*."
Grandfather and grandson—see " *CHAIR* "
If fathers cultivate, children can glean—see " *CULTIVATION*."
Lama Hamy's child—see " *DEATH* "
Man who threatened to eat his own child—see " *CANNIBAL*."
Meaning of marriage when children cry—see " *MARRIAGE*."
Old people in a house without infants—see " *OLD*."
Placing logs before mothers—see " *MOTHER*."
The mother's milk when the child cries—see " *MOTHER*."
The parent crab and its young ones—see " *CRAB*."
The young of the Loris—see " *LORIS*."
Youngest in a family worse than a slave—see " *SLAVE*."

CHUNAM

Carrying a winnow of chunam—see " *LADDER*."
Chunam in every one's betel pouch—see " *BETEL*."

CIGAR

Like trying to light your cigar from another man's flaming beard.

රැවුල පත්තුවෙද්දී සුරුට්ටුව පත්තුකරගන්ට ආවා වගෙයි.

[Callous to other people's sufferings.]

CIVET-CAT—See " *CAT*."

CLAWS

A tiger without claws—see " *TIGER*."
What use being a tiger without claws ?—see " *TIGER*."

CLAY

The cat and the rat of clay—see " *RAT*."

CLEANING

Killing the fowl for the fox to clean—see " *FOWL*."

CLEANLINESS

The prawn's pretensions to cleanliness —see " *PRAWN*."

CLEVERNESS

The cleverest man will find his match one day.

හපනාටත් හපනා සම්බවෙනවාලු.

CLIMBING

Making ladders for monkeys to climb—see " *MONKEY*."

CLINGING

Clinging to a thorny branch when about to fall—see " *FALL*."
When the " dimiya " clings in anger —see " *ANT*."

CLOTH

A gift of cloth to the dancer—see " *DANCER.*"
The cloth hired out by a dhoby—see " *DHOBY.*"
Though the " kachchiya " goes for a pice—see " *DOG.*"
Woman wearing cloth upon cloth—see " *WOMAN.*"

CLUB

Like (my) club for (your) scythe.

කැත්තට පොල්ල වගෙයි.

No club when there's a dog—see " *DOG.*"
The club for a strong man—see " *STRENGTH.*"
The man with a club in hand—see " *POTTER.*"
The use of the club in others' villages—see " *VILLAGE.*"

COAST

Starving men even on the coast of Soli—see " *GILIMALE.*"

COBRA—(See also " *SNAKE.*")

It is impossible to make a young cobra a rat-snake.

නයාගේ පැටියා ගැරඩියා කරන්ට බැරිලු.

Like missing the blow (lit. " stick ") at a cobra.

නයාට පොල්ල වැරැද්දුවා වගෙයි.

[It would be a fatal miss.]

Like throwing a stone at a cobra.

නයාට ගල ගැහුවා වගෙයි.

[A dangerous proceeding, since the cobra, which is said to be very vindictive, is certain to take revenge on its assailant.]

On seeing the cobra spread out its hood, the rat-snake also danced with a potsherd in its mouth.

නයා පෙණේ කරනවා දැක ගැරඩියත් කැබලිත්තක් ඩැහැගෙන නැටුවාලු.

[An ineffective imitation.]

The cobra will bite you, whether you call him " Nayá " or " Nayihámy " (" Snake " or " Lord Snake.")

නයා කීවත් කනවා, නයි හාමි කීවත් කනවා.

[This is said in ridicule of the national love of flattering terms of address.]

When the cobra meets the polonga—see " *FIGHTING.*"

COCHIN-LEG

Dispelling the fear of the " Cochin-leg "—see " *LEG.*"

COCK—See " *FOWL.*"

COCONUT

Eat coconuts while you have your teeth.

දත් ඇති දා පොල් කන්ට කීවාලු.

[Cf. Eng. " Make hay while the sun shines."]

"I have coconuts in my bag," answered the man who was asked whither he was going.

යන්නේ කොහාට දැයි ඇහුවාම මල්ලේ පොල්ය කීවාලු.

[A pointless answer.]

Like distributing the thousand coconuts among a thousand friends.

යාළුවෝ දහට පොල් දහ බෙදුවා වගෙයි.

Like giving coconut trees from the river bottom.

ගඟට යටින් පොල්ගස් දෙන්නා වගෙයි.

[An unsubstantial gift.]

Like saying, "I did not steal the coconuts, but simply brought them down the tree."

පොල් හොරකම් කළා නොවෙයි, එල්ලන් බැස්සයි කීවා වගෙයි.

Like the man who flung the coconut half at the thieving dog.

හොර බල්ලාට පොල් බෑයෙන් ගැහූ මිනිහා වගෙයි.

[The dog was carrying away half a coconut that was lying outside the house; so the angry man threw at the animal the other half that was inside the house. Cf. Eng. "Throwing good money after bad."]

Black crow on a "ran-tembili" bunch—see "*CROW*."
Eating even iron coconuts—see "*TEETH*."
Eating my coconut and eloping—see "*HOSPITALITY*."
Giving an unhusked coconut to a dog—see "*DOG*."
Grimacing at a coconut slice—see "*GARDEN*."
If the grinding-stone is good—see "*GRINDING-STONE*."
Jaggery and coconut in hand—see "*JAGGERY*."
"*Kaha-kurulla*" *on a king-coconut*—see "*KAHA-KURULLA*."
Learning to scrape coconuts—see "*MÁTARA*."
The fox with a coconut husk in mouth—see "*FOX*."
To eat the coconut of that tree—see "*EAT*."
Toddy-drinking cup of coconut shell—see "*TODDY*."

COCONUT-SCRAPER

Even if you take it overseas, the "hiramanaya" is for scraping coconut.

රට ගෙනගියත් හිරමණය පොල් ගාන්ඩයි.

The coconut-scraper will know (its owner's) former sorrows.

වරක් විඳි දුක් හිරමණේ දනී.

COIN

The frog upon a silver coin—see "*FROG*."

COLD

Firebrand in cold water—see "*FIREBRAND*."

COLOUR

Crow on a rock of golden colour—see "*GOLD*."

COMB

The comb of a cock seen twice a day seems as white as a conch-shell.

දෙවේලේ දකින කුකුළාගෙ කරමලා, එවේලේ පෙනෙයි සකසේම සුදුවෙලා.

COMBINATION

Thief and master of house combining—see "*THIEF.*"

COMFORT

Sleepiness unaware of comfort—see "*SLEEPINESS.*"

COMMUNITY

One man can ruin a whole community—see "*ONE.*"

COMPLAINT

The poor man, his wife and the king—see "*POOR.*"
If both fence and dam eat up the crop—see "*CROP.*"

CONCH-SHELL

Cock's comb as white as the conch-shell—see "*COMB.*"
Milk poured into a conch-shell—see "*PURITY.*"

CONGEE

One cannot drink as it is hot, and one cannot throw it away as it is congee.

උණු හන්දා බොන්ටත් බෑ, කැඳ හන්දා අහක දමන්ටත් බෑ..

[This is sometimes said of a relation who has disgraced the family, but who has still claims as a member of it ; the point being that, while association is no longer desired, the relationship cannot be denied.]

The congee and the beard are both necessary.

කැඳත් ඕනෑලු, රැවුලත් ඕනෑලු.

CONSISTENCY

The "Undupiyali" leaf—see "*UNDUPIYALI.*"

CONSOLATION

Consolation begotten by patience—see "*PATIENCE.*"

CONSTRUCTION

The construction of sheds and pavilions—see "*BRIDE.*"

CONTEND

Contending against fortunate men—see "*FORTUNATE.*"

CONVERSATION—(See also "*TALK.*")

Conversation is a ladder to the traveller.

කතාව ගමනට ඉණිමගලු.

COOKING

Quarrel till the rice-pot is boiled—see "*MARRIAGE.*"

CORN

Elephants eating up the corn in the field—see "*ELEPHANT.*"
When deer eat up the corn in the field—see "*DEER.*"

CORNER

Door-frame for every corner—see "*DOOR.*"
Woman's fortune in corner of winnowing fan—see "*WOMAN.*"

CORPSE

The corpse of a Korava—see "*KORAVA.*"

COTTON

Can you find "imbul" cotton in a house where iron has been consumed by fire ?

යකඩ දැව්ච ගෙයි ඉඹුල් පුලුන් කොයින්ද ?

[*Imbul* (Lat. *Eriodendron anfractuosum*, Sansk. *Salmali*, Tam. *Illanku*) is the white silk cotton tree of the Sinhalese and yields Kapok or pillow cotton.]

Poverty lighter than "imbul" cotton—see "*POVERTY.*"

COUNTRY

Can you rear chicks in a country where children are eaten ?

ළමයි කන රටේ කුකුල් පැටවුන් ඇතිකළ හැකිද ?

In a country of palaces, there are humble little hovels, too.

මාලිගා ඇති රටේ දිළිඳු පැලුත් තිබෙනවාලු.

In one country you cannot yawn ; in another you cannot clear your throat.

එක රටකදී ඇනුම් අරින්ට බැහැ, වෙන රටකදී කාරන්ට බැහැ.

Your language must fit the country you are in.

දේසේ හැටියටයි බාසේ.

Fencing a country, but not the tongue—see "*GARRULITY.*"
No country is foreign to the learned—see "*EDUCATION.*"
The country for those who have the mouth—see "*MOUTH.*"
The Paduva and the white man's rule—see "*PADUVA.*"

COURAGE

No helpful friend like courage—see "*FRIEND.*"

COW

The short-tailed cow and the runners—see "*RUNNING.*"

COW-DUNG

Putting cow-dung into a pot of milk—see "*MILK.*"

CRAB

Like the crab's gambols till the water gets hot.

කකුළුවා දිය රත් වෙන කල් කරන සෙල්ලම වගෙයි.

[It is the practice to boil crabs alive in a pot, for food. The proverb is applied to any short-lived enjoyment which is succeeded by much suffering, especially to the enjoyment of sensual pleasures.]

The parent crab, walking crookedly, tells its young ones to go straight.

කකුළුවා පැත්තෙන් පැත්තට යමින් පැටවුන්ට කෙළින් එන්ට කියනවාලු.

[The Tamils say : "If a crab gets fat, it will not stay in its hole." The Jamaicans say : "When crab no hab hole, him nebber get fat" —i.e. a steady home life is best.]

CRANE

If there is a time for the "koká," there will be one for the "tittaya," too.

කොකාට වාරයක් නම් තිත්තයාටත් වාරයක්ලු.

[The *tittayá* is a very small river fish on which the *koká* feeds frequently. The *koká* (order *Herodiones*) is the crane or heron, of which there are many species in Ceylon, such as—

Beli-koká—muscle coloured crane
Sudu-koká—white coloured crane
Kana-koká—dun coloured crane
Karavel-koká—long-necked crane
Manan-koká—spreading crane]

Like the crane waiting for the river to dry up.

කොකා දිය සිඳෙන කල් බලා උන්නා වගෙයි.

[Cf. Lat. "*Rusticus expectat dum defluat amnis.*"]

The white of a "kana-koká" appears only when it flies.

කණ කොකාගේ සුදු පෙනෙන්නේ ඉගිලුණාමලු.

[The upper part of the body of the *kana-koká* is dun-coloured, and the lower is white.]

Going after cranes for clothes given to dhoby—see "*DHOBY.*"

CRAWLING

Old people crawling on their knees—see "*OLD.*"

CREDITOR

Debtor the slave of the creditor—see "*DEBTOR.*"

CREEPER

Its own fruit not a burden to the creeper—see "*FRUIT.*"
Placing the "messa" the way the creeper goes—see "*MESSA.*"

CREEPING

The jungle to the man who can creep—see "*JUNGLE.*"

CROCODILE

Like the arrangement of a "match" for the crocodile.

කිඹුලාට මඟුල් ජෝඩු කළා වගෙයි..

[The folklore story is that a cunning jackal, who had seen the carcase of an elephant on the bank of a river, crossed the river every day on the back of a crocodile, on the pretence of going there to arrange a marriage for the crocodile. The jackal maintained the deceit for some days, telling the crocodile that the bride's father was away one day, and the uncle on another, etc. On the day he ate the last of the carcase he ran away to the jungle, saying, in answer to the inquiries of the crocodile, "What marriages for crocodiles that live in the river?"]

Though you escape the Crocodile, you will find the Lizard at home.

කිඹුලාගෙන් ගැලවුණත් හූනා ගෙදරලු.

[In Sinhalese folklore, the crocodile, the lizard and the cheetah were three brothers, herdsmen, skilled in necromancy. According to Perera's *Sinhalese Folklore Notes*, as the animals they were looking after refused to yield milk, the eldest transformed himself into a cheetah, and the evil nature of the beast asserting itself, he began to destroy the flock and attack the brothers. The youngest took refuge on a tree, transforming himself into a lizard, and the other, who had the magical books, turned himself into a crocodile and jumped into a river. These three have ever since lived in friendship, and a person who escapes a crocodile is killed if a lizard urinates on him when sleeping. A crocodile's victim can free himself by tickling its stomach and trying tc take away the books concealed there."]

You can endure the crocodile's teeth, but not the thorns of the "Kohila."

කිඹුලා අල්ලනවා ඉවසතත් කොහිල කටු ඇණෙනවා ඉවසන්ට බැරිලු.

[The *Kohila* (Lat. *Lasia spinosa*, Sansk. *Abhiru*) is a plant both the leaves and root of which are edible. Its thorns are among the sharpest in the vegetable world.]

CROOK

The crook in the dog's tail—see "*DOG.*"

CROP—(See also "*HARVEST*" and "*THIEF.*")

If both the fence and the dam eat up the crop, to whom shall (the owner) complain ?

වැටත් නියරත් ගොයම් කානම් කාට පවසමු ඒ අමාරුව ?

[That is, its protection has proved its destruction. Note the Tamil saying, "The thief is found to be the gardener."]

No crop without sowing—see "*SOWING.*"

CROW

"I eat the flesh of every one, but no one eats my flesh," said the crow.

"හැමෝගේම මස් මම කනවාය, මගේ මස් කවුරුත් කන්නේ නැත" කියා කපුටා කීවාලු.

[As no one eats its flesh it sorrowfully cries out : *Kát-ká* ("I eat everybody"), according to Sinhalese Folklore.]

Like a black crow alighting on a "ran-tembili" bunch.

කළු කපුටා රත්තැඹිලි වල්ල පිට වැහුවා වගෙයි.

[The *Tembili* is a species of coconut tree which produces nuts of a light-yellow or "golden" colour, commonly called "King-coconuts." The water of the *tembili* is a cooling and refreshing beverage.]

Like crows flocking round the carcase of a bull.

ගෙරි කුණට කපුටෝ වහන්නා වගෙයි.

The pain of the wound (of an animal) is of no consequence to the crow.

කපුටාට වණේ කැක්කුම මොටද ?

[Which keeps pecking at the wound callously.]

Dead crow not to be thrown away—see "*DEATH.*"
The crow and the Moorman ubiquitous—see "*MOORMAN.*"
The crow on a golden rock—see "*GOLD.*"
The crow's pain and that of the bull—see "*BULL.*"
Unrelished food is like crow flesh—see "*EATING.*"
When crow flesh is better than peacock flesh—see "*FLESH.*"

CROWN

Is the crown, which ought to be worn on the head, to blame if it be put on the feet ?

හිසේ පළඳින ඔටුන්න පයේ ලා ගැනීම ඔටුන්නේ වරදද?

CRUPPER

A crupper as a cure for dysentery—see "*DYSENTERY.*"

CRYING

For those who cried standing we should cry standing ; for those who cried sitting we should cry sitting.

හිට ඇඬුවන්ට හිට ඇඬීමත්, ඉඳ ඇඬුවන්ට ඉඳ ඇඬීමත් නිසිලු.

A deer's cry in Sabaragamuva—see "*TALK.*"
Children crying and marriage—see "*MARRIAGE.*"
Cry not for the lost jaggery—see "*JAGGERY.*"
The cat taken to Europe—see "*CAT.*"
Grandfather who weeps for nothing—see "*GRANDFATHER.*"
Your finger in an eye ready to cry—see "*EYE.*"

CULTIVATION

If fathers cultivate, children will have a chance of gleaning.

පියවරු ගොසිතැන් කළොත් දරුවන්ට කරල් ඇහිඳීමට ඉඩ ඇතිලු.

CUNNING

Cunning people can escape hell—see "*HELL.*"

CUP

Toddy-drinking cup as Buddha's target—see "*TODDY.*"

CURD

Like the description of curd given to a blind man.

අන්ධයකුට දී කිරිවල සුද කීවා වගෙයි.

[A person, being asked by a blind man what curd was like, said it was white. On being asked what white was like, he said it was like a conch-shell. When asked again by the blind man what a conch-shell was like, he said it was like the kernel of a coconut. "What is a coconut like," then asked the blind man. "It is like a crane," was the reply. "What is a crane like ?" was the next question. The man thereupon bent his hand into the shape of a crane and asked the blind man to feel it. The blind man felt the hand and said : "Oh, after all, curd is exactly like the hand."]

Even cats will testify in favour of curd.

බළල්ලුත් දී කිරට සාක්කිසි.

CURE

Eating "bali" will not cure illness—see "*ILLNESS.*"
Wearing a crupper to cure dysentery—see "*DYSENTERY.*"

CURRY

A curry without cummin is no curry—see "*CHILDREN.*"

CURSE

Where is the curse that is not the consequence of sin ?

පාපයක් නැතුව සාපයක් කොයින්ද ?

He is under a curse who is legless.

ගාතයක් නැති එකාට සාපයක් ඇතිලු.

CUTTING

Like cutting hedge-stakes on to a river.

ගඟට ඉණි කැපුවා වගෙයි.

Like cutting the throat while eating together.

එක්ක කකා බොටුව කපනවා වගෙයි.

Andrisa and hair-cutting—see "*HAIR.*"
Kissing the hand that cannot be cut off—see "*HAND.*"
Story of the lime-cutting ceremony—see "*LIME.*"
To cut "jak" with the sword—see "*SWORD.*"
The cutting down of the drum-stick tree—see "*DRUM-STICK.*"
The scythe cuts sharply—see "*SCYTHE.*"

DAM

If both fence and dam eat up the crop—see "*CROP.*"
Relations who do not help—see "*RELATIONS.*"

DAMBULLA-VIHARA—(see also "*BUDDHA.*")

Like asking you to worship at Dambulla Vihára and, when returning, kill and bring some "talagoyi."

දඹුල්ලත් වැඳගෙන තලගොයිත් මරාගෙන එන්ට කීවා වගෙයි.

[Dambulla Vihára is the name of a famous rock temple of Ceylon to which thousands of Buddhist pilgrims go yearly. The *talagoya* is a land lizard called "Iguana" (Lat. *Varanus dracoena*, order *Sauria*) whose flesh is a delectable dish to epicures.]

DANCE

Though you mask in secret, you must dance in public.

හංග හංගා කෝලම් බැන්දත්, එළියේලු නටන්නේ.

Devil-dancing and the "Kattadiyá"—see "*KATTADIYÁ.*"
Devil-dancing and tom-toming—see "*TOM-TOMING.*"
Making bears dance—see "*TIGER.*"
Resin and coal for a dancing devil—see "*DEVIL.*"
The dance and somersault for Kapurála—see "*RICE.*"
The dance of the rat-snake—see "*COBRA.*"
Tiger-dancing at a Pinkama—see "*TIGER.*"
Woman dancing like a celestial—see "*WOMAN.*"

DANCER

Even the fall of a dancer is a somersault.

නැට්ටුවා වැටුණත් අඩව්වලු.

[At least, that is how it looks like to the admiring gaze of the average onlooker. The reference here, of course, is to the Eastern dancer moving nimbly or merrily, tripping, gliding, and leaping rhythmically.]

Is a gift of cloth a trifling thing to the straw-covered dancer masquerading like a dog ?

පිදුරු වෙනිය ඇඳ කුකු නටන කිඩින්ට වත් කාරියක් ලද නොසියාඩම කැයි කීවාසේ.

"It is not that I cannot dance, but the floor is not level," said the dancer.

නටන්න බැරුවා නොවේ, පොළොවේ ඇද.

[This was the excuse of the dancer who fell during his dance. The Jamaicans say: "If man can't dance him say de music no good." In Ashanti, "If you cannot dance, you will say the drum is not sounding sweetly."]

DARKNESS

Like darkness, out of enmity to the moon, becoming helpful to the thieves.

සඳට වෛරව සොරුන්ට අඳුර පිහිටවූ මෙනි.

DAUGHTER

A daughter with beauty—see "*CHILDREN.*"

DAUGHTER-IN-LAW—(See "*MOTHER-IN-LAW.*")

DAY

Fish on a lucky day—see "*FISH.*"
One day's heavy rain—see "*RAIN.*"

DAYLIGHT

Falling in daylight into a pit—see "*PIT.*"

DEAF

Like blowing a chank to a deaf man.

බීරි අලියාට වීණා ගානවා වගෙයි.

Like saying: "The deaf man, on hearing the song of the dumb man, clapped his hands for joy."

"ගොළුවාගේ සින්දුව බිහිරාට ඇසී අත් පොළොසන් දුන්නාය" කියන්නා වගෙයි.

Music to a deaf man—see "*MUSIC.*"
Fiddle-playing to a deaf elephant—see "*FIDDLE.*"

DEAF PERSONS

Like the story of the four deaf persons.

හතර බිහිරි කථාව වගෙයි.

[In a certain family the father and the mother were both deaf, as well as their son and daughter-in-law. One day, when the wife took the old man's breakfast into the field, the old man asked her where their son was. The old woman, however, replied:

"It is no fault of mine. It is the daughter-in-law who delayed cooking."

On returning home she told her daughter-in-law, who happened to be spinning at the moment, that the old man had blamed her for being late. The daughter-in-law, thinking that her mother-in-law was finding fault with her spinning, said:

"I spin as best as I can."

When, however, the daughter-in-law a little later told her own husband, who was then warming himself near the fire-place, that her spinning was found fault with, he swore that he had not roasted a single potato.]

[The Jamaicans say : "Deaf ear gi' story-carrier trouble."]

DEATH

Like asking, "Is Lama Hamy's child the personification of death to me ?"

ලම හාමිගේ දරුවා මගේ මරුවාදැයි කීවා වගෙයි.

Neither a dead child nor a dead crow should be thrown away.

දරු කුණත් කපුටු කුණත් අහක ලන්ට එපාලු.

The bear's death is the lamb's salvation.

වලසාගේ මරණය බැටළු පැටවාගේ සරණය.

The pains of death on top of lameness.

කොරේ පිටට මරේ.

[That is, crippled and then brought to the pass of death.]

There is no kind of death without a cause.

ලැවැන්නක් නැති මරණයක් නැතිලු.

There is no death without lamentation.

ලයත්නක් නැති මරක් නැ.

When a man with projecting teeth dies, you feel doubtful of his demise.

බොල්ලැවා මළත් අදව් නැතිලු.

[Because of the grin of his unclosed lips.]

When death comes, there is no let or hindrance.

මරුවා ආ දාට බාදා නැතිලු.

A dead man's horoscope—see "*HOROSCOPE.*"
A thousand though dead—see "*THOUSAND.*"
A tear for the mother-in-law—see "*MOTHER-IN-LAW.*"
A thing grows quickly to end in death quickly—see "*SCYTHE.*"
A voice after Andare's death—see "*VOICE.*"
Death to the rat and play to the cat—see "*RAT.*"
Death-agony smile of the trapped fox—see "*FOX.*"
Fame abroad and death-agony at home—see "*FAME.*"
Man who goes from tree to tree—see "*MAN.*"
On mother's death, father becomes uncle—see "*MARRIAGE.*"
The day the grand-mother died—see "*GRAND-MOTHER.*"
The death of the grand-son—see "*GRAND-FATHER.*"
The fish dies because of its mouth—see "*FISH.*"
The "Máraya" who gives work—see "*FRIEND.*"
The Moorman's manner of dying—see "*MOORMAN.*"
The old man does not die—see "*OLD.*"
The soles of your feet and fatal spots—see "*SOLES.*"
What avails the father when mother dies—see "*MOTHER.*"

DEBTOR

The debtor is the slave of the creditor.

නය ගත් අය නය දුන් අයගේ වාලාලු.

[There is a story concerning the two. There was a certain debtor who had evaded a creditor for a long time in order to escape the payment of his debts. Seeing the creditor come one day to the house, he pretended to be dead. The wife of the supposed dead man, in order to carry through the fiction, began to yell out for grief. The creditor, who was by no means deceived by all this, waited till in due time the body was placed on the funeral pyre, and then jumped on the supposed dead body, saying, "I, too, will die with my friend." Thereupon the supposed dead man got up and promised to pay off the amount due with compound interest.]

[The Jamaicans say : "Man in debt like bird in net."]

DECEPTION—(See "*TRICK.*")

DECOY

Killing animals behind buffalo decoy—see "*BUFFALO.*"

DEER

Like beating the elk-skin at home because deer ate up the corn in the field.

කෙතේ මුවෝ කෑවාට ගෙදර තිබුණ ගෝණ හමට තඩිබෑවාලු.

Like the deer which has seen a tiger.

දිවියා දුටු මුවා වගෙයි.

Throw not the herbs you have plucked at the sight of running deer.

දුවන මුවන් දැක නොදමන් නේලු පළා.

Will the spots of a deer vanish by jumping from one jungle to another ?

ඒ කැලෙන් මේ කැලේට පැන්නාම මුවාගේ තිත් මැකේද?

A deer in Sabaragamuva—see "*TALK.*"
"*Ánam*" *and deer-hunting*—see "*ÁNAM.*"

DEFEAT

Defeat is three-legged.

පරාදෙට අඩු තුනයි.

[Thus enabled to come quicker than with one or two legs.]

Defeat is the portion of the devil-server—see "*DEVIL.*"
Defeating a 100 *Pandits but not a single fool*—see "*FOOL.*"

DEFECTS

Getting one's defects exposed by talking nonsense.

අනං මනං දොඩවා වනම් පනම් අහගන්නා වගෙයි.

DEPRAVITY

Depraved children and parents—see "*CHILDREN.*"

DESCRIPTION

Description of curd to a blind man—see "*CURD.*"
Elephant described by four blind men—see "*ELEPHANT.*"

DESERTS

One's hopes and deserts—see "*FATE.*"

DESIRE

Desire alone insufficient to learn language—see "*LANGUAGE.*"

DESTITUTE

The destitute brings forth a female child—see "*CHILDREN.*"

DESTRUCTION

Pride precedes destruction—see "*PRIDE.*"

"DEVALA"

The God and the Kapurála's son—see "*KAPURÁLA.*"

DEVIL—(See *also* "*IMAGE.*")

An image is like an "aggaláva" to the Devil who has gulped down a Buddhist priest.

ගණේ ගිල්ල යකාට පිළිමේ අග්ගලාවලු.

[See under "IMAGE" for the variant: "An image is like an *aggaláva* to the man who has swallowed a Vihára." The *aggaláva* is a kind of sweetmeat—a globe-cake or ball of dough made of flour and jaggery.]

An offering is a "sine qua non" to the Devil.

යකාට දොළ නොදී බැහැ.

Defeat, never victory, is the portion of those who serve the Devil.

යකුන් සේවය කළෝ ඇත්නම් පැරදුණෝ මිස දිනුවෝ නැත.

Like offering burning resin and coal to a Devil who dances even otherwise.

නිකම් නටන යකාට අඟුරු දුම්මල ඇල්ලුවා වගෙයි.

[Unnecessary and superfluous ceremonial.]

The departing Devil smashed even the "Koraha" as he went.

යන යකා කොරහත් බිඳගෙන ගියාලු.

[A veritable vandal in his anger at his forced departure. The *koraha* is a large pan or chatty used for washing rice preparatory to cooking—therefore a necessary utensil in every household. The cihatty was regarded as so essential for cooking purposes that the Tamils have a saying, "Everything wanted is in the box, but there is no chatty in which to make a curry," the implication being that there was great preparation for the meal, when in fact the host had nothing in the house, or only an excuse that he had lost the key of the box!]

[Say the Jamaicans: "It hard fe keep out de debil, but it wus fe dribe him out." Cf. the Scotch proverb: "Better keep the deil oot than hae to turn him oot."]

This, sure, is a Maha Sohona killing.

මේක නම් මහසොන් මැරිල්ලක්.

[Maha Sohona is the chief of the important spirits of disease. In Sinhalese Folklore, he is said to be 122 feet high, has the head of a bear with a pike in his left hand, and in his right an elephant, whose blood he squeezes out to drink. He inflicts cholera and dysentery, and presides over graveyards and junctions where three roads meet.

He is said to appear riding on a pig. In ancient times two giants, Jayasena and Gotimbara, met in single combat. Gotimbara knocked off the head of Jayasena, whereupon the god, Senasura, tore off the head of a bear and placed it on the body of Jayasena, who then rose up alive as the demon Maha Sohona. The Sinhalese believe that a man struck down by this demon would exhibit, on the back of his body, the mark of a hand with the palm and fingers standing out of the flesh, embossed as it were.]

Devil-dancing and the "kattadiyá"—see "*KATTADIYÁ.*"
Devil-dancing and too much tom-toming—see "*TOM-TOM.*"
Fear of the Devil—see "*HOUSE.*"
The Devil as god-father—see "*HELL.*"
The Devil a hermit in old age—see "*HERMIT.*"
Twins of opposite sex are Devils—see "*TWINS.*"

DEW

Tanks are filled by rain, not dew—see "*TANKS.*"

DHOBY

Like a cloth hired out by a dhoby.

රදා පිරුවටය වගෙයි.

[The *piruvata* is a cloth or dress either lent by a dhoby to a person to wear while his own is being washed, or hired by the dhoby to a person needing it to wear for some function or ceremony. Whatever is lent or hired in this manner, is, of course, not the dhoby's but other people's clothes.]

Like going after cranes, after giving your clothes to the dhoby.

රදවුන්ට රෙදි දීලා කොක්කු පාරේ යන්නා වගෙයි.

[Pursuing a wrong direction or person.]

Like the way the Lady gave rice to the dhoby.

රදවාට හාමිනේ බත් දුන්නා වගෙයි.

[When the dhoby had come during meal time, on more than one occasion the Lady of the house had said to him : "Washerman, there is rice and there is curry, but I am sorry I am unable to give you to eat, since there is no plantain-leaf available." One day the dhoby put a plantain-leaf in his bundle of clothes, and, when the Lady made the usual excuse, he produced it, saying : "Here is one, Lady; I brought it with me." "Upon my word, Washerman," she thereupon said, "all these days I told you the truth, but to-day I meant it in fun." (The necessity for the plantain-leaf is this. In a respectable Sinhalese household, when a low-caste man is given to eat, his food is served not on a plate but on a plantain-leaf.)]

The "ins and outs" of the women are best known to the village dhoby.

ස්ත්‍රීන්ගේ වගතුග ගමේ අපුල්ලන රදවා දනී.

[Tamil sayings in regard to the dhoby are :

(*a*) "The washerman knows the poor of the village, the goldsmith knows whose ornaments are made of fine gold."

(*b*) "The tricks of a goldsmith and a weaver are not equal to those of a dhoby."

(c) "Employ a new dhoby but an old barber."]

The affection of a dhoby—see "*BARBER.*"

DHONEYS

Great dhoneys founder through one small leak.

සුළු සිදුරෙන් ලොකු හම්බන් කිඳා බහිනවාලු.

DIFFICULTY

Every difficulty is to the poor—see " *POVERTY.*"

DIGGING

Like digging where it resists.

හේබෙන තැන හාරනවා වගෙයි.

Earth in the digger's loin-cloth—see " *HOE.*"

" DIMBUL "—(See *also* " *ATTIKKÁ.*")

Like watering a " dimbul " tree in order to get flowers.

දිඹුල් මල් ලබමැයි සිතා දිය ඇද්දා වගෙයි.

[The *Dimbul* here is not the " Wood-apple " tree (*Feronia Elephantum*), but a species (*Ficus Carica*) of the Fig tree which never flowers.]

" DIMIYA "—(See " *ANT.*")

" DISAVA "

" *Disáva* " *friendly*, " *dasáva* " *unlucky*—see " *RANK.*"

DISEASE—(See *also* " *ILLNESS,*" " *SICKNESS.*")

The iron's purging disease—see " *IRON.*"

DISHONEST

Be dishonest to the deceitful—see " *UPRIGHTNESS.*"

DISLOCATION

Boxing and a dislocated hip—see " *BOXING.*"

DISTANCE

The Valave-ganga seven " *gavvas* " *away*—see " *AMUDE.*"

DISTRESS

Fame abroad and distress at home—see " *FAME.*"

DISTRIBUTION

The distribution of 1,000 *coconuts*—see " *COCONUTS.*"

DIVINATION

The sluggard and the gift of divination—see " *PROPHECY.*"

DIVORCE

Marrying a divorced woman forbidden—see " *MARRIAGE.*"

" DIYA-KAVA "

Like hiding salt in the back of the " diya-kává."

දිය කාවාගේ පිටේ ලුණු හංගුවා වගෙයි.

[The *Diya-kává* is a bird called the Little Cormorant (Lat. *Phalacrocorax pygmoens*). The term is applied also to a bird called the Darter (Lat. *Plotus melanogaster, Pelecanidae,* order *Steganopodes*). It frequently dips into water—which makes it a bad preserver of the salt hidden on its back.]

DOGS

Barking dogs do not bite.

බුරන බල්ලෝ හපා කන්නේ නැහැ.

Dogs bark even at the moon.

හඳටත් බල්ලෝ බුරනවා.

Even though the "kachchiya" goes for a "pichchiya," the dog goes naked.

කච්චිය පිච්චියට ගියත් බල්ලා හෙලුවෙන්.

[*Kachchiya*, according to Clough, is "a piece of linen cloth no part of which has been torn off"—generally 40 yards in length. *Pichchiya* is a pice, one and a half cents in Ceylon currency to-day. Cf. the Jamaican proverb: "Darg say no care how clot' a sell cheap, him no wear none."]

If you get ready for a dog-masquerade, you must be prepared to go where the fingers are snapped.

බලු කෝලමට හැරහුණොත් අඟුර ගහපු තැනට යන්ට ඕනෑලු.

Like giving an unhusked coconut to a dog.

බල්ලාට ලෙලි පොල් දුන්නා වගෙයි.

[A useless gift]

Like the barking of familiar dogs.

අඳුනන බල්ලෝ බුරන්නා වගෙයි.

Like the dog that was getting lean through lack of food.

කෑම හිඟයෙන් කෙට්ටු වෙච් සිටි බල්ලා වගෙයි.

[The story is that a friendly dog, who had observed the dog owned by a certain Brahman to be very lean, asked the latter to come to his master's house where abundance of food could be had. The lean dog replied: "I am living in a Brahman's house, and when the Brahman gets angry he calls his wife a bitch, and thus she is my daughter and the Brahman my son-in-law. On this account I cannot leave the Brahman's house." The dog thus died of starvation through his love of vainglory.]

Like the friendship of the short (-tailed) dog.

කොට බල්ලාගේ හාදකම වගෙයි.

[Unable to wag its tail to show its affection.]

The barking of dogs will not frighten elephants.

බල්ලන් බිරුවාට අලි භය නොවෙත්.

Like the dog in the heap of straw.

පිදුරු ගොඩේ ඉන්න බල්ලා වගෙයි.

The barking of dogs will not make the mountain collapse.

බල්ලන් බිරුවාට කන්ද කඩා වැටෙන්නේ නැහැ.

The barking of dogs will not cease at the gate so long as the smell of meat remains within the house.

ගෙයි මස් ගඳ තිබෙනතෙක් දොරකඩ බලු හඬ තොර නොවෙයි.

The crook in the dog's tail can never be straightened, even though you put the tail within a bamboo.

බලු වල්ගේ උණ බම්බුවේ දැම්මත් ඇද ඇරෙන්නේ නැහැ.

The dog always runs even though he has no work to do.

බල්ලාට ඇති වැඩකුත් නැහැ, හෙමින් ගමනකුත් නැහැ.

The dog, even if he becomes a King, bites sandals.

රජවුණත් බල්ලා සෙරෙප්පු විකනවාලු:

The dog reared in a blacksmith's forge is not afraid even of thunder.

කම්මලේ ඇතිවෙච්ච බල්ලා හෙණේටත් භය නැතිලු.

The dog wanted the order given to him to be given to his tail.

බල්ලාට කීවාම බලු වල්ගෙට කියන්ට කීවාලු.

The moon is not ruffled by the barking of dogs.

බල්ලන් බිරුවට චන්ද්‍රයා නොසලකයි.

[Cf. the Jamaican proverb: "Darg bark nebber frighten moon"—applied to one who uses futile threats.]

The tail-less dog cannot show his affection.

වල්ගේ නැති බල්ලාගේ ආදරේ පෙන්වන්ට බැරිලු.

The teeth will fall of the dog who barks at fortunate people.

පිනැත්තන්ට බුරන බල්ලාගේ කටේ දත් වැටෙනවාලු.

Though a dog bites your leg, do you bite its leg in return?

බල්ලා කකුල කෑවාට උගේ කකුල කපාකන්නේ නැහැ.

When there is a dog, you have no club; when you have the club, there is no dog.

බල්ලා ඉන්න විට පොල්ල නැහැ, පොල්ල තිබෙන විට බල්ලා නැහැ.

Will the dog that has eaten a shipload of dung be troubled by a little bad smell?

අසූචි කප්පරක් කෑ බල්ලාට සුළු ගඳක් මොකක්ද?

Like the dog-flea which the blind man has got hold of.

කණාට අහුවුණු බලු මැක්කා වගෙයි.

[He can not see what exactly it is and does not let it off for that reason.]

Curs and hunting dogs—see "*HUNTING.*"
Dog left to starve at wedding—see "*WEDDING.*"
Driving dogs away from a stranger's house—see "*HOUSE.*"
No lack of dogs in a Rodiya's hut—see "*RODIYA.*"
The dog-masquerading dancer—see "*DANCER.*"
Threw half a coconut at a dog—see "*COCONUT.*"
The stay-at-home foot worse than a dog's—see "*TRAVEL.*"

"DOLE"

Monkeys playing the "dōlé"—see "*MONKEY.*"

DOOR

Make a door-frame for every corner you see.

දුටු දුටු අස්සට ගස උළුවස්සා.

DOTING

Doting on a spouse betokens that widowhood is near.

ඉතා වැවෙන්නේ කනවැන්දුම් වෙන්ටලු.

Excessive fondness precedes a quarrel—see "*FIGHTING.*"

DOVE

A "kobeyiyá" (dove) though fried in oil—see "*KOBEYIYÁ.*"

DOWRY

The gift of a horse as dowry—see "*KALUHÁMY.*"
The girl who received a nuptial present—see "*MARRIAGE.*"

DRAWING

Drawing water to wedding house—see "*WATER.*"

DREAM

The dumb man's dream—see "*DEAF.*"

DRESS

The "Sinno" and his hat—see "*HAT.*"

DRINK

A congee-drinking house—see "*HOUSE.*"
A rat drunk on toddy—see "*RAT.*"
Drinking muddy water—see "*WATER.*"
Drinking river water—see "*WATER.*"
Eaten the earth and drunk all the water—see "*EARTH.*"
Gruel that cannot be drunk or thrown away—see "*GRUEL.*"
Jaggery in hand, water from any well—see "*JAGGERY.*"
Moorman dying of drinking—see "*MOORMAN.*"
One cannot drink as it is hot—see "*CONGEE.*"
Poor Moorman and toddy drinking—see "*MOORMAN.*"
The place where the ox drank water—see "*OX.*"
The man whose arrack was drunk—see "*ARRACK.*"
Toddy-drinking-cup as Buddha's target—see "*TODDY.*"

DROP

Drop of quicksilver on your palm—see "*HAND.*"

DROPSY

No amount of water can quench the thirst of a dropsical man.

මහෝදර ලෙඩා කොතරම් දිය බීවත් ඇතැයි යන තෘපතියට නොපැමිණෙයි.

DROUGHT

Long drought ended by one day's rain—see "*RAIN.*"

DRUM

You must beat the drum which you have tied on.

බැඳ ගත්ත බෙරේ ගහන්ඩ ඕනෑ.

DRUMSTICK

Keeping on a "Murungá" branch.

මුරුංගා අත්තේ තියනවා.

[The same significance as the English, "Lauding to the skies." The *murungá* is the horse-radish, commonly called drum-stick tree (Lat. *Moringa pterygosperma*).]

Like the cutting down of the drum-stick tree.

මුරුංගා ගහ කැපූ කථාව වගෙයි.

[There was a person who had a *murungá* (drum-stick) tree in his garden. When one day he saw the first blossoms on it, he fell to thinking about the way in which the drum-sticks they would produce should be tied into bundles. From that he passed on to a speculation about the profits that would accrue to him by selling them, the trade he could carry on with this money, the extensive commerce which in course of time he would be able to maintain with foreign countries with the help of ships of his own, and the store-houses that should be built for foreign goods. And as the *murungá* tree seemed to obstruct the way to the store-houses, he cut it down.]

DRUNKARD

The drunkard and his toddy-cup—see " *TODDY.*"

DRY-FISH

The dry-fish seller and sandalwood—see " *FISH.*"

DUCK

The hen hatching duck eggs—see " *HEN.*"

DUMB MAN

Like the dumb man's dream.

ගොළුවා දුටු ස්වප්නය වගෙයි.

[Indescribable.]

The song of the dumb man—see " *DEAF.*"

DUNG

The dog and a shipload of dung—see " *DOG.*"

DUNUGAMUVA

The bow at Dunugamuva—see " *TALK.*"

DUST

If you raise the dust, it will rise up to your own head.

දූවිලි ඇවුස්සුවොත් හිසට දූවිලි නගියි.

Dust and the illiterate man—see " *EDUCATION.*"
Pilfering gold dust from his mother—see " *BADÁLÁ.*"

DWARF—(See " *SHORTNESS.*")

DYSENTERY

Like wearing a crupper to cure dysentery.

අතිසාරෙට අමුඩෙ ගහනවා වගෙයි.

EACLE-BOW

The eye and an eacle-bow—see " *EYE.*"

EACLE-BROOM

A new eacle-broom sweeps well.

අලුත් ඉළප්පතෙන් හොඳට පිහ දැමෙන වාලු.

[The *ilapota* is a small broom made of the strong fibres (eacle or ekels) of the coconut leaf. In Sinhalese households it is generally used to sweep the kitchen and compound.

The Jamaicans say: "New broom sweep clean, but de ole broom know de carner."]

EAR

Like the recently sprung horn grown longer than the older ear.

ඉස්සර වෙලා ආ කනට වඩා පස්සේ ආ අඟ දික්වුණා වගෙයි.

[The new acquaintance preferred to the older friend.]

Feeding on the ear—see " *FEED.*"
Pouring honey into the ear—see " *HONEY.*"

EAR-RING

Chameleon and a gold ornament—see " *CHAMELEON.*"

EARTH

Like (a man who had) eaten the whole earth and drunk all the water.

ලෝකෙ කාලා වතුර බීලා වගෙයි

[Like the man who had " escaped all seven gallows."]

Earth from the hoe—see " *HOE.*"

EATING

It is only the eater who knows the taste.

කාපු එකයි රස දන්නේ

Though eating together, the stomachs are different.

එක්ක කතත් බොක්ක වෙනලු

[What is consumed together, though eaten out of the same plate, goes into different stomachs. The Tamils say: " When plates are interchanged, inter-marriages take place "—in other words, if persons can eat together, they can inter-marry, commensality being confined to persons of the same caste.]

To eat the jak of that tree, you want the coconut of that tree.

ඒ ගහේ කොස් කන්න ඒ ගහේ පොල් ඕනේ.

[Boiled *jak* is usually eaten with the scraped coconut, either in the raw or made into *sambol.*]

What avails the inclination to eat, if the quantity (of rice in the plate) is small ?

හිත තිබුණට මොකටද පත කුඩානම් ?

What you relish to eat is like peacock flesh, otherwise it is crow flesh.

කතොත් මොනර මාලු, නොකතොත් කපුටු මාලු.

You call a " kabaragoyá " a " talagoyá " when you want (to eat) it.

ඕනෑකමට කබරගොයත් තලගොයාලු.

[The flesh of the *kabaragoyá* or large spotted lizard (*Hydrosaurus salvator*, order *Sauria*) is generally not eaten. For previous reference to *talagoyá*, see under " Dambulla." A variant of the above is, " Upon emergency, you can make a *Talagoyá* of even *a Kabaragoyá.*"]

A country where children are eaten—see "*COUNTRY.*"
A house where inmates do not eat—see "*HOUSE.*"
Child's desire to eat with his father—see "*CHILDREN.*"
Dog that has eaten a shipload of dung—see "*DOG.*"
Eat coconuts while you have teeth—see "*COCONUTS.*"
Eat like a Lord—see "*WORK.*"
Eaten salt out of one bag—see "*SALT.*"
Eating "ánam" and deer-hunting—see "*ÁNAM.*"
Eating "bali" will not cure illness—see "*ILLNESS.*"
Eating beef that dangles from your neck—see "*BEEF.*"
Eating even iron coconuts—see "*TEETH.*"
Eating in milk and washing your hand in honey—see "*MILK.*"
Eating my coconut and eloping—see "*HOSPITALITY.*"
Eating the rice of the Gods—see "*RICE.*"
Eating without salt—see "*SALT.*"
Eating together and cutting the throat—see "*CUTTING.*"
Evacuating on the plate out of which you ate—see "*PLATE.*"
Even eat up a part of me after telling the truth—see "*TRUTH.*"
"*Kabaragoyás*" *eating "anjila" fish*—see "*KABARAGOYÁ.*"
Licking may cost you the eating—see "*LICKING.*"
Like having eaten "kalu-nika"—see "*KALU-NIKA.*"
Man who had eaten the whole earth—see "*EARTH.*"
Man who threatened to eat his child—see "*CANNIBAL.*"
Moorman dying of too much eating—see "*MOORMAN.*"
Move the hands to move the mouth—see "*HAND.*"
My fire-place knows how I eat—see "*FIREPLACE.*"
Return from wedding without eating cake—see "*CAKE.*"
The cat which has eaten chameleons—see "*CATS.*"
The crow and flesh-eating—see "*CROWS.*"
The monkey that has eaten "goraka"—see "*MONKEY.*"
The way Andaré ate sugar—see "*SUGAR.*"
The way Múchi ate "kevum"—see "*MUCHI.*"
When deer ate up the corn—see "*DEER.*"
When did pigs eat saffron—see "*PIG.*"
When elephants eat up the corn—see "*ELEPHANTS.*"
When even a small piece of cake is acceptable—see "*CAKE.*"

EBONY

When ebony furniture is a necessity—see "*ADVERSITY.*"

"EDANDA"

The too-erudite Pandit cannot even cross an "édanda."

වැඩි පණ්ඩිතයාට ඒදණ්ඩෙන් යන්ටත් බැරිලු.

[An *édanda* is a plank or beam laid across a river or brook to serve as a bridge.]

EDUCATION—(*See also* "*LEARNING.*")

Education is an indestructible form of wealth.

ඉගෙනීම නොනැසෙන ධනයකි.

The learned wise sit proudly over all,
The proud jump up and precipitately fall,
බණ දන්නෝ ආසන වල වැඩ හිඳී ති
උඩ පැන්නෝ ඒ සැණෙකින් බිම වැටෙ ති

To be educated at Mátara—see "*FATE.*"
Woman educated to write is undesirable—see "*WOMAN.*"

[The Tamil sayings in this connection are:

(*a*) "A well-instructed youth is an old man."
(*b*) "The illiterate who boast of high rank may be compared to dust mixed with paddy (unhusked rice)."
(*c*) "The poverty of the learned is better than the wealth of the unlearned."
(*d*) "Though of low origin, the learned rank with the highest caste."
(*e*) "Wealth without learning is like beauty without chastity."
(*f*) "What country is foreign to a man of learning?"
(*g*) "The king who had learnt his letters tore and threw away his *ola*."

This, as Denham explains, ridicules the idea of any one believing that he has no longer any need of records, when he has once completed his education, but it also reveals the point of view from which education is regarded.]

EEL

Like eating "ánda" flesh with an eacle.
ආඳ මාළු ඉරවුවෙන් කන්නා වගෙයි.

[That is, getting a task, which is repugnant to us, performed by others. The *ánda* is the eel.]

EFFORT

One's own effort is the best effort.
තමන්තෙ මට්ටම් තම්මට්ටම්.

EGG-LAYING

Like coming to lay eggs between two stones.
දෙගල් අස්සෙ බිජු දාන්ඩ ආවා වගෙයි.

[When there is so much more room outside.]

Like the egg-laying of the "kesbá" and hen respectively.
කැස්බාගෙත් කිකිළිගෙත් බිජු දැම්ම වගෙයි.

[The *kesbá* (female of Indian edible turtle, *cholonia virgata*) is said to make no noise even after laying hundreds of eggs, but the cackling of a hen, which has laid one single egg, can be heard in the whole neighbourhood.]

"EHELA"

Rooting out "Ehela" trees—see "*TREE.*"
Tom-toming at "Ehela" Perahera—see "*PERAHERA.*"

EIGHT

Eight brinjals but nine taxes—see "*BRINJALS.*"

ELBOW

The host and the guest's elbow—see "*RICE.*"

ELEPHANTS

Bullocks, too, in addition to elephants.

අලි මදිවට හරක්.

[Something more than a surfeit.]

Is it of any use to take to herb-selling after failing in the trade in elephants ?

අලි විකුණලා බැරිවෙලා තම්පලා විකුණලා හරියයිද ?

Do you want spectacles to distinguish the footprints on the track of elephants ?

අලි ගිය මග අඩි පාර සොයා යන්ට කණ්ණාඩි ඕනෑයෑ ?

Like saying that your hand got raised after shooting at (and missing) the elephant.

ඇතාට විදලාත් අත උස් වුණයි කීවා වගෙයි.

Like the four blind men's description of the elephant.

අන්ධයින් හතර දෙනා ඇතාගෙ ලක්ෂණ කීවා වගෙයි.

[He who felt the leg said the elephant was like a rice-pounder (mortar): he who felt the trunk said the elephant was like the stem of the Papaw tree (*Carica papaya*) ; he who passed his hand over the ear said the elephant was like a bamboo-tree ; and he who felt the tail said the elephant was like a dried coconut flower.]

Like the wood-apple swallowed by the elephant.

ඇතා ගිල්ල දිවුල් ගෙඩිය වගෙයි.

[The wood-apple (Sinh. *Divul*, Sansk. *Kapittha*, Tam. *Nilavilam*, Lat. *Feronia elephantum*) is also known as the elephant-apple. It is a curious fact that a wood-apple swallowed by an elephant passes out absolutely hollow, *i.e.*, without any kernel, the shell being intact.]

Like tying up the mortars (paddy-pounders) of the village because elephants ate up the corn in the field.

කුඹුරේ අලි කෑවාට ගමේ තිබුණ වංගෙඩි බැන්දෙව්වා වගෙයි.

Snipe also go on the same path as elephants

ඇතුන් යන පාරෙ වටුවොත් යනවාලු.

[See under " Sea ' for the similar saying : " Small boats, too, venture upon the sea where big ships sail."]

You cannot bathe an elephant in a " koraha," even when he gets lean.

ඇතා වැරුණත් කොරහේ නාවන්ට බැරිලු.

[For previous reference to the " *koraha*," see under " *DEVIL*."]

When an elephant is stuck in the mud, you want another of stronger and nobler breed to pull him out.

මඩේ හිලුණු ඇතා ගොඩ ගන්ට ඊට වඩා බලසම්පන්න ගජේන්ද්‍රයෙක් ඕනෑ කෙරෙයි.

When elephants fight (lit. "give their tusks") the "tóra" plants in between them are ruined.

ඇත්තු දළ දෙනකොට මැද තිබෙන තෝර ගැටෙනවාලු.

[The *tóra* is the cassia plant of which there are many species in Ceylon.]

Will you have to labour for breath if an elephant tramples you ?

ඇතා පෑගුවාම හුස්ම ගන්ට අමාරුවේද ?

[This saying has been slightly changed to modify the vulgarism of the original.]

A mountain road to bury an elephant—see "*ROAD.*"
Elephants and past wisdom—see "*WISDOM.*"
Elephants unaffrighted by dogs barking—see "*DOG.*"
Elephant-face and rice-face—see "*KINDNESS.*"
Fiddle-playing to a deaf elephant—see "*FIDDLE.*"
Give an elephant to a Pandit—see "*KORAVA.*"
Spreading mats for elephants—see "*PASDUN KORALE.*"
The morrow's elephant—see "*TO-DAY.*"

ELEPHANTIASIS

The fear of the "Cochin-leg"—see "*LEG.*"

ELK-SKIN

Beating the elk-skin at home—see "*DEER.*"

ELOPING

My coconut and my mother—see "*HOSPITALITY.*"

EMERGENCY

When a "kabaragoyá" becomes á "talagoyá"—see "*EATING.*"
When even Mathe Appu is a Vedarála—see "*VEDARALA.*"

EMIT

If you swallow, you'll have to emit—see "*SWALLOWING.*"

EMPLOYMENT

Employ new dhoby, but old barber—see "*DHOBY.*"
The master who gives employment—see "*FRIEND.*"

ENEMY

A wise enemy and a foolish friend—see "*RESPECT.*"

ENMITY

Darkness in enmity to the moon—see "*DARKNESS.*"

ENTRAILS

Giving entrails to a fox to wash—see "*FOX.*"

ENVY

The curse of the envious eye—see "EYE."

ERA

"*Labu-gediya*" *in Buddha-less era*—see "*LABU.*"
In the Kaliyuga age—see "*KALIYUGA.*"
This is not a Vessantara era—see "*VESSANTARA.*"

ESCAPE

You may escape God Saman, but not (his servant) Amangalla.

සමන් දෙවියන්ට හැංගුණත් අමංගලට හැංගෙන්ට බැරිලු.

[Saman Deviyo is the deified half-brother of Rámá, who conquered Ceylon in prehistoric times, and is the guardian-spirit of Adam's Peak. Pilgrims, while climbing the Sacred Hill to worship Buddha's footprint, call on him to aid their ascent. Amangalla is the name of his servant.]

Best jugglery is escape from trouble—see "*JUGGLERY*."
Escaped all seven gallows—see "*GALLOWS*."
Even the Tamby next door will not escape—see "*MOORMAN*."

"ETA-KEHEL"

The wild cat and the "eta-kehel"—see "*PLANTAIN*."

EUROPE—(*See also "OVERSEAS*.")

The cat taken to Europe—see "*CAT*."

EVACUATE

Like evacuating on the plate out of which you eat —see "*PLATE*."
The cat which has evacuated on a rock—see "*CAT*."

EVIDENCE

Cat's evidence in favour of curd—see "*CURD*."
Evidence given by the priest—see "*PRIEST*."

EVIL

No good can come out of evil.

නොහොඳින් හොඳක් නොවේලු.

Forest life in evil times—see "*LIFE*."
Good and evil both come from the mouth—see "*MOUTH*."
Good and evil are like the cart wheel—see "*WHEEL*."

EXCEL

Each man excels in one thing or another—see "*MAN*."

EXTRACT

Trying to extract oil from sand—see "*OIL*."

EYE

Like patting the head and gouging out the eye.

ඉස අතගා ඇහැ උලුප්පනවා වගෙයි.

Like knocking your finger into the eye which is ready to cry.

අඬන්න තියෙන ඇහට ඇඟිල්ලක් ඇන්නා වගෙයි.

The eye gets blinded if you shoot even with a bow of eacle.

ඉරටා දුන්නෙන් විද්දත් ඇහැ කණ වෙනවා.

[The Tamils have a saying, "You may escape the cast of a stone but not the glance of an evil eye." The Sinhalese term for the latter is *es-vaha* (lit. "eye poison")—a curse supposed to be produced by an envious eye.]

The eye will be blinded from the prick even of a golden needle.

රත්රන් ඉඳිකටුව වුණත් ඇනේ ඇනුණොත් කණවෙයි.

The eye will benefit as often as the face is washed.

මුහුණ සේදු තරමට ඇසට සනීපලු.

When one eye is pricked, tears flow from the other eye also.

එක ඇහැකට ඇන්නාම අනිත් ඇහෙනුත් කඳුලු එනවාලු.

[Sympathy between members of one family or community.]

Ghee for a she-buffalo's eye disorder—see "*BUFFALO.*"
The cat's young ones without eyes—see "*CAT.*"

EYE-FLIES.

Oil of eye-flies—see "*MEDICINE.*"
The solitary eye-fly and the "jak" fruit—see "*JAK.*"

FACE

Eye benefited when face is washed—see "*EYE.*"
Rice-face overcomes elephant-face—see "*KINDNESS.*"
Spittle on your own face—see "*SPITTLE.*"

FALL

Like clinging to a thorny branch when about to fall.

වැටෙන්න යනකොට කටු අත්ත අල්ලනවා වගෙයි.

Falling into river to drink strained water—see "*RIVER.*"
If you jump up, you will also fall—see "*JUMPING.*"
Man fallen from all seven gallows—see "*GALLOWS.*"
Pushing one who is about to fall—see "*PUSHING.*"
Saturn's fall into the beggar's bowl—see "*BEGGAR.*"
The fall of fruit from the tree—see "*FRUIT.*"
The proud jump up to fall—see "*EDUCATION.*"
Will the mountain collapse because a dog barks ?—see "*DOG.*"

FAME

Fame abroad and distress (lit. "death-agony") at home.

ලොවට ප්‍රකාශෙ, ගෙදරට මරගාතේ.

A shrine without fame—see "*CHILDREN.*"

FAMILY

Youngest in family worse than slave—see "*SLAVE.*"

FAMILY-NAME

"*Ge-nama*" *the test of respectability*—see "*NAME.*"

FAN

A fan is a luxury in adversity—see "*ADVERSITY.*"

FANAM

Lend a fanam to make friend unfriendly—see "*FRIEND.*"

FATAL

The soles of your feet and fatal spots—see "*SOLES.*"

FATE—(*See also* "*MÁTARA.*")

Having been born for a quarter measure (of rice), can you expect to sift a half-measure ?

පතට ඉපදිලා දෙපතක් ගරන්ට පිළිවන්ද ?

To be born at Kalutara and educated at Mátara is the best fate a man could ever have.

කළුතර උපදින්මත් මාතර ඉගෙනගන්මත් ඇත්නම් මදැයි.

[Lit. "Is it not enough to be born at . . ." Kalutara and Mátara are sea-coast towns of Ceylon, 25 and 100 miles respectively from Colombo. Kalutara has always borne a high reputation for its healthiness, while Mátara has long been famous amongst the Sinhalese for the learning of its priests. See under "MÁTARA" for the saying, "Even after going to Mátara, have you learnt only to scrape coconuts ?"]

Though your hopes are as high as Meru, yet you will get only your deserts.

හිතුවත් මෙර උසට, ලැබෙයි තම කළ කුසල් පමණට.

[Meru is the sacred mountain of mythology, whose height is said to be 168,000 *yojanas* (a *yojana* is about nine miles), 84,000 of which are below the surface of the earth.]

Doctoring for a child born to misery—see "*CHILDREN*."
Sleeping on the road because Gods exist—see "*GOD*."

FATHER

On mother's death, father becomes uncle—see "*MARRIAGE*."
The devil as God-father—see "*HELL*."
The son who does not do what his father did—see "*SON*."
The young silversmith and his father—see "*BADÁLÁ*."
What avails the father when mother dies—see "*MOTHER*."

FATHERLESS

The fatherless child's cry—see "*CHILDREN*."

FAULT

One's own fault is invisible, that of others apparent.

තමා වරදස නොදිස්-නේ, මෙරමා දොස් දිස්නේ.

One's own Meru-like fault appears to him as a mustard seed, while another's mustard-like fault appears to him as Meru.

පර අබසා දොස මෙරසා පෙනෙත් දැයි
තම මෙරසා දොස අබසා පෙනෙත් දැයි

[For previous reference to Meru, see under "FATE."]

FAVOUR

Favour of Kings cannot be an inheritance—see "*KING*."

FEAR

For fear of the master, he (servant) goes to the watch-hut, but for fear of the wild-boar he dares not come out.

හාමුදුව බයේ පැලට යනවාලු, ඌරාට බයේ බිමට බහින්නේ නැතිලු.

[Cf. Eng. "Between the devil and the deep sea."]

Blacksmith's dog has no fear of thunder—see "*DOG*."
Dispelling the fear of the "Cochin-leg"—see "*LEG*."
House-building and the fear of the devil—see "*HOUSE*."

FEAST

Feast time of " haban-kukulo "—see " *BOAR*."
Funereal fare at wedding feast—see " *FOOD*."

FEATHERS

Asking feathers from a tortoise—see " *TORTOISE*."

FEEDING

Sitting on the horn and feeding on the ear.

අඟේ ඉඳගෙන කන කනවාලු.

[This is what the crow does to the ox with a wound in its ear. Its application to human life is obvious—the guest who insults or maltreats his host, for example.]

Is it you who first fed me ?—see " *RICE*."
The pig fed on foeces—see " *PIG*."

FEET

Crown put on the feet—see " *CROWN*."

FEMALE

The destitute brings forth a female child—see " *CHILDREN*."

FENCE

Bunch of plantains jumping over fence—see " *PLANTAINS*."
Cattle in a fenceless garden—see " *CATTLE*."
Fencing a country, but not the tongue—see " *GARRULITY*."
If both the fence and the dam eat up the crop—see " *CROP*."

FERRY

Will the ferry be washed away with bridge ?—see " *BRIDGE*."

FERVOUR

The fervour of hypocrisy—see " *HYPOCRISY*."

FEVER

Like the man in fever asking for water.

උණ කාරයා වතුර ඉල්ලනවා වගෙයි.

FEZ

The Tamby's fez—see " *MOORMAN*."

FIDDLE

Like playing the fiddle to a deaf elephant.

බිහිරි අලියාට වේණා ගාන්නාක් මෙනි.

FIELD

Deer eating up the corn in the field—see " *DEER*."
Elephants eating up the corn in the field—see " *ELEPHANT*."
Scarecrow in a paddy field—see " *PADDY*."

FIEND—(*See " DEVIL."*)

FIG

Watering the unflowering fig—see " *DIMBUL*."

FIGHTING

A struggle on a rock is no friendly struggle.

ගලපිට පොර හාද පොර නොවෙයි.

[In regard to fighting, the Tamils have a saying, "If it can be reached, seize by the *kudumi* ; if not cling to the feet." The *kudumi* is the tuft of hair on the back of the head. This is fast disappearing, especially among the younger generation of present-day Tamils, with whom the short crop has become more fashionable. The point of the above Tamil saying will, therefore, soon be lost. The advice is to submit, if you find you cannot get the better of it. When a fight took place between Tamils, each tried to seize the other by the *kudumi*. The clinging to the feet was not intended to be a wrestler's trick, but an act of submission.]

Like the cobra meeting the "polonga."

නයාට පොළඟා හම්බවුණා වගෙයි.

[A fight to the death is the result. In Sinhalese folklore, the story of the origin of the bitter feud between the two is as follows : During a certain hot season a child was playing inside a tub full of water, and a thirsty cobra drank of it without hurting the child. A thirsty *polonga* (viper) met the cobra and was told where water was to be found, on the *polonga's* promise that it would not injure the child. As the *polonga* was drinking the water, the child playfully struck it and the *polonga* bit him to death. The cobra, who had followed the *polonga*, there and then killed it for breaking its promise. From which day there is said to be bitter hatred between the two.]

Like the Rodiya meeting the Kinnará.

රොඩියාට කින්නරා හම්බවුණා වගෙයි.

[The feud between members of these two low castes is explained in the Rodiyás' own account (as given by Nevill) of their degradation. At Parákrama Báhu's court the venison was provided by a certain Vedda archer, who, during a scarcity of game, substituted the flesh of a boy he met in the jungle, and provided it as venison for the Royal Household. Navaratna Valli, the beautiful daughter of the King, discovered the deception and, impelled by a sudden longing for human flesh, ordered the hunter to bring this flesh daily. The Vedda accordingly waylaid youths in the woods and disposed of their flesh to the Royal kitchen. Tho whole country was terrified by the constant disappearance of youths and maidens. It happened one day that a barber came to the palace to complain of the disappearance of his only son. While waiting for an audience he was given, by the servants at the Royal scullery, a leaf of rice and venison curry. Just as he was about to eat he noticed on his leaf the deformed knuckle of the little finger of a boy. Recognizing it by the deformity as that of his son, he fled from the palace and spread the alarm that the King was killing and eating the youths of the city. The facts then came to light ; and the King, stripping his daughter of her ornaments, and calling up a scavenger then sweeping in a neighbouring yard, gave her to him as wife, and drove her out to earn her living in her husband's class. The Princess and the scavenger fled from the town, and, as night came on, asked for shelter from a Kinnará, but were angrily repulsed. The Kinnará, who was the first person to repulse the founders of the race, is regarded as their hereditary enemy ; and so strong is the feeling between them, that a meeting between the two means a veritable death struggle, in fact "Like the cobra meeting the *polonga*."]

Arguments and umbrella-handles—see "*UMBRELLA*."
Nondi and Siman Pancha after toddy—see "*TODDY*."
Sword not available for battle—see "*SWORD*."

FIGURES

Woman skilled in figures—see " *WOMAN*."

FILE

Trying your teeth upon a file—see " *TEETH*."

FINGER

Are the five fingers of the same length ?

ඇඟිලි පහම එක වාගෙද ?

The swelling of the finger must be proportioned to its size.

ඇඟිල්ලේ තරමට ඉදිමෙන්ට ඕනෑලු.

[Cultivate a sense of proportion.]

A dog masquerade and finger snapping—see " *DOG*."
Hand with a gold ring on finger—see " *RING*."
Knocking your finger into an eye—see " *EYE*."

FINGER-NAIL

The tree that might have been nipped with the nail—see " *TREE*."

FIRE

Like adding straw to a raging fire.

ඇවිළෙන ගින්නට පිදුරු දමන්නා වගෙයි

Like pushing into the fire a sun-scorched man.

අව්වෙන් දැවිච මිනිහා ගින්නට පෙරළුවා වගෙයි.

[Cf. Eng. " Out of the frying pan into the fire."]

Like throwing worms into a fire.

ගින්දරේ පණුවන් දැම්මා වගෙයි.

The bamboo jungle sets itself afire.

උණ වනේ උණ වනෙත්ම ගිනිගන්නවාලු.

[Fires are often caused in bamboo jungles by the friction of the bamboo trees against each other.]

There cannot be smoke without fire.

ගින්නක් නැතිව දුමක් නැතිලු.

A "Pànmaduva" mid "Ginimaduva"—see " *PÁNMADUVA*."
Bubbling gravy does not burn a house—see " *HOUSE*."
Cats taking " jak" seeds out of the fire—see " *CAT*."
Cotton in a house where iron is burnt—see " *COTTON*."
Lighting a cigar from a flaming beard—see " *CIGAR*."
No ash left where camphor is burnt—see " *CAMPHOR*."
Warmed himself to make up for vigil—see " *HOUSE*."

FIREBRAND

It's the same whether you dip a firebrand in hot or cold water.

හුළු අත්ත උණුවතුරෙ දැම්මත් එකයි ඇල්වතුරෙ දැම්මත් එකයි

FIRE-CHARM

Like Isvarayá giving the fire-charm to Bakmasuraya.

ඊශ්වරයා බක්මාසුරයාට අගනි සෑරේ දුන්නා වගෙයි.

[The point of the saying—the confounding of an ungrateful man who seeks to injure his benefactor—will be apparent from the story, which is as follows: Isvarayá (another name for God Siva) had a beautiful spouse named Umayanganávi. She was passionately loved and desired by Bakmasuraya, who had served like a slave under Isvarayá for a period of some seven years. In order to achieve his ignoble purpose, which was possible only by killing Isvarayá, he went to the latter one day, and, as a sort of reward for his years of faithful service, asked Isvarayá for the gift of the knowledge of the "fire-charm." Isvarayá was reputed to be able, after uttering a certain charm over the palm of his hand, to scorch to death immediately any one whose body was touched by that palm, and it was this charm which Bakmasuraya wanted to learn in order to use it against Isvarayá himself. The obliging Isvarayá imparted the required knowledge to Bakmasuraya, who, without delay, uttering the charm over his own hand, approached Isvarayá in order thus to kill him and then possess the beautiful Umayanganávi. The knowing Isvarayá, however, suddenly becoming conscious of the approaching danger, fled with Bakmasuraya in pursuit, and, disappearing from the pursuer's sight for a few seconds, appeared in the guise of a heavenly maid of indescribable beauty, seated on a swing and moving gracefully up and down. Bakmasuraya straightway fell head over ears in love with the seductive maid, whom he there and then asked to marry him, all thought of Isvarayá having fled from his mind. "Men are deceitful creatures," said the maid. "Swear on your head that you will never discard me and I will marry you." Bakmasuraya swore with his hand on his head, and instantaneously the "fire-charm" worked and he was reduced to ashes.]

FIREFLY

Even the firefly frightens the man who has been thrashed with a fire-brand.

ගිනිපෙණෙල්ලෙන් බැටකාපු එකා කනමැදිරියාටත් භයලු.

[Cf. Eng. "A burned child dreads the fire."]

How can a firefly shine in the sun ?

දිවසුරු ඉදිරියේ-කොසේ බැබලෙද කනමැදිරියේ.

FIRE-PLACE

My fire-place knows exactly how I eat.

මා කන හැටි ලිපා දනී.

Andiyás cnd ash from your own fire-place—see "ASH."

FIREWOOD

Sugar-canes to warm yourself when teethless—see "*TEETH.*"

FISH

Like catching a big fish with a small bait.

කුඩා ඇමක් දාලා මහාමාලු මරන්නාවගෙයි.

On a lucky day you can catch fish with twine; but on an unlucky day the fish will break even chains of iron.

වාසනාව තියෙන දවසේදී නූල් පටිනුත් මාලු අල්ලන්ට පුළුවනි, වාසනාව නැති දවසේදී මාලු යකඩ දම්වැලුත් කඩනවාලු.

The fish dies because of its mouth.

මාලුවා නසින්නේ කට නිත්දසි.

[This applies, of course, to fish caught by bait.]

What has the dry-fish seller to do with the price of white sandal-wood?

කරවල වෙළඳාමේ ඇවිත් සුදු සඳුන්වල ගණන් කුමටද?

[Eng. "Let the cobbler stick to his last."]

"Kabaragoyás" eating "Anjilá" fish—see "*KABARAGOYÁ.*"
Putting your hand into a "hunga" hole—see "*HAND.*"
The "Kanaya" and the "Lúla" in the pit—see "*PIT.*"
The "Lúla" that got away—see "*LÚLÁ.*"
Padda-boatman's Maldive fish—see "*UMBALAKADE.*"
The "Tittaya's" day—see "*CRANE.*"

FLEA

The dog-flea in blind man's hand—see "*DOG-FLEA.*"

FLESH

Crow flesh at hand is better than peacock flesh afar off.

ඈත තිබෙන මොනර මසට වඩා ළඟ තිබෙන කපුටු මස හොඳලු.

Like the leaf in which putrid meat had been wrapped up.

කුණු මාලු ඔතාපු කොළේ වගෙයි.

Give a cat to a "Korava"—see "*KORAVA.*"
Man who threatened to eat his child—see "*CANNIBAL.*"
Pig's flesh chopped on its own back—see "*PIG.*"
The crow and flesh-eating—see "*CROW.*"
The crow and peacock flesh—see "*EAT.*"

FLIES

Oil of eye-flies—see "*MEDICINE.*"

FLIGHTINESS

Senile flightiness vaults o'er house-top—see "*OLD.*"

FLOOR

Dancer and floor that was not level—see "*DANCER.*"

FLOWER

Like a flower blossoming among brambles.

කටු ගාලේ පිපුණු මල වගෙයි.

Like flowers blossoming on an "attikká" tree.

අට්ටික්කා ගහේ මල් පිපුණු වගෙයි.

[The *attikká* (*Ficus Glomerata*) never flowers, like the *dimbul*, q.v.]

Like saying of the flower which could not be plucked: "May Buddha accept it as an offering."

කඩන්ට බැරි මල බුදුන්ගේ නමට පූජාවෙච්චාවේ කිව්වාලු.

[Lit. "Let it be offered to the name of Buddha."]

Garlands for monkeys—see "*MONKEY*."
Lotus flower and its stalk—see "*LOTUS*."
The "Labu" flower unfragrant—see "*INGRATITUDE*."
The tavern-keeper's "mal-baliya"—see "*BALI*."
Watering the fig for flowers—see "*DIMBUL*."

FLYING

The white of a crane seen only when flying—see "*CRANE*."

FOLD

Tigers where there's no cattle in the fold—see "*TIGER*."

FOOD

Like going to a wedding feast and receiving funereal fare.

මගුල් කෑමට ගොස් ඉලව් කෑම ලැබුණු වගෙයි.

A curry without cummin—see "*CHILDREN*."
If you must eat beef—see "*BEEF*."
Search for good food in Uva—see "*KURAKKAN*."
Starving though named Hetuhamy—see "*NAME*."
The dog become lean for want of food—see "*DOG*."
The house and bubbling gravy—see "*HOUSE*."
The Vedda and "Goraka" as meat—see "*VEDDA*."

FOOLS

He who cries for mercy the more he is beaten, and he who beats the more the other cries for mercy, are both fools.

ගහන්ට ගහන්ට වඳින එකාත්, වඳින්ට වඳින්ට ගහන එකාත්, දෙන්නම මෝඩයෝලු.

Like the way in which a certain fool tied his "amude."

එක මෝඩයෙක් අමුඩෙ ගැහුවා වගෙයි.

[A fool of a Gamarála, who had gone out one night to catch thieves, sat on a stile and unconsciously tied his truss so as to get entangled in it. Being, however, unable to get away when he attempted to run after the thieves when they came, and thinking that he was held down by someone, he yelled out, "Let me go, Let me go!"]

Though you defeat a hundred Pandits (in argument), you cannot defeat a single fool.

පණ්ඩිතයන් සියෙකුගෙන් දිනතත් මෝඩයකුගෙන් දිනන්ට බැහැ.

A fool and woman's advice—see "*WOMAN*."
The man named "Arrant Fool"—see "*MAN*."
Wise enemy and foolish friend—see "*RESPECT*."
You must be foolish to learn wisdom—see "*WISDOM*."

FOOT

Branch on which your foot had rested—see "*BRANCH*."
The gem which the blind man kicks—see "*GEM*."
Soles of your feet and fatal spots—see "*SOLES*."
Touch foot first to touch the head—see "*HEAD*."

FOOTPRINTS

Looking for footmarks in rapids—see "*WATER*."
Spectacles for elephant footprints—see "*ELEPHANT*."

FORCE

Anger evaporates against 1,000 men—see "*ANGER*."
Ant-eater in the porcupine's hole—see "*ANT-EATER*."

FOREST—(*See also "JUNGLE."*)

Axe-heads and the forest's cry—see "*AXE*."
Civet-cats in sandal-wood forest—see "*CAT*."
The jungle a Royal highway—see "*JUNGLE*."
The forest life in evil times—see "*LIFE*."

FORGE

The dog reared in a forge—see "*DOG*."

FORTUNATE

You cannot contend against the fortunate man.
පිනා එක්ක වතන්න බැහැ.

Dog that barks at fortunate people—see "*DOG*."

FORTUNE

Beauty and fortune of owl—see "*OWL*."
When good fortune comes—see "*PROSPERITY*."
Women's good fortune—see "*WOMAN*."

FOULING—(*See "BEFOULING."*)

FOWL

A wet cock does not feel the cold.
තෙම්වච කුකුළාට සීත නැතිලු.

Like a wet fowl.
තෙම්වච කුකුළා වගෙයි.

Like killing the fowl and handing it to the fox to clean.
මරාපු කුකුළා සුධකරන්ට නරියාට භාරදුන්නා වගෙයි.

Like the fowl of the ancient Capitals.
අනුරාධපුරේ කුකුළා වගෙයි.

[Lit. "Like the fowl of Anurádhapura." There is a Sinhalese saying that, in ancient days, "A fowl could pass from the roof of a house in Polonnaruva to the roof of a house in Anurádhapura without descending to the ground," so thickly was Tamankaduva peopled in those days.]

Like the tail running before the fowl.

කුකුළාට ඉස්සර වෙලා පෙඳේ දිව්වා වගෙයි.

Feast time of "haban-kukulo"—see "*BOAR*."
The comb of a cock seen daily—see "*COMB*."
The fox hides the fowl in the jungle—see "*FOX*."

FOX

"He is smiling" was said of the fox, even when caught in a trap, its mouth twitched in death-agony.

උගුලේ අසුවී නරියා කට ඇරගෙන පණයන්ට එද්දිත් මේක සිනාවෙයි කීවාලු.

Like giving entrails to a fox to wash.

නරියාට බොකු හෝදන්ට දුන්නා වගෙයි.

Like Mr. Fox entangled in a "pamba" thicket.

පඹ ගාලේ පැටලුණ නරි නයිදෙ වගෙයි.

[*Pamba* is a kind of brushwood.]

The fox hides the fowl in the jungle and runs about, dangling a coconut husk from its mouth.

නරියා කුකුළා කැලේ සඟවා පොල්ලෙල්ල ඩැහැගෙන දුවනවාලු.

[To disarm suspicion and put any possible pursuers off the scent.]

Killing the fowl for the fox to clean—see "*FOWL*."
The fox's claim to knowledge of Law—see "*LAW*."

FRAGRANCE

The "Labu" flower unfragrant—see "*INGRATITUDE*."

FRICTION

Charcoal and friction against a stone—see "*CHARCOAL*."

FRIEND

If you want to make a friend unfriendly, lend him a "fanam."

මිත්‍රයෙක් අමිත්‍ර කරගන්ට මනාපනම් ඔහුට පණමක් ණයට දෙන්ටලු.

[A *fanam* is three half-pence or six and a quarter cents.]

The friend who confers happiness is the "Máraya" who gives work.

සැප දෙන මිත්‍රයා වැඩදෙන මාරයාලු.

[For previous reference to *Máraya*, see under "*BUDDHA*."]

The master who gives employment is the friend who gives happiness.

වැඩදෙන ස්වාමියා සැපදෙන මිත්‍රයාලු.

There is no helpful friend like courage.

වීර්‍යය හා සමාන උදව්කාර මිත්‍රයෙක් නැතිලු.

A foolish friend and wise enemy—see "*RESPECT*."
1,000 *coconuts among* 1,000 *friends*—see "*COCONUT*."

FRIENDSHIP

Thing for thing and no friendship besides.

දේට දේ මිසක් වැඩි හාදකම් නැත.

Friendship of short-tailed dog—see "*DOG.*"

FRIGHTEN

Dog barking will not frighten elephants—see "*DOG.*"

FROGS

Even in the lotus pond there are frogs.

මහනෙල් මල් විලෙත් මැඩියෝ ඉන්නවාලු.

[You find the vulgar even in good society, and the cad even among the high-born.]

However high the water may rise, it will only be up to the neck of the frog.

කොපමණ වතුර ගැලුවත් ගෙම්බිත්තාගේ කරවටලු.

Like measuring frogs with a "láha."

ගෙම්බි ලාහෙන් මනින්නා වගෙයි.

[*Láha* is a basket used in measuring paddy.]

Like the frog in a well.

ළිඳේ ඉන්න ගෙම්බා වගෙයි.

[Sees and knows nothing of the world outside.]

The frog, which got upon a silver coin, opened its mouth with the threat to gulp down the elephant.

රිදී කාසිය පිට නැගුණු මැඩියා ඇතා ගිලිම්සි කියා කට ඇරියාලු.

The story of the melted gold frog—see "*MELTING.*"

FRUIT

Its own fruit is not a burden to the creeper.

වැලේ පලගත් ගෙඩිය වැලට බර නැතිලු.

Like a fruit grown out of season.

අකලට පලගත් ගෙඩිය වගෙයි.

Like breaking open a hollow fruit.

පුස්ස බින්දා වගෙයි.

Like the fall of the unripe fruit while the dried one remains on the tree.

වේලිච්ච කෙඩිය ගහේ තිබෙද්දී අමුගෙඩිය වැටුණක් මෙනි.

[The death of an infant, for instance.]

FRYING

An "alu-kobeyiyá" though fried in oil—see "*PIGEON.*"
Frying one's honour—see "*HONOUR.*"

FUNERAL

Funereal fare at a wedding feast—see "*FOOD.*"

FURNITURE

Ebony furniture a necessity in prosperity—see "*ADVERSITY*."

GAIN

Gain by selling camphor—see "*TODDY*."

Losers and gainers among King's servants—see "*KING*."

GAJA-BAHU

King Gaja-Báhu's walking stick—see "*PEN*."

GALLOWS

Like a man who had escaped (lit. "fallen from") a seven gallows.

පෝරක හතෙන්ම වැටිච්ච මිනිහෙක් වගෙයි.

[See under "EARTH" for reference to a man of similar type.]

Woman is a ladder to the gallows—see "*WOMAN*."

GAMA-MAYIYA

Like the "Gama-máyiyá's" hair-cut.

ගමමායියා කොණ්ඩෙ කැප්පුවා වගෙයි.

[A *Gama-máyiyá* is the wife of a *Gama-rála*, i.e., village chief of headman. A certain *Gama-rála* used to give his barber a bag of paddy every year for shaving him. When the barber came to the house one day during the absence of the *Gama-rála*, the *Gama-máyiyá* got her own head shaved in place of her husband's beard, and boasted of her wise act on her husband's return.]

Like the two "Gama-máyiyás'" praise of the cleverness of their respective husbands.

ගමමායියාලා දෙන්නා රාළලාගෙ සමර්ථකම් කීවා වගෙයි.

[When one of them said, "My husband is very clever, for it is a fact that what he writes nobody can read," the other observed, "My husband is cleverer still, for I assure you that what he writes he himself cannot read."]

GAMA-RALA

Like the Gama-rála who got his axe made after tricking the blacksmith.

ආචාරියා රවටා ගමරාළ කැත්ත හැදෙව්වා වගෙයි.

[A Gama-rála went to a blacksmith to get an axe made and gave the latter only the iron, keeping back the steel, thinking by that means to deceive him.]

Like the Gama-rála's "vangediya."

ගමරාළගෙ වංගෙඩිය වගෙයි.

[A *vangediya* is a large wooden mortar used to clean the husk from the rice. A certain young man, visiting his intended bride's house for the first time, was offered a mortar to sit upon by his mother-in-law. A little while after, the mother-in-law wanted the mortar in order to stand on it and get some paddy down from the loft. So she asked the young man to get up for a while, and, after finishing her business, allowed the young man to resume his seat. After the paddy was dried in the sun, the mortar was wanted a second time to pound the paddy in. The young man, on being asked a second time to get up, left the house, in disgust, observing that there was but one mortar to sit upon, to stand on, to pound paddy in, etc.]

Like the " Gama-rála's " shot from his gun.

ගමරාළුගෙ වෙඩිල්ල වගෙයි.

[The wife of a certain Gama-rála was in the habit of hiding herself in the jungle whenever she happened to fall out with her husband. In order to make her give up the habit, the Gama-rála thought out a plan and made her believe that he could shoot anything with his gun, wherever it might be. Having shot an animal at a distance, he hid it in a jungle. After returning home he fired his gun and ordered his servant to go to a certain place and fetch the animal that was killed by the shot. The servant went to the place he was directed to go to and brought back the animal. Never after this did the *Gama-máyiyá* resort to her old habit of hiding herself in the jungle.]

Like the way the Gama-rála went to Heaven.

ගමරාළු දිව්‍ය ලෝකෙ ගියා වගෙයි.

[A certain Gama-rála found one morning his paddy field badly trampled about and traces everywhere of large feet which looked like the impressions made by mortars on the ground. Thinking that the village mortars had run riot in the night on his property, he went to each villager's house and asked as a favour that every mortar should be tied up for the night. This was done but in vain, for the next morning the paddy field was again in a mess, with the same traces of feet as before. That night the Gama-rála kept watch on a tree, and he saw a large white elephant—a creature from Heaven—come on the scene. The Gama-rála hastily clambered down and, as the elephant started running away, he sped behind and clung to his tail. In this way the Gama-rála was taken to Heaven, which he saw was a very wonderful place, and the next day he was brought down to earth by the elephant in the same fashion. Speeding home he related to his wife the tale of his experiences, and she was herself fired to make the trip to Heaven. She sent for the dhoby to bring her clothes quickly, and the dhoby came with his wife. This pair, too, wished to accompany the Gama-máyiyá, and all arranged to meet the elephant in the paddy-field. When at night the animal came the Gama-rála clung to its tail as at first, and his wife, the Gama-máyiyá, clung to her husband's legs. The dhoby woman in her turn clung to the Gama-máyiyá's leg and the dhoby to his own wife's. In this fashion they travelled up through the air, and midway the dhoby woman was struck by an idea. She was curious to find out how dhobies were paid their hire in Heaven, and she inquired whether the Heavenly measure with which they would be paid their *divel* (hire) was larger than the earthly one. " Oh, it is as large as this," said the Gama-rála as he stretched out his hands to show her, and the whole party came down to earth like a bolt from the blue, and died on the spot.]

The " Gama-rála " who has "kurahan" can be made out from his teeth.

ගමරාළට කුරහන් ඇතිබව දතෙන් පෙනේ.

[*Kurahan* or *Kurakkan* (Sansk. *Ragi*, Tam. *Kayur*, Lat. *Eleusine Coracana*) is a food grain used by the poorer classes of the Sinhalese. Being richer in nitrogenous elements than rice, it is a good substitute for it in the case of diabetic patients. It is cooked in the same way as rice. The habitual *Kurakkan* eater has blackish teeth.]

Siman Gama-rála's request to his wife—see " *TOBACCO*."
Story of the Gama-rála's mortar—see " *MORTAR*."
The Gama-rála and his "amude"—see " *FOOL*."
The Gama-rála who went to Ruhuna—see " *KURAKKAN*."

GAME

The kind of game good for Kotte—see "*SPORT.*"
That kind of game won't do—see "*SPORT.*"
That is a hell of a game—see "*SPORT.*"

"GAMPOLAYA"

Like "Gampolaya" and "Rayigamaya."

රයිගමයා සහ ගම්පොළයා වගෙයි.

[*Gampolaya* was the name of a man of Gampola (the ancient capital town near Kandy), and *Rayigamaya* that of a man of Rayigama (a village in the Kalutara district). The two were fast friends. One night they robbed a house, took away a box of jewellery which they carried to the seashore, where they buried it in the sand, and slept over it for safety. Before dawn Gampolaya rose up stealthily, dug up the box quietly, buried it in the sea floor above which the water reached up to his neck, and, returning to his place, slept again. Rayigamaya, awakening a little later and discovering the disappearance of the box, noted that his companion's body was wet. Licking the sleeping man's body, Rayigamaya found that the salt taste stopped at the neck, whereupon he made for the sea, stopped where the water reached his neck, dived, and, scraping the sea floor near his feet, found the precious box. Fleeing from the place with the box in his hand, he hid himself in a big bundle of straw he saw lying in an outhouse near by. Gampolaya, waking soon after and realising the situation, gave chase. Seeing the straw bundle, he guessed that his friend lay hidden within. He saw a *sokade* ("clappers tied around the necks of cattle"), which he put round his neck, and tugged at the bundle of straw. The sound of the clappers made the concealed Rayigamaya believe that it was a bull or cow come to eat the straw. So he jumped out, shouting "*Jah, Jah, Tiger,*" only to be clasped in the arms of Gampolaya. The pair thereupon became friends again, divided the jewellery equally between them, and, hand in hand, started on the homeward journey.]

GARDEN

Like leasing out the garden and grimacing at a coconut slice.

වත්ත බදු දීලා ඇස්සට දත නියවනවාලු.

Cattle in a fenceless garden—see "*CATTLE.*"
Nettles in your own garden—see "*NETTLES.*"

GARDENER

If a thief and gardener combine—see "*THIEF.*"
Thief found to be the gardener—see "*THIEF.*"

GARLAND

What garlands for monkeys—see "*MONKEY.*"

GARRULITY—(See also "*TALK.*")

You can fence even a whole country round, but you cannot fence the tongue.

රට වටකර වැට බඳිතත් කට වටකර වැට බඳින්ට බැරිලු.

GATE

Barking of dogs at the gate—see "*DOG.*"

“GAVVA ”

The “ gavva ” and the “ ambalama ”—see “ *AMBALAMA*.”
The “ labba ” two “ gavvas ” away—see “ *LABBA*.”
The Valave-ganga seven “ gavvas ” away—see “ *AMUDE*.”

GAZING

Gazing at clear water—see “ *WATER*.”

GEM

Can a blind man make out and pick up the gem which his foot strikes against ?

මැණික් ගලේ පය හැපුණට කණා ඇහිඳලා ගනීද ?

Though it lie in a heap of filth, a gem is a gem for all that.

කසළ ගොඩේ තිබුණත් මැණික මැණිකමයි.

The Tamby who sees gems—see “ *MOORMAN*.”
The young of the Loris a gem to her—see “ *LORIS*.”

“ GE-NAMA ”

“ Gé-nama ” as test of respectability—see “ *NAME*.”

“ GERANDIYA ”

No charms for the “ gerandiyá ”—see “ *SNAKE*.”

GHEE

Like applying (buffalo) ghee on both sides.

දෙපැත්තේ දුන්තෙල් ගාන්නා වගෙයි.

[Cf. Eng. “ To butter both sides of one's bread ”—to gain advantages from two parties at one time.]

The ghee of a she-buffalo—see “ *BUFFALO*.”

GIFT

The gift of a gift is the best of all gifts.

තෑග්ගෙන් තෑග්ග උතුම් තෑග්ගලු.

A gift of cloth to a dancer—see “ *DANCER*.”
A son with the “ gift of the gab ”—see “ *CHILDREN*.”
Gift of coconut trees from river bottom—see “ *COCONUT*.”
Kaluhámy's father's gift—see “ *KALUHÁMY*.”
Sluggard's gift of prophecy—see “ *PROPHECY*.”

GILIMALE

Even on the coast of Soli there are starving men, and even in Gilimale there are white-teethed people.

සොලී කරෙත් ඇතිලු බඩ පුප්පන්නෝ, ගිලිමලෙත් ඇතිලු දත සුද්දෝ

[The “ coast of Soli,” or the Coromandel coast, was reputed for its prosperity. Gilimale, a village in the Ratnapura district, was remarkable for the excellence (and quantity) of the betel it produced. No persons who habitually chew betel are white-teethed.]

GIRL

A girl, after ten, must be affianced—see “ *MARRIAGE*.”
The verses of the Ranchagoda girl—see “ *VERSES*.”

GIVING

Giving coconut trees from river bottom—see "*COCONUT.*"
Giving entrails to a fox to wash—see "*FOX.*"
Giving milk to a venomous serpent—see "*MILK.*"
Giving the hand and mocking—see "*MOCKING.*"

GLEANING

Time when children can glean—see "*CULTIVATION.*"

GLITTER

The fault of the other man glitters—see "*FAULT.*"

GOAT

The goat and the lowly barber—see "*BARBER.*"

GOD

Like sleeping on the road because Gods exist.

දෙසියන්නේ පලියට පාරේ බුදියාගන්නා වගෙයි.

[That is, to protect you.]

Eating the rice of the Gods—see "*RICE.*"
Escape from God Saman—see "*ESCAPE.*"
Snake on God Saman's neck—see "*SNAKE.*"
The God and the Kapurála's son—see "*KAPURÁLA.*"

GOD-FATHER

The devil as God-father—see "*HELL.*"

GOLD

Even the crow on a golden rock has a golden hue.

රන් පව්වේ සිටින කපුටත් රන් පැහැයලු.

A gold vessel for the lion's grease—see "*LION.*"
Eye blinded by a golden needle—see "*NEEDLE.*"
Gold on a pig's snout—see "*PIG.*"
Hand with a gold ring—see "*RING.*"
"*Masuran*" *in bread for the sinner*—see "*SINNER.*"
Pain of stab with a golden weapon—see "*WEAPON.*"
The chameleon with gold ornament—see "*CHAMELEON.*"
The needle changed into gold—see "*NEEDLE.*"
The parrot's cage of gold—see "*PARROT.*"
The story of the melted gold frog—see "*MELTING.*"

GOLDSMITH

The associate of a goldsmith—see "*BADÁLÁ.*"
The goldsmith and his mother—see "*BADÁLÁ.*"
The goldsmith and ornaments of fine gold—see "*DHOBY.*"
Tricks of a goldsmith and weaver—see "*DHOBY.*"

GONAGALA

The "Gónagala" does not feel the beating of the waves.

ගෝනගලට රළ ගැහුවාට නොදැනේලු.

[*Gónagala* is a small rock at the mouth of the Pánadura river.]

GOOD

Good and evil are like the cart wheel—see " *WHEEL.*"
Good and evil both come from the mouth—see " *MOUTH.*"
No good can come out of evil—see " *EVIL.*"

" GORAKA "

The monkey that ate " goraka "—see " *GORAKA.*"
The Vedda and " goraka "—see " *VEDDA.*"

GOSSIP

Scratching begets more scratching, and gossip begets more gossiping.

කසිත් කසිත් කස් බෝවේ, බසිත් බසිත් බස් බෝවේ.

GOURD

" *Labu-gediya " in Buddha-less era*—see " *BUDDHA.*"
Lime-cutting within the gourd—see " *LIME-CUTTING.*"
The hand that plucks the long gourd—see " *HAND.*"

GRANDFATHER

Like the death of a grand-son to a grand-father who weeps for nothing.

නිකම් හඬන මුත්තාට මුනුපුරෙක් මැරුණා වගෙයි.

On a wedding day, even the grand-father is a stranger.

මඟුල් දාට මුත්තත් අමුත්තයි.

[That is, his relationship must not be held to deprive him of any of the ceremony and courtesy due to the stranger guest. In other words, everybody must be treated alike on such a day.]

Even the grand-father talks " Bana."

මුත්තා කියන්නෙත් බණ.

[The grand-children naturally expect the grand-father to talk to them about other things than *Bana* ; but when even he begins preaching, they feel it is going beyond their endurance.]

Like the day the grand-mother died.

ආච්චි මැරිච්ච දවස වගෙයි.

[A great day for those who had long been looking forward to the distribution of her rich hoard of accumulated savings and other valuables—a hoard invariably more precious than grand-father's.]

Grand-father and grand-son—see " *CHAIR.*"
Grand-father Lavanchi's last advice—see " *LAVANCHI.*"

GRASS

Lion never eats grass, however hungry—see " *LION.*"
Where there is grass no cattle graze—see " *CATTLE.*"

GRATITUDE

The Kevula shows no gratitude—see " *INGRATITUDE.*"

GRAVY

The house and bubbling gravy—see " *HOUSE.*"

GREASE

A gold vessel for the lion's grease—see " *LION.*"

GREAT MEN

Great men and good qualities—see "*MAN.*"

GRIMACE

Making grimaces at a coconut slice—see "*COCONUT.*"

GRINDER

If the grinder is good, so will the coconut be.

ගල හොඳනම් පොලුත් හොඳලු.

[As being well ground.]

When one blow follows another, even the grinder begins to run.

එක පිට එක වදින කොට මිරිස් ගලත් දුවනවාලු.

[The grinder is a heavy stone.]

GROUND

The screw-pine on the ground—see "*PINE.*"

GROWING

A thing grows quickly to die quickly—see "*SCYTHE.*"
Non-growth is due to "Karma"—see "*KARMA.*"

GRUEL—See also ("*MILK.*")

As it is hot it cannot be drunk, and being gruel it cannot be thrown away.

උණු නිසා බොන්ටත් බැහැ, කැඳ නිසා අහක ලන්ටත් බැහැ.

[In a variant, "milk" is substituted for "gruel."]

GUARDING

Guarding deserted huts—see "*HOUSE.*"

GUEST

Host's sincerity towards guest—see "*RICE.*"

GUM

The gum of one's own teeth is better than another's axe.

අනුන්ගේ පොරවට වඩා තමන්ගේ විදුරු මස හොඳලු.

GUN

The Gama-rála's shot from his gun—see "*GAMA-RALA.*"

GUNNY BAG

Like covering the new (article) with a gunny bag.

අලුත් පිටට ගෝණිය කැදලුවා වගෙයි.

"GURU"

The way the wilful "guru" goes—see "*OBSTINACY.*"

"GURUNANSE"

The Palliye-gurunánse and his fee—see "*PALLIYE.*"

GYPSIES

The gypsy tribe of Áhikuntakayás—see "*KORAVA.*"

"HABAN-KUKULO"

Feast time of "haban-kukulo"—see "*BOAR.*"

HABIT

(One's) Habit is greater than (one's) nature.

ජම්මෙට වැඩිය පුරුද්ද ලොකුයි.

HAILSTORM

There is certain to be a hailstorm when the unlucky man gets his head shaved.

කාලකණ්ණියාගේ ඉසකේ බානකොට ගල් වර්ෂාව සත්තකයි.

[A variant is, " It hailed on the day the sinner's head was shaved.]

Wherever the sinner goes, there is hailstorm—see " *SINNER.*"

HAIR—(See also "*FIGHTING.*")

Andrisa is Andrisa even if his hair is cut.

කෙස්ස කැපුවත් අන්දිරිසා අන්දිරිසාමයි.

If you have hair, you can tie it up in all four directions.

කොන්ඩේ ඇත්නම් හතරඟටම බැන්දෑකිලු.

[A variant is, " If you have hair, what way can you not tie it"?]

A single hair of cattle and the tiger—see " *TIGER.*"

" HAL "—(See " *RICE.*")

" HAMY "

The " Pidi-bat " Hámy is bigger than the " Geyi-Hámy."

ගෙයි හාමිට වඩා පිඩි බත් හාමි ලොකුයි.

HAND

Getting your hand burnt whilst having the pincers.

අඬුව තිබෙද්දී අත පුලුස්සා ගන්නා වගෙයි.

It is the same hand that plucks the " Labba " as well as the " Puhula "

ලබ්බට තිබු අතලු පුහුලටත් තියන්නේ.

[The *labba*, *labu-gediya*, or *diya-labu* is the fruit known as the " Long Gourd," " Bottle Gourd " and " Calabash Cucumber " (Lat. *Lagenaria Vulgaris*, Sansk. *Alabu*, Tam. *Shorakai*). The fruit grows to a considerable size and the dried fruit, cleaned of its contents, serves as a good vessel for carrying fluids, and is used as such especially by toddy-drawers, who find it a convenient vessel in which to bring toddy down from the trees. The *Puhula* (Sansk. *Kushmanda*, Tam. *Kumbuli*) is of two varieties, the " Pumpkin " or " Vegetable marrow " (*Cucurbita pepo*) and the " Ash-pumpkin " (*Benincasa cerifera*, Tam. *Punchini*), which is the *Alu-puhul* of the Sinhalese.]

Kissing the hand that cannot be cut off.

කපන්ට බැරි අත සිඹින්නා වගෙයි.

Like putting your hand into a " hungas' " hole.

හුංගේ ඇති වලේ අත දමුවා වගෙයි.

[The *hunga* is a small sort of prickly fish found in rivers.]

Like the drop of quicksilver poured into the palm (of your hand).

අල්ලේ වක්කරපු රසදිය බින්දුව වගෙයි.

The light (i.e. life) of this "magul-sakvala" is good enough even for the brief moment that it takes one to stretch out a bent hand.

වක්කළ අත දික්කරන තුරු මගුල් සක්වළ එළිය හොඳලු.

[*Magul* "fortunate," *sakvala* "universe," is an epithet applied to this world by Buddhists, in consequence of its being favoured with the religion of the Buddha.]

What you have not in your hand may as well be (looked for) beyond the seas.

අතේ නැත්නම් මූදින් එතර තිබුණත් එකයි.

You cannot expect to move the mouth without moving the hands.

අත හොලවන්නේ නැතුව කට හොලවන්ට බලාපොරොත්තු වෙන්ට බැහැ.

[One cannot obtain a living without working for it.]

Your hands and feet are the same, even if you go to Tuttukudi.

තුත්තුකුඩි ගියත් ඒ අත පයමයි.

[Tuttukudi, on the southern coast of India, is another form of Tuticorin.]

Your own hand is the shelter (protection) for your own head.

තමා හිසට තම අතමය සෙවණැල්ල.

A bee-hive breaker will lick his own hand—see "*BEEHIVE.*"
A knock from a hand having a gold ring—see "*RING.*"
Congee and the short-spoon in hand—see "*SPOON.*"
Giving your hand and mocking—see "*MOCKING.*"
Hand getting raised when shooting—see "*ELEPHANT.*"
Hand in "Koraha" in a hurry—see "*HURRY.*"
Hand-clapping of the deaf man—see "*DEAF.*"
Hand-holding and host's sincerity—see "*RICE.*"
Jaggery and coconut in hand—see "*JAGGERY.*"
Man with a club in hand—see "*POTTER.*"
Washing your hand in honey—see "*MILK.*"
Water from any well with jaggery in hand—see "*JAGGERY.*"

HAPPINESS

Employer who gives happiness—see "*FRIEND.*"
Friend who confers happiness—see "*FRIEND.*"

HARE

Shot at hare but hit the bush—see "*SHOOTING.*"

HAT

You can know the " Sinno " by his hat.

සිඤ්ඤොගෙ හැට් තොප්පියෙන් දනේ.

[*Sinno*, a corruption of *Signor*, is to-day a contemptuous term among the Sinhalese for anybody who wears trousers and a hat. As Mr. Donham observes in his *Report on the Census*, the saying has no point to-day when Sola topees, bowlers and straw hats are common wear, and at village weddings the bridegroom frequently appears in a high hat.]

The Tamby's hat—see " *MOORMAN*."

HEAD

If you dash your head against a rock, what will get smashed is not the rock but the head.

ගලේ හිස හැපීමෙන් හිස පොඩිවෙනවා මිස ගල පොඩි නොවෙයි.

If you want to touch the head, first touch the foot.

ඉස අල්ලන්ටනම් පළමුවෙන් කකුල අල්ලන්ටලු.

[Cf. Eng. " Stoop to conquer."]

Ant-eater's life is in its head—see " *ANT-EATER*."
Crown which ought to be worn on head—see " *CROWN*."
Dust rising up to one's own head—see " *DUST*."
Is there a mouth above the head ?—see " *MOUTH*."
Patting the head to gouge out the eye—see " *EYE*."
Temple crashing over man's head—see " *RELIGION*."
The shade for your own head—see " *HAND*."
When the sinner's head was shaved—see " *SINNER*."
When the unlucky man shaves his head—see " *HAILSTORM*."

HEADACHE

Even the headache of another is good.

අනුන්ගේ හිස රදෙත් හොඳලු.

More common than the yam is " Kos," commoner still is the headache.

අලට වැඩිලු කොස්, ඊටත් වැඩිලු හිස රදේ.

[*Kos* here is the seed of the fruit of the Jak tree (*Artocarpus integrifolia*), the wood of which is so much valued as timber for building purposes and also for making furniture of all sorts. The seed provides a popular food.]

Like changing your pillow to ease your headache.

හිස රදේට කොට්ටෙ මාරු කළා වගෙයි.

HEADMAN

Eight brinjals and nine taxes—see " *BRINJALS*."
Good to be a Headman even in Hell—see " *RANK*."
Lamp lit for the Headman's use—see " *LAMP*."

HEALING ART

If you cannot be a King—see " *KING*."

HEART

He has a heart of stone who is unable to run.

දුවන්ට බැරි අයගේ ලය ගලලු.

How can there be a heart if there's no bile ?

පිත් නැත්නම් හිත් කොයින්ද ?

Poison in the heart—see " *HONEY.*"

HEAVEN

The way the Gama-rála went to Heaven—see "*GAMA-RÁLA.*"

HELL

The road to Hell is easy if the Devil becomes your god-father.

යක්ෂයා පක්ෂවුණොත් නරකාදි යාම ලේසියි.

The wily can escape Hell.

උපා දන්නෝ අපා නොවැටෙත්.

[Tactful people will not " put their foot into it."]

Good to obtain rank even in Hell—see " *RANK.*"

HELP

Darkness helpful to thieves—see " *DARKNESS.*"
Relations who do not help—see " *RELATIONS.*"

HEMP

Prosperity and ropes of hemp—see " *PROSPERITY.*"

HEN

Like the hen hatching duck eggs.

කිකිළි තාර බිත්තර රැක්කා වගෙයි.

[As soon as they grow a little, the ducklings abandon the chickens and take to their own brood.]

Hen reared by talkative woman crows—see " *WOMAN.*"
Egg-laying of the tortoise and the hen—see " *EGG-LAYING.*"

HERBS

" If we are of one mind let us live even on boiled herbs ; otherwise let us separate," said a certain woman.

"එක හිත්නම් තම්බා කමු පලාවත්, වෙන හිත්නම් යමු කාවත් බලාවත්" කියා ගෑණියක් කීවාලු.

Herb selling after failure in elephant trade—see " *ELEPHANT.*"
Mad woman's basket of herbs—see " *MAD.*"
Throw not the herbs you have plucked—see " *DEER.*"

HERD

Herd of cattle entrusted to care of tiger—see " *TIGER.*"

HERMIT

Even the devil wants to be a hermit in old age.

මහලු වුණම යකාත් තපස් රකින්ට කැමතිලු.

" HETU-HAMY "

Starving though named Hétu-hámy—see " *NAME.*"

HIDING

Hiding jaggery in a water course—see " *JAGGERY.*"
Hiding one's own fault—see " *FAULT.*"
Hiding salt on the back of a "Diya-kává"—see "*DIYA-KÁVÁ.*"
When respectability hides itself in the jungle—see " *MONEY.*"

HIGHWAY

When the jungle is a Royal highway—see " *JUNGLE.*"

HINDRANCE

No hindrance when death comes—see " *DEATH.*"

" HINGURU "

In cases of necessity, even the " Hinguru " creeper is good to cling on to.

අසීරුවට හිඟුරු වැලෙත් එල්ලෙන වාලු.

[The *Hinguru* is a climbing prickly plant with saponaceous legumes (Lat. *Acacia concinna—Leguminosae*).]

HIP-BONE

Boxing cannot cure dislocated hip—see " *BOXING.*"

" HIRALUVA "

" *Sangha's* " *language and ex-priests*—see " *BUDDHISM.*"
Two wives to atone for ex-priest's celibacy—see " *BUDDHISM.*"

HIRING

The cloth hired out by a dhoby—see " *DHOBY.*"

HOE

Like saying the earth from the hoe (mammoty) reaching (no further than) the loin-cloth (of the digger.)

උදැල්ලේ පස් බඩ තුරටසි කිවා වගෙසි.

HOLE

Basket full of holes—see " *WATER.*"

HONEY

Like pouring honey into the ear.

කනෙත් මීපැණි වක්කරනවා වගෙසි.

[Praising a man highly within his hearing.]

Though there is honey at the root of the tongue, yet there is poison in the heart.

දිව මුල මීපැණි තිබුණත් හෘදය තුළ විෂලු.

Where there is honey, there is no lack of ants.

පැණි තියෙන තැන ඇඹිලියෝ හිඟ නැහැ.

Ant in a pot of honey—see " *ANT.*"
Washing your hand in honey—sce " *MILK.*"

HONOUR

Like frying one's honour.

වංශය කබල් ගෑවා වගෙයි.

[The parents, who had given away their daughter in marriage to a poor man on account of his high birth, went to see the daughter some time after the marriage. The daughter had nothing in the house to offer her parents to eat. So, in a fit of rage, she went and placed an old frying-pan over the fire and pretended as if she were stirring up its contents. When asked by the old pair what she was doing, she replied : " I am trying to fry the honour you got for me."]

HOOK

Iron hook for tamarind fruit—see " *TAMARIND*."

HOPE

Will bridge and ferry be both washed away ?—see " *BRIDGE*."
Hopes as high as Meru—see " *FATE*."

HORN

Giving horns to a horse—see " *HORSE*."
Horn grown longer than ear—see " *EAR*."
Horse not getting horns—see " *HORSE*."
Sitting on horn and feeding on ear—see " *FEED*."

HORNET

Like throwing stones at the nest of the hornet.

දෙබරෙට ගල් ගැහුවා වගෙයි.

[The nest of the hornet (*debaraya*) is usually built of clay, is attached to the branches of trees and is as large as a common basket or beehive. The sting of the *debara*, a large species of the wasp or hornet (Lat. *Spea ferruginea*, order *Hymenoptera*) is so exceedingly poisonous that the Sinhalese will sooner forfeit the fruit of a tree where this nest is built than attempt to destroy it.]

HOROSCOPE

What's the use of consulting the horoscope when the man is dead ?

මළගිය අයගේ කේන්ද්‍රය බැලුවාසින් කවරනම් ප්‍රයෝජනද ?

HORSE

Like giving horns to a horse.

අශ්වයාට අං දුන්නා වගෙයි.

Like the horse not getting horns.

අශ්වයාට අං නොලැබුණා වගෙයි.

You want both to buy a horse for two pice and also one that could jump over the wall.

තුට්ටු දෙකට අශ්වයා ගන්නත් ඕනෑ, තාප්පෙට උඩින් පනින්නත් ඕනෑ.

Gift of a horse as dowry—see " *KALUHÁMY*."

HOSPITALITY

Like eating my young coconuts and even running away with my mother to the bargain.

වැවරයත් කාලා අම්මත් කැටුව ගියා වගෙයි.

[This remark—to illustrate gross abuse of hospitality—was uttered by a man. of whom permission was asked by a stranger to break a young coconut in order to assuage his hunger and thirst. The permission was granted. The stranger ate and drank his fill and then persuaded the other's mother, who happened to be in the garden at the moment, to run away with him.]

Like showing your hospitality at another's wedding.

අනුන්ගෙ මගුල් දාට තමුන්ගෙ ආදරේ පෙන්වන්නා වගෙයි.

[Liberality at the expense of others. Cf. Eng. "Cocks are free of horse-corn."]

Letting you go and holding you by elbow—see "*RICE.*"

HOST

Host's sincerity towards guest—see "*RICE.*"
The host and the guest's elbow—see "*RICE.*"

HOT

Firebrand in hot water—see "*FIREBRAND.*"

HOUSE

A congee-drinking house is better than a non-eating house.

නොකා ඉන්න ගෙදරට වඩා හොඳයි කැඳ බොන ගෙදර.

[That is, it is better to live in a house where at least congee is drunk rather than in a house where the inmates starve.]

Do not build your house in a cemetery if you are afraid of the Devil.

යකාට බය නම් සොහොනේ ගෙය නොසාදනු.

Like guarding deserted huts.

පාලු පැල් රැක්කා වගෙයි

Like leaving your own doors open and chasing dogs from another's house.

තමන්ගේ ගෙයි දොර ඇර තබා අනුන්ගේ ගෙදර බල්ලන්ට ගහන්ට ගියා වගෙයි.

The house will not catch fire if the gravy (soup) bubbles over.

හොදි උතුරා ගෙය ගිනි නොගනී.

The lowliest thing in a house is the threshold.

ගෙට නිවට එලිපත්තලු.

[Because everybody tramples it, even the low-caste beggar who comes for alms.]

Warmed himself (at the fire) to make up for his vigil in the watch-hut.

පැල් ලැග්ගා ගිනි තැප්පාට හිලව්ලු.

A house without an infant—see "*CHILDREN.*"
A tank-breach and a widow in the house—see "*WOMAN.*"
Cotton in a house where iron is burnt—see "*COTTON.*"
Fame abroad and death-agony at home—see "*FAME.*"
Nothing to sit upon in carpenter's house—see "*CARPENTER.*"
Old people in a house without infants—see "*OLD.*"
Returning from wedding-house—see "*CAKE.*"
Senile flightiness vaults o'er house-top—see "*OLD.*"
Size of house does not indicate "Walauwa"—see "*RANK.*"
Smell of meat in house and dogs—see "*DOG.*"
Staple for a bolt in the house—see "*CHILDREN.*"
The fowl of the ancient capitals—see "*FOWL.*"
The "Geyihámy" and "Pidibat Hámy"—see "*HÁMY.*"
The tiger on the roof—see "*TIGER.*"
Thief and master of house combining—see "*THIEF.*"
Veddas speaking of building houses—see "*VEDDAS.*"
Water-drawing to wedding-house—see "*WATER.*"
"We earn our living in the same house"—see "*MARRIAGE.*"
Winnowing-fans for the house—see "*WINNOWING-FAN.*"

HOUSE-NAME

"Ge-nama" the test of respectability—see "*NAME.*"

HOVELS

Hovels as well as palaces in every country—see "*COUNTRY.*"

HUE

The crow on a golden rock—see "*COLOUR.*"

HUNCHBACK

Can a hunchback be forced to walk erect ?

කුදු මිනිහාට කෙළින් වෙලා යන්ට කියා බලකළාට යන්ට පිළිවන්ද?

HUNGER

Hunger knows no taste.

බඩ ගින්න රස නොදනීලු.

HUNTING

Like going to the chase with curs when you have hunting-dogs tied up at home.

දඩයම් බල්ලන් බැඳ තබාගෙන මගෝඩි බල්ලන් ගෙන ගියා වගෙයි.

A python hunt—see "*SNAKE.*"
"Ánam" and deer-hunting—see "*ÁNAM.*"
Killing animals behind decoy—see "*BUFFALO.*"
Killing iguanos after worship at Dambul—see "*DAMBULLA.*"

HURRAH

Hurrah for the winning side—see "*VICTORY.*"

HURRY

In a hurry you sometimes cannot put your hand even into a "Koraha."

ඉක්මනට කොරස් කටෙත් අතලන්ට බැරිලු.

[The *Koraha* is a large chatty.]

The cat in a hurry to bring forth—see "*CAT.*"
Silversmith taking up hurried work—see "*BADÁLÁ.*"

HUSBAND

A husbandless woman like sand in river—see "*MARRIAGE.*"
A Korava as husband—see "*KORAVA.*"
Husband's poverty or age immaterial—see "*MARRIAGE.*"
Quarrel between husband and wife—see "*MARRIAGE.*"
The husband at Migamuva—see "*TALK.*"
Two Gama-máyiyás' husbands—see "*GAMA-MÁYIYÁ.*"

HUSK

Fox with a coconut husk in mouth—see "*FOX.*"

HUT

The servant and the watch-hut—see "*FEAR.*"

HYPOCRISY

Hypocritical fervour is a three-fold sin.

ප්‍රයෝග භක්තිය තුන් ඉරට්ට පාපය වේ.

[In application for a hypocrite, the Jamaicans say "Some people clean a top (i.e. on top) an' dutty underneat'.]

IGUANOS

Hunting iguanos on return from worship—see "*DAMBULLA.*"

ILLITERATE

Advice by the illiterate—see "*ADVICE.*"
Illiterate Tamby Appu as Vedarála—see "*VEDARÁLA.*"
Illiterate who boast of high rank—see "*EDUCATION.*"
Wealth of the unlearned—see "*EDUCATION.*"

ILLNESS—(See also "*SICKNESS.*")

It is not by eating "bali" that illness is cured.

ලෙඩ හොඳ වෙන්නේ බලි කාලා නොවෙයි.

Medicine before illness—see "*MEDICINE.*"
The tail is the illness—see "*TAIL.*"
The thirst of a dropsical man—see "*DROPSY.*"

IMAGE

An image is like a sweetmeat to the man who has swallowed a "Vihára."

වෙහෙර ගිල්ල මිනිහාට පිළිමේ අග්ගලාවක්ලු.

[A variant (see under "Devil") is "An image is like an *aggaláva* to the Devil who has gulped down a Buddhist priest." A *Vihára* is, of course, a Buddhist temple.]

“ IMBUL ”

“ Imbul ” cotton in house where iron is burnt—see “*COTTON.*”
Poverty lighter than “ imbul ” cotton—see “ *POVERTY.*”

“ INAGGODA ”

Marriage proposed by Inaggoda people—see “ *MARRIAGE.*”

“ INAME ”

Andiyás of the same “ iname ”—see “ *ANDIYÁS.*”

INFANTS

Old people in a house without infants—see “ *OLD PEOPLE.*”

INGRATITUDE

Ungrateful is the “ Kevulá,” and unfragrant the “ Labu-mala.”

කෙවුලා ගුණේ නැත, ලබු මල සුවඳ නැත.

[*Kevulá* is a contemptuous term for a man of the “ Fisher ” caste. *Labu-mala* is the “ flower of the *Labu* tree,” q.v.]

INHERITANCE

Favour of Kings cannot be an inheritance—see “ *KING.*”

INJUSTICE

Same treatment to water-drawer and pot-breaker—see “ *MAN.*”

INSOLENCE

Insolence in others' villages—see “ *VILLAGE.*”

INVITATION

Sincerity of host's invitation to eat—see “ *RICE.*”

IRON

Like the iron kept for safe custody getting a sort of purging disease.

පුවෙසමට තැබූ යකඩේ ඇලියාවට හිටියා වගෙයි.

[The term rendered by “ purging disease ” is *eḷiyáva*, which is really “ a disease in which the belly is swelled.”]

Cotton in a house where iron is burnt—see “ *COTTON.*”
Eating even iron coconuts—see “ *TEETH.*”
Fish breaking iron chains—see “ *FISH.*”
The blacksmith and the malleable iron—see “ *BLACKSMITH.*”
The iron hook for the tamarind—see “ *TAMARIND.*”
The iron style of the writer—see “ *PANHINDA.*”

JACKAL—(See also “ *FOX.*”)

Like the jackal entrapped in the Island.

දූවට අසුවුණු හිවලා වගෙයි.

JAGGERY

Cry not for the lost jaggery, but preserve the jaggery you still have.

ගිය හකුරට නාඬන්නේ, තිබෙන හකුර රැක ගන්නේ.
[Cf. Eng. “ To cry over spilt milk.”]

If I have jaggery and coconut in my hand, what does it matter of what river I drink ?

අතේ හකුරුත් පොලුත් තිබෙනවානම් කොයි ගඟෙන් වතුර බිව්වත් මොකද?

[Note its application in the following verse :

නයි වගේ වයිර අප දුටුවාම කිතේ
ලෙයි තිගේ කොහෙත්වත් කරුණාව නැතේ
ඇයි මගේ හකුරු පොල් තිබුණි නම් අතේ
කොයි ගඟේ දියත් දියවර නොවෙද කතේ

" Like a cobra thou art angry, when thou seest me,
No pity whatever dwells in thy breast ;
Why, O woman, what matters of what river I drink,
So long as I have jaggery and coconut in my hand ?"

Jaggery in hand, you can get water from any well.

අතේ හකුරු ඇත්නම් කොයි ළිඳෙන් දිය ඇතිලු.

Jaggery on top, scissors underneath.

උඩින් හකුරු යටින් කතුරු.

Like hiding jaggery in a " vakkade."

වක්කඩේ හකුරු හැංගුවා වගෙයි.

[A *vakkade* is a hole or opening in a dam to let off the water from the paddy-fields. It may, therefore, be translated here as "water-course."]

Like the remark of the " Sudu-hakura."

සුදු හකුරාගෙ කීම වගෙයි.

[To the query as to the way in which the jaggery was prepared for the use of the Sinhalese King, the answer was : "A white canopy above, a carpet on the floor, a screen of white cloth all round ; the workers first bathe, then wear a clean white dress, and, after tying a white cloth over their mouths to prevent their breath contaminating the preparation in hand, they sit to their work." Investigation as to whether the man's deeds were as good as his words showed, however, a different picture. The man who went to see the jaggery-makers at work saw instead only the jaggery-boys sprawling about, licking the pots, pans and other vessels used in the preparation.]

Cake costing nothing in jaggery—see "*CAKE.*"
Loading a bull with jaggery—see "*BULL.*"

JAK

Like a solitary eye-fly, flying away from the core of a mellow jak fruit.

වැල වහල්ලෙන් කෝදුරුවෙක් ඉගිලුණා වගෙයි.

[The one which flew away was one out of ten thousand or more.]

" Jak " also (goes to the place) where there is rice.

බත් ඇති තැනටමයි කොසුත්.

Cats taking roasted " jak " seeds out of fire—see "*CAT.*"
Headache commoner than yams and "jak"—see "*HEADACHE.*"

"Jak" becomes bitter when rice is seen—see "*RICE.*"
No "jak" to eat, though named Kosvatta—see "*KOSVATTA.*"
The thunderbolt and "sweet-jak"—see "*THUNDERBOLT.*"
To cut "jak" with the sword—see "*SWORD.*"
To eat the "jak" of that tree—see "*EAT.*"

JAR

Like a lid that just suits the jar.

ජාඩියට මූඩිය වගෙයි.

JUDGMENT

A woman's judgment second-rate—see "*WOMAN.*"

JUGGLERY

The best jugglery is the jugglery of escape from trouble.

හැම විජ්ජාවට වඩා ගැල විජ්ජාව හොඳයි.

JUMPING

If you jump up, you will also fall down.

උඩ පැන්නොත් බිම වැටෙ විලු.

A horse to jump over a wall—see "*HORSE.*"
Bunch of plantains jumping over fence—see "*PLANTAIN.*"
Chameleon jumping on a heap of straw—see "*CHAMELEON.*"
If you jump into a well on one provocation—see "*WELL.*"
Senile flightiness vaults o'er house-top—see "*OLD.*"
Tiger jumping before the bear—see "*BEAR.*"
The proud jump up to fall—see "*EDUCATION.*"
Will the spots of a deer vanish—see "*JUNGLE.*"

JUNGLE

The jungle is a Royal highway to the man who can creep through.

රිංගන්ට පිළිවන්නම් බැද්ද රජ මාවතලු.

Axe-heads and the forest's cry—see "*AXE.*"
A jungle without the sandal-wood tree—see "*SANDAL-WOOD.*"
Civet-cats in sandal wood forest—see "*CATS.*"
Fire in bamboo jungle—see "*FIRE.*"
Fox hides fowl in the jungle—see "*FOX.*"
Fox's knowledge of law in the jungle—see "*LAW.*"
Monkeys clearing jungles—see "*MONKEY.*"
Moon shining on a jungle—see "*MOON.*"
Respectability hiding itself in jungle—see "*MONEY.*"
Wild cats who eat jungle plantains—see "*PLANTAINS.*"
Will the spots of a deer vanish—see "*DEER.*"

JUSTICE

Justice of the King of Kekilla—see "*KEKILLA*"

" KABARAGOYA "

When did " Kabaragoyás " eat " Anjilá " fish ?

කබරැ අඤ්ජිලා මාලු කෑවේ කවදද ?

[*Anjilá* is a kind of seer fish which makes a delectable dish.]

" *Kabaragoyá* " *turned into a* " *talagoyá* "—see " *EATING.*"

" KAHA-KURULLA "

Like the " kaha-kurulla " sitting on a king-coconut.

කහ කුරුල්ලා තැඹිලිගෙඩිය උඩ වාඩිවුණා වගෙයි.

[Both " golden-coloured " and therefore well-matched. The *kaha-kurullá* (lit. " yellow bird ") is the bird called either black-headed Oriole (Lat. *Oriolus melanocephalus*) or the black-headed Bulbul (Lat. *Rubigula melanictera*, order *Passere.*]

" KAHAMBILIYA "

The " *Kahambiliya* " *in your own garden*—see " *NETTLES.*"

" KALAM "

Gain a " *kalam* " *by selling toddy*—see " *TODDY.*"

KALIYUGA

In the Kaliyuga age, dry cow-dung sinks below and the " Tiriváne " stone comes up (to the surface of the earth.)

කලියුගේ ගොමරිටි යට යනවා, තිරිවාණ ගල් උඩ එනවා.

[*Kaliyuga* is the fourth age of the world. According to the Hindus, it corresponds with the Iron Age or Age of Vice. The commencement of the Kaliyuga Age is placed about 3,101 years anterior to the Christian Era. The number of its years is 432,000, at the expiration of which the world is to be destroyed. The *Tiruvána-gala* is white stone, quartz.]

" KALLAN "

A Kallan may become a Máravan—see " *RANK.*"

" KALUHAMY "

Like Kaluhámy's father's gift of his horse as dowry.

කළුහාමිගෙ අප්පොච්චි අශ්වයා දෑවැද්දට දුන්නා වගෙයි.

[The gift in effect was " making a virtue of necessity." The Sinhalese story is as follows :—Once upon a time there lived in a certain village a Gama-rála and his wife, whose only child was a daughter by name Kaluhámy. It happened that this daughter died a premature death, not long after which sad event there came a lean beggar to the house when the Gama-rála was away. The sorrowing mother of Kaluhámy, pitying the wretched condition of the beggar, asked him how he had got so lean. " *E-lova gihin me-lova ává* " (" I have just returned from the other world "), replied the beggar, meaning of course that he had been very ill recently and had narrowly escaped death. The foolish mother, however, taking the beggar's reply literally, asked him if he had seen Kaluhámy there. The beggar, perceiving that the woman was a simpleton, determined to take advantage of the occasion. " It is I who married her in the other world," said he in reply to her question. Thereupon Kaluhámy's mother affectionately embraced the beggar as her son-in-law, and gave him all the jewels and silk that were in the house to be taken to the other world for the use of Kaluhámy and her husband. Shortly after the beggar had gone away the Gama-rála returned home. The wife then related to him what had happened during his absence and he was highly incensed at what he heard. After severely rebuking the wife for her folly, he mounted his horse and rode off in the same direction as the beggar had gone, with the object of capturing him. The beggar, on seeing the Gama-rála at a distance, went up a tree. The Gama-rála, too, came up to the tree, and, tying his horse at the foot, began climbing up. The beggar, however, getting down by a branch, untied the horse and rode off on it as fast as possible. The unfortunate Gama-rála, who was still on the tree, seeing that nothing could be done, shouted out "Son-in-law! Tell Kaluhámy that the jewels and clothes are from the mother, but the horse is from me."]

"KALU-NIKA"

Like having eaten "kalu-nika."

කළු නික කාලා වගෙයි.

KALUTARA

To be born at Kalutara—see "*FATE.*"

"KALUVA"

Like Kaluva's trip to Márapona.

කළුවා මාරපන් ගියා වගෙයි.

[A certain Nilame (a Sinhalese nobleman) told his servant, Kaluva, that he was to go to the village of Márapona, intending to send a letter by him. Before, however, the Nilame could fetch the letter, Kaluva started off. Being asked, on his return, why he went away in that manner, Kaluva repled that he only did what he was told. He was asked to go to Márapona, and he did so.]

"KANAYA"

The "Kanaya" in the pit—see "*PIT.*"

"KANA-KOKA"

The white of the "kana-koká"—see "*CRANE.*"

"KAPURALA"

The God does not get angry when the Kapurála's son befouls the Déválaya.

කපුවාගෙ පුතා දේවාලේ කැත කළාට දෙවියෝ තරහ වෙන්නේ නැහැ.

[A *Devála* is a temple dedicated to some Hindu God or local divinity. A *Kapurála* is the officiating priest of a *Devála.*]

Dance and somersault for Kapurála—see "*RICE.*"

"KAPURU-HAMY"

His mouth stinks, though his name is "Kapuru-Hámy."

නමින් කපුරු හාමි නමුත් කට ගඳලු.

[*Kapuru* means "Camphor." An English equivalent for the above would be, for example. "He is a drunkard (sot) though his name is Mr. Drinkwater."]

"KARIVILA"

Like the "karivila" creeper twining round the "kohomba" tree.

කොහොඹ ගහට කරවිල වැල ගියා වගෙයි.

[It is "Like meeting like," bitterness being characteristic of both. The *Karivila* (Lat. *Memordica Charantia*, Sansk. *Ugralata* or *Kandira*, Tam. *Pakal*, *Nuti-pakal*) is a creeping plant, the fruit of which is used in making curry. For the *kohomba*, see under "KOHOMBA."]

" KARMA "

Non-growth is due to "Karma."

නැඟැදෙන්නේ කරුමෙටයි.

Doctoring for a child born to misery—see "*CHILDREN*."

" KATARAGAMA "

If you go knowingly, it is Kataragama—see "*TRAVEL*."

" KATTADIYA "

When the "devil-dancing" is ended, the "kattadiyá" is useless even as a calf-post.

යකුන් නැටුවාට පසු කට්ටාඩියාව වහු කණුවටත් එපාලු.

["Devil-dancing" (*Yakun-netima*) is a ceremonial dancing to propitiate the demons. The *Kattadiyá* is a "sorcerer, enchanter, magician, expeller of devils, devil priest or dancer." "Calf-post" is a log or post to which calves are tied.]

" KAVALU "

"*Kávalu*" *blossom before* "*Amu*"—see "*AMU*."

" KEHEL "

Failing "*alu-kehel*"—see "*PLANTAIN*."

" KEKILLA, KING OF "

Like the justice of the King of Kekilla.

කැකිල්ලේ රජ්ජුරුවන්ගෙ නඩුව වගෙයි.

[Certain thieves burgled a house, and, while engaged in their nefarious work, a wall collapsed and killed one of them. The rest of the thieves made complaint to the King of Kekilla, who, enquiring as to the person responsible for this loss of life, was told that it was presumably the house-owner, who had no business to live in so dilapidated a building. The house-owner was sent for, but he protested that the blame was not his, but the mason's who was responsible for the construction. The mason in turn repudiated guilt and fastened it on the plasterer, who had probably added an excessive quantity of water to his mortar-mixture. The plasterer, on being sent for, admitted the excess of water, but attributed it to the fault of the water-pot, which had had an unusually large mouth. The potter was then brought up, but he had his own valid excuse. He admitted the largeness of the mouth of the pot, but the blame for that lay with a certain beautiful woman who had passed by while he was moulding the vessel. Her beauty had distracted his attention and he had, while gazing at her, unconsciously fashioned a mouth too large for the pot. The woman was then haled up before the King, but she had herself a good and ready excuse. She had not been out to distract the potter at all. She had given some sovereigns to the village goldsmith to make some jewellery for her, and as the man had delayed to complete the work, she had gone out to remonstrate with him. They brought up the goldsmith then—a lank, bony individual—and he had no excuse to give at all. The King thereupon ordered him to be killed on the spot in the usual way, viz. to be gored by the Royal Tusker (elephant). The man, however, demurred, not because he feared to die, but because the King would thus do himself irreparable damage. "How?" asked the ruler, whereupon the goldsmith replied, "Your Majesty can see for yourself what a scarecrow of a man I am—a skeleton, no more than skin and bone. The tusk of the elephant will pierce through me easily, but break when it strikes the rock behind me, and the Royal Tusker will be disfigured for all time." "But, man, how can I avoid it?" asked the King, and the goldsmith replied, "There lives next door to me, Your Majesty, a fat Moorman who can take my place without injury to the Royal Elephant, and I pray that he be substituted for me." "That is an excellent suggestion," commented the King, who thereupon had the fat Moorman brought and gored to death in his presence. In such wise was the responsibility for the death of the burglar fixed on the fat Moorman, who was punished "according to the justice of the King of Kekilla."]

"KEKUNA"

When wild boars smash "kekuna"—see "*BOAR.*"

"KEMANA"

The "kemana" after adoring Buddha—see "*BUDDHA.*"
Shrimps in the "kemana" on the loft—see "*MARRIAGE.*"

"KENDETTA"

However much rain there may be, the "Kẹndettá" is always thirsty.

කොපමණ වර්ෂාව තිබුණත් කෑදැත්තා දිය පිපාසයෙන්ලු.

[The *Kéndettá* (Lat. *Tockus gingalensis*) is the Ceylon Hornbill. He is a bird with a long bill, the two parts of which are curved inwards—hence, according to the popular belief, he is never able to take in a sufficient amount of water to quench his thirst. He is a bird with a peculiarly plaintive or begging cry. He is supposed, when crying, to be begging water from the clouds, the sole source of the fluid that this bird drinks. In Sinhalese folklore, the great difficulty of the *kéndetta* to drink water is due to its refusal to give water to a thirsty person in a previous existence.]

"KEVULA"

The ingratitude of the "Kevulá"—see "*INGRATITUDE.*"

"KEVUM"

Small "kevum" piece that is acceptable—see "*CAKE.*"
Smaller "kevum" after Auntie's arrival—see "*AUNT.*"
The way "Múchi" ate "kevum"—see "*MÚCHI.*"

KILLING

A Maha-Sona killing—see "*DEVIL.*"
Killing animals behind decoy—see "*BUFFALO.*"
Killing fowl for the fox to clean—see "*FOWL.*"
One who has killed a 1,000 patients—see "*VEDARÁLA.*"
There's the creature, here's the stick to kill—see "*PANSIL.*"
This is a great "Yon" slaughter—see "*YONAS.*"

KINDNESS

The rice-face overcomes the elephant-face.

බත් මුණෙන් ඇත් මුණ බිඳෙනවාලු.

Be kind to the kind—see "*UPRIGHTNESS.*"

KINGS—(See also under " *VEDARÁLA.*")

If you cannot be a King, then take to the healing art.

රජකම් කරන්ට බැරිනම් වෙදකම් කරන්ටලු.

Poor men, too, travel on the same road as Kings.

රජුන් යන මග දිළින්දොත් යනවාලු.

The favour of Kings cannot be an inheritance (*i.e.* hereditary property).

රජුන්ගේ කරුණාව උරුමයක් නොවෙයි.

There are losers as well as gainers among those who serve Kings.

රජුන් සේවය කලෝ දිනුවොත් ඇති, පැරදුණොත් ඇති.

King Gaja Báhu's walking stick—see " *PANHINDA.*"
The dog, though made King, bites sandals—see " *DOG.*"
The King who had learnt his letters—see " *EDUCATION.*"
The parrot's golden cage in Palace—see " *PARROT.*"
The pigeon of the King's Palace—see " *PIGEON.*"
The poor man, his wife, and the King—see " *POOR.*"

KING-COCONUT

A black crow on a king-coconut bunch—see " *CROW.*"
The " kaha-kurullá " on a king-coconut—see " *KAHA-KURULLÁ.*"

" KINNARA "

Rodiya meeting the Kinnará—see " *FIGHT.*"

KISSING

Kissing the hand you cannot cut off—see " *HAND.*"

" KITALAGAMUVA "

The arrows at Kitalagamuva—see " *TALK.*"

KNEES

Old people crawling on their knees—see " *OLD.*"

KNIFE

He has neither cloth nor knife—see " *POVERTY* "

KNOCK

Like knocking tho milky tree with a pestle.

කිරි ගහට මෝල් ගහෙන් ඇන්නා වගෙයි.

A knock from a hand with a gold ring—see " *RING.*"
Knocking your finger into an eye—see " *EYE.*"

" KOBEYIYA "

It is still a " kobeyiyá," though fried in oil.

තෙලෙන් බැද්දත් කොබෙයියා කොබෙයියාමයි.

[The *kobeyiyá* is the common Indian dove (Lat. *Turtur risorius*). The *alu-kobeyiyá* is the spotted dove (Lat. *Turtur suratensis.*)]

" KOHILA "

Thorns of the " kohila " unendurable—see " *CROCODILE.*"

" KOHOMBA "

Though you wash a "kohomba" seed (with water), where will its bitterness go ?

කොහොඹ ඇටේ හෑදුවාට තිත්ත රසේ කොහිබ යාද ?

[The *Kohomba* (Lat. *Azadirachta Indica*, Sansk. *Nimba*, Tam. *Vembu*, *Veppan*) is the well-known Margosa or Nim-tree of the East. It has been used medicinally from the remotest times.]

" KOKA "—(See " *CRANE.*")

" KOKKANAM-PAYIYA "

The " kokkanam-payiya " of the Ándiyás—see " *ANDIYÁS.*"

" KORAHA "

Bathing an elephant in a " koraha "—see " *ELEPHANT.*"

Putting your hand in a " koraha "—see " *HURRY.*"

The departing devil and the "koraha"—see " *DEVIL.*"

" KORAVA "

It's all the same whatever animal is caught in the " Korava's " trap.

කොරවගෙ උගුලේ මොකා අසුවුණත් එකලු.

[In a variant saying " *Beravdyá* " is substituted for " *Korava.*" The *Koravas* are not rice eaters, and will eat the flesh of most animals. The Tamils say, " Give an elephant to a Pandit and a cat to a Korava." The Sinhalese speak of this tribe of Gypsies as *Ahikuntakayás*, which means those who play with the mouth (*tunda*) of serpents or who sport with or make serpents dance. In the *Bhuridatta Játaka*, it is said that the Bódhisat, in one birth, was a cobra with 1,000 hoods, and an *Ahikuntakayá* caught the cobra and played tricks with it. The Gods, being angry at this, cursed the *Ahikuntakayá*, and ever since the tribe has been nomadic. Though the *Koravas* or *Ahikuntakayás* now claim to be of Vedda descent and to have come from *Támankaduva*, they are in reality descendants of a gypsy tribe found all over the Tamil country, originally from Telugu. In Ceylon as in India, these people never come into Court. They settle their disputes among themselves, and have their own Headmen and Court, who inflict fines, usually paid in arrack consumed by the gang. They have a bad character for squabbling and fighting amongst themselves, so much so that the Tamils, among whom they mostly live, have the following sayings about them :

(*a*) " Koravas' justice is the ruin of the family."

(*b*) " The *Kolukattai* (a kind of rice cake) is neither one thing nor the other, so are Koravas neither virtuous nor well behaved."

(*c*) " Disputes amongst scavengers are easier settled than those amongst Koravas." The Tamil proverb, " If the wife of the Korava is brought to bed, her husband takes the prescribed stimulant," refers to the practice of *couvade* or custom in accordance with which the father goes to bed and is doctored until the child is born. Denham, who records the above, gives another Tamil saying, " No one ever saw the dead body of a monkey or the corpse of a Korava," in reference to the fact that, when a Korava dies, the body is buried as quickly as possible. The grave is covered with the leaves of the hut occupied by the deceased, and the camp is broken up at once. A small quantity of arrack, with some cooked rice and curry, is placed over the grave.]

" KOSVATTA "

Though named " Kosvatta," it hasn't even a single young " jak " to boil and eat.

නමින් කොස්වත්තේ, තම්බා කන්ට පොලොසුත් නැත්තේ.

[*Kos* means "*Jak*" and *Vatta* "garden."]

" *Kos* " *more common than yams*—see " *HEADACHE.*"

" KOTTE "

Like the Parangiyá going to Kótte—see " *PARANGIYÁ.*"
That kind of game is good for Kótte—see " *SPORT.*"

" KOTTORUVA "

Like the " Kottóruvá " coming across a plantain trec.

කොට්ටෝරුවාට කෙහෙල් ගහ හම්බවුණා වගෙයි.

[The *Kottóruvá* is the Ceylon barbet.]

" KULLA "—(See " *WINNOWING-FAN.*")

" KURAKKAN "

Like the Gama-rála who went to Ruhuna because he could not eat " kurakkan."

ගමරාළ කුරක්කන් කන්ට බැරුව රුහුණු ගියා වගෙයි.

[He went to Ruhuna in search of better food. On going there, however, he found that the fingers of its inhabitants had wasted by their constantly handling *kurakkan* porridge, this being the staple food of the people there. *Ruhuna* (including the Southern Province of to-day) represented an ancient division of Ceylon. For fuller reference to *kurakkan*, see under " GAMA-RÁLA."]

Like thc man who, fed up with " kurakkan talapa," went to Maha Bintenna to eat " kurakkan roti."

අකුරම්බඩයාලාට හලප කාලා ඇති වෙලා මහ බින්තැන්නට කුරක්කන් රොටි කන්ට ගියා වගෙයි.

[This seems to be a variant of the above. *Kurakkan talapa* is a kind of porridge made of this grain, while the *kurakkan roti* is a baked cake of the same grain. The point of the saying is that this particular pudding or porridge (*talapa*), though unappetising, is preferable to the cakes (*roti*) eaten in Maha Bintenna, which is the Uva of to-day. This proverb shows that the Province of Uva was regarded as even worse off than still wilder Districts, and migration to Uva would be regarded as an act of folly.]

Having gone to do hired " kurakkan " work, why inquire about the boundaries of the village ?

කුලී කුරක්කනට ගොස් ඉම් ගම් කුමටද ?

The Gama-rála and his " *kurakkan* "—see " *GAMA-RÁLA.*"

" LABBA " (LABU)

The "labba" is two "gavvas" away, the "labu" creeper one " gavva."

ලබ්බ දෙගව්වයි, ලබු වැල ගව්වයි.

[The *labba* is, of course, the *gediya*, fruit.]

Lime cutting ceremony in "labu-gediya"—see "*LIME.*"
The "labu-gediya" in Buddha-less era—see "*BUDDHA.*"
The "labu-mala" unfragrant—see "*INGRATITUDE.*"
The same hand for "labba" and "puhula"—see "*HAND.*"
Water of celestial river in "labu-gediya"—see "*CHANDÁLA.*"

LABOUR

Hired "kurakkan" work—see "*KURAKKAN.*"
Labour for breath under an elephant's legs—see "*ELEPHANT.*"
Move the hands to move the feet—see "*HANDS.*"
Six months' labour of the potter—see "*POTTER.*"

LADDER

Can you carry a winnow of chunam up a ladder which you cannot scale even without such a burden ?

නිකම් යන්න බැරි ඉණිමගේ හුණු කුල්ලක් බඳගෙන යන්නෙ කොහොමද?

[A variant substitutes *umageya* (subterranean passage) for *inimaga* (ladder), and reads : "Can you carry a winnow of chunam through a subterraneous passage (vault) which you cannot traverse even without such a burden ?" The chunam would choke you if you knocked against an obstacle while groping your way in the dark.]

Like setting up ladders to reach the sky.

අහසට ඉණිමං බඳිනවා වගෙයි.

A ladder to the traveller—see "*CONVERSATION.*"
Making ladders for monkeys—see "*MONKEY.*"
Woman is a ladder to the gallows—see "*WOMAN.*"

LADY

The way the lady gave rice to the dhoby—see "*DHOBY.*"

"LAHA"

Like going to get the "láha" made bigger.

ලාහ ලොකු කරගන්න ගියා වගෙයි.

[The *láha* is, of course, a grain measure—one-eighth of a bushel or four seer. The story is that there was strong feeling in a certain village about the King's portion of paddy, which was considered to be too large. An assembly of the villagers decided to make respectful representations to the King, and one man was deputed to wait upon His Majesty and explain the situation. The man set forth bravely enough, but when he got near the neighbourhood of the palace his courage had oozed out a bit. As he crossed the palace gates he was quite nervous about his business, and when, in due course, he was ushered into the King's presence, he was absolutely sick with fear. "Why have you come, Sirrah ?" asked the King, somewhat sternly, and the poor yokel, now quaking about his knees, stuttered feebly, "I came, Your Majesty, to get the *láha* (measure) made bigger"—which was exactly the opposite of what he had come to beseech His Majesty. The King, now quite pleased, readily agreed and immediately gave instructions that the contribution from the man's village should be increased thenceforth—a circumstance which convinced the villagers that they would have done better to have let things well alone.]

A "láha" is a "thimba"—see "*MEASURE.*"
Like measuring frogs with a "láha"—see "*FROGS.*"

" LAMA HAMY "

Lama Hámy's child—see " *DEATH.*"

LAMB

The bear's death and the lamb's salvation—see " *DEATH.*"

LAMENESS

The pains of death on top of lameness—see " *DEATH.*"

LAMENTATION

No death without lamentation—see " *DEATH.*"

LAMP

The lamp lit for the Headman's use gives light to the Lascarin, too.

ගමේ රාළට ඇවුලු පහනෙන් සේවකයත් එළිය බලනවාලු.

[The Lascarin was the ordinary Sinhalese soldier or private.]

A "Pánmaduva" midst a "Ginimaduva"—see "*PÁNMADUVA.*"

Lamp-light to the blind man—see " *BLIND MAN.*"

LANGUAGE

Desire alone will not suffice to learn a language.

භාෂාව ඉගෙනීමට ආසාව තිබූ පමණින්ම පිළිවන්ද?

The language used by the " Sangha "—see " *BUDDHISM.*"

Your language according to your country—see " *COUNTRY.*"

LASCARIN

The lamp for Headman and Lascarin—see " *LAMP.*"

" LAVANCHI "

Like Grandfather Lavanchi's last advice.

ලවන්චි සීයාගෙ අන්තිම අවවාදය වගෙයි.

[Coffee seeds and the seeds of the Croton oil plant (Sinh. *Jápála,* Lat. *Croton tiglium,* Tam. *Nervalam*) were in two bags side by side upon the loft. One night Grandfather Lavanchi had a splitting headache. " Here, you wenches, pour me a little coffee, will you ? " he shouted from his bed, and a little girl of the house clambered up to the loft, and, in the pitch darkness, felt for the coffee-seed bag. Unfortunately for the old man, she got hold of the wrong bag and what she brought down were, not coffee seeds but the seeds of the *Jápála.* These she hastened to fry and pound and then, pouring what she thought was coffee, gave the old man to drink. Quickly the beverage did its purgative work. Like the breakdown of a *vakkade* (" hole or opening in a dam to let off the water from the paddy-fields,") Lavanchi began squirting out coffee from mouth and bowels, till in a short time the man, who had normally been " with one foot in the grave," was brought to Death's door. " Unless you want to be human spouts, drink no coffee, ye fools " was his last advice to the children and grandchildren, who had hastily assembled by his bedside, after which he surrendered himself to the *Máraya* (Death) who finds no let or hindrance when he comes.]

LAW

The fox claimed to know Law though he lived in the jungle.

වනන්තරේ ඉඳිතත් නඩු ක්‍රමය දනෙනවයි කියා නරි නසිදෙ කීවාලු.

LAZINESS

Laziness is the original father of sin.

කම්මැලි කම පාපයේ මුල් පියාලු.

Lazy man has the gift of prophecy—see "*PROPHECY.*"
The pen of the man too lazy to write—see "*PANHINDA.*"

LEAK

Baling vessel for unleaky boat—see "*BOAT.*"

LEAPING—(See also "*JUMPING.*")

Ladders for leaping monkeys—see "*MONKEY.*"

LEARNING—(See also "*EDUCATION.*")

Learning a language by desire only—see "*LANGUAGE.*"
Learning to scrape coconuts—see "*MÁTARA.*"
Low rank and the learned—see "*EDUCATION.*"
No country foreign to learned man—see "*EDUCATION.*"
The King who learnt his letters—see "*EDUCATION.*"
The learned and the proud—see "*EDUCATION.*"
The poverty of the learned—see "*EDUCATION.*"
Wealth without learning—see "*EDUCATION.*"
You must be foolish to learn wisdom—see "*WISDOM.*"

LEASING

Leasing out the garden—see "*GARDEN.*"

LEAVEN

(Like the man who) refused a little leaven but promised to send a she-calf.

මුහුන් ටික නොදී වැස්සී පස්සෙ එවන්නයි කීවාලු.

LEAVES

What is the use of breaking and showing the leaves to one who knows the tree ?

ගහ දන්නාට කොළ කඩා පාන්නේ කුමටද?

"*Andu*" *leaves and the snake*—see "*SNAKE.*"
Leaves which show the growing tree—see "*TREE.*"
The leaf for wrapping putrid meat—see "*FLESH.*"

LEECH

The leech lets go his hold of one place only when he has secured another.

කූඩැල්ලා එක පළක් අල්ලාගනයි අනිත් පළ අත්හරින්නේ.

Will a leech remain on a mattress even though you place it there ?

කූඩැල්ලා මෙත්තේ ඉන්දුවාට ඉදීද?

Like squeezing lime into the face of a leech.

කූඩැල්ලාගෙ මූණට දෙහි ඇඹුල් මිරිකුවා වගෙයි.

LEG

Like dispelling the fear of the "Cochin-leg."

බරවා කකුලේ හැක ඇරියා වගෙයි.

[What is meant by "Cochin-leg" is Elephantiasis. One's first feeling is that a blow from an Elephantine leg would be a smashing blow. In fact, for purposes of kicking, such a leg is helpless, comparatively speaking,—a bugbear, nothing to be afraid of.]

A legless man is under a curse—see "*CURSE.*"
Defeat is three-legged—see "*DEFEAT.*"
If the dog bites your leg—see "*DOG.*"

LENDING

A friend made unfriendly by lending—see "*FRIEND.*"

LETTERS—(See also "*EDUCATION.*")

The King who had learnt his letters—see "*EDUCATION.*"
Woman skilled in letters—see "*WOMAN.*"

"LEVAYA"

No salt though living in the "Leváya"—see "*SALT.*"
Going to the "Leváya" to buy salt—see "*SALT.*"

LICKING

Licking may cost you the eating.

ලෙවිල්ලෙත් කැවිල්ල නැතිවෙනවාලු.

[Cf. Eng. "Losing the substance by grasping at the shadow."]

Breaking a bee-hive and licking your hand—see "*BEE-HIVE.*"
Licking up anything running to waste—see "*WASTE.*"

LID

The lid that just suits the jar—see "*JAR.*"

LIE

A lie has no life.

බොරුවට පණ නැහැ.

The tongue and the mouth for lying—see "*TONGUE.*"

LIFE

(Seek) the forest life in these evil times.

අතේ කාලේ වනේ වාසේ.

A lie has no life—see "*LIFE.*"
Life in this world—see "*HAND.*"
Secrets are never long-lived—see "*SECRETS.*"
The ant-eater's life—see "*ANT-EATER.*"
Wishing "Long Life" to the ocean—see "*WATER.*"

LIGHT

The light of this world—see "*HAND.*"

LIGHTING

Lighting a cigar from a flaming beard—see "*CIGAR.*"

LIKE

Like a black crow on a "ran-tembili" bunch—see "*CROW.*"
Like a bone going out of one's body—see "*BONE.*"
Like a bull butting a man fallen from a tree—see "*BULL.*"
Like a certain man's description of candy—see "*CANDY.*"
Like a cloth hired out by a dhoby—see "*DHOBY.*"
Like a flower blossoming among brambles—see "*FLOWER.*"
Like a line drawn on water—see "*WATER.*"
Like a Lord, eat your food—see "*WORK.*"
Like a man who had eaten the whole earth—see "*EARTH.*"
Like a man escaping all seven gallows—see "*GALLOWS.*"
Like a python hunt—see "*SNAKE.*"
Like a slave, do your work—see "*WORK.*"
Like a snake that bit without discrimination—see "*SNAKE.*"
Like a tiger without claws—see "*TIGER.*"
Like a wet fowl—see "*FOWL.*"
Like adding straw to a raging fire—see "*FIRE.*"
Like adorning the chameleon with a gold ornament—see "*CHAMELEON.*"
Like an unseasonable fruit—see "*FRUIT.*"
Like "andu" leaves to the snake—see "*SNAKE.*"
Like applying ghee on both sides—see "*GHEE.*"
Like arranging a match for the crocodile—see "*CROCODILE.*"
Like asking a tortoise for lock-stitches—see "*TORTOISE.*"
Like asking the thief's mother about the stolen goods—see "*THIEF.*"
Like "bana" preaching by Veddás—see "*ADVICE.*"
Like barren women getting children—see "*WOMAN.*"
Like beating the elk-skin at home—see "*DEER.*"
Like being put in turbid water—see "*WATER.*"
Like blowing a chank to a deaf man—see "*DEAF.*"
Like blowing on a beehive—see "*BEEHIVE.*"
Like breaking Buddha's bowl—see "*BUDDHA.*"
Like breaking open a hollow fruit—see "*FRUIT.*"
Like buying for 1,000 and selling back for 500—see "*TRADE.*"
Like catching a big fish with a small bait—see "*FISH.*"
Like catching hold of an animal's tail—see "*TAIL.*"
Like catching hold of a tiger's tail—see "*TIGER.*"
Like changing pillow to ease headache—see "*HEADACHE.*"
Like chopping a pig's flesh on its back—see "*PIG.*"
Like clinging to a thorny branch when about to fall—see "*FALL.*"
Like coming to lay eggs mid two stones—see "*EGG-LAYING.*"

Like commencing a " Pánmaduva " in the midst of a " Gini-maduva "—see " *PÁNMADUVA.*"
Like covering a pig's snout with gold—see " *PIG.*"
Like covering the new with a gunny bag—see " *GUNNY.*"
Like crows flocking round the carcase of a bull—see " *CROWS.*"
Like cutting hedge-stakes on to a river—see " *CUTTING.*"
Like cutting the throat after eating together—see " *CUTTING.*"
Like darkness becoming helpful to thieves—see " *DARKNESS.*"
Like digging where it resists—see " *DIGGING.*"
Like dispelling the fear of the " Cochin-leg "—see " *LEG.*"
Like drawing water in a basket full of holes—see " *WATER.*"
Like drinking muddy water while gazing at clear water—see " *WATER.*"
Like drinking river water and wishing " Long life " to the Ocean—see " *WATER.*"
Like eating eel fish with an eacle—see " *EEL.*"
Like eating in milk and washing your hand in honey—see " *MILK.*"
Like eating my coconut and eloping with my mother—see " *HOSPITALITY.*"
Like eating without salt though living in the "Leváya"—see " *SALT.*"
Like emptying the pit just in the nick of time—see " *PIT.*"
Like flowers blossoming on an "attikká" tree—see " *FLOWERS.*"
Like frying one's honour—see " *HONOUR.*"
Like getting cats to take roasted "jak" seeds out of the fire—see " *CAT.*"
Like getting the hand burnt whilst having the pincers—see " *HAND.*"
Like giving an unhusked coconut to a dog—see " *DOG.*"
Like giving coconut trees from the river bottom—see " *COCONUT.*"
Like giving entrails to a fox to wash—see " *FOX.*"
Like giving horns to a horse—see " *HORSE.*"
Like giving milk to a venomous serpent—see " *MILK.*"
Like going after cranes after giving your clothes to the dhoby—see " *DHOBY.*"
Like going to get the "láha" made big—see " *LÁHA.*"
Like going to the "Leváya" to bring salt—see " *SALT.*"
Like going to start tiger-dancing at a " Pinkama "—see " *TIGER.*"
Like Grandfather Lavanchi's last advice—see " *LAVANCHI.*"
Like guarding deserted huts—see " *HOUSES.*"
Like having eaten "kalu-nika"—see " *KALU-NIKA.*"
Like having eaten the rice of the Gods—see " *RICE.*"
Like hiding jaggery in a water-course—see " *JAGGERY.*"
Like Kaluhámy's father's gift of his horse as dowry—see " *KALUHÁMY.*"
Like Kaluvá's trip to Márapona—see " *KALUVA.*"

Like killing animals behind decoy buffalo—see "*BUFFALO.*"
Like killing the fowl to give to the fox—see "*FOWL.*"
Like knocking your finger into the eye which is ready to cry—see "*EYE.*"
Like leading an ascetic's life on the point of a needle—see "*NEEDLE.*"
Like leasing out the garden—see "*GARDEN.*"
Like leaving your own doors open to drive away dogs from a stranger's house—see "*HOUSE.*"
Like letting off the bird in your clutch—see "*BIRD.*"
Like letting you go and then holding you by the elbow—see "*RICE.*"
Like lighting your cigar from another man's flaming beard—see "*CIGAR.*"
Like loading a bull with jaggery—see "*BULL.*"
Like losing the village one has by going to get others—see "*VILLAGE.*"
Like making ladders for monkeys to climb—see "*MONKEY.*"
Like measuring frogs with a "láha"—see "*FROGS.*"
Like men who had eaten salt out of one bag—see "*SALT.*"
Like missing the blow at a cobra—see "*COBRA.*"
Like missing the target of the elephant because your hand got raised—see "*ELEPHANT.*"
Like mocking at a man after giving him your hand—see "*MOCKING.*"
Like Mr. Fox in a "pamba" thicket—see "*FOX.*"
Like my club for your scythe—see "*CLUB.*"
Like not washing your body out of consideration to the river—see "*RIVER.*"
Like opening up a road to a mountain to bury an elephant—see "*ROAD.*"
Like placing logs of wood before mothers (of children)—see "*MOTHER.*"
Like placing quarter cents among the rupees—see "*RUPEES.*"
Like placing the "messa" in the direction in which the creeper goes—see "*MESSA.*"
Like planting potato leaves with the tongue—see "*TALK.*"
Like playing the fiddle to a deaf elephant—see "*FIDDLE.*"
Like pouring honey into the ear—see "*HONEY.*"
Like preaching to the wind—see "*WIND.*"
Like pushing one about to fall—see "*PUSHING.*"
Like pushing into the fire a sun-scorched man—see "*FIRE.*"
Like putting a little cow-dung into a pot of milk—see "*MILK.*"
Like putting your hand into a "hungá" hole—see "*HAND.*"
Like returning from the wedding house without eating rice-cake—see "*CAKE.*"
Like ripening before matnrity—see "*RIPENING.*"
Like rooting out "Amu" plants—see "*PADDY.*"

Like rooting out " Ehela " trees to stamp out the Ehelapola race —see " *TREE*."
Like running after runners—see " *RUNNING*."
Like Saturn falling into the bowl of the beggar—see "*BEGGAR*."
Like scalding with cold water—see " *WATER*."
Like serving soup to the unwanted lover—see " *SOUP*."
Like setting up ladders to reach the sky—see " *LADDER*."
Like shooting from under water—see " *SHOOTING*."
Like showing your hospitality at another man's wedding—see " *HOSPITALITY*."
Like Siman Gamarála's chew of tobacco—see " *TOBACCO*."
Like sinning by killing rat-snakes—see " *SINNING*."
Like sleeping on the road because Gods exist—see " *GOD*."
Like sowing on a rock—see " *SOWING* "
Like stepping into the rapids and looking for footmarks—see " *WATER*."
Like swinging about and shooting—see " *SHOOTING*."
Like taking medicine in anticipation of illness—see " *MEDICINE*."
Like teaching the alligator's young to swim—see " *TEACHING*."
Like the ant which fell into a pot of honey—see " *ANT*."
Like the arecanut caught in the cutter—see " *ARECANUT*."
Like the barking of familiar dogs—see " *DOG*."
Like the blind tortoise peering at the sky—see " *TORTOISE*."
Like the cakes being made small even after Auntie's arrival see " *AUNT*."
Like the cart running before the bull—see " *BULL*."
Like the cat on the doorstep—see " *CAT*."
Like the cat which has evacuated on a rock—see " *CAT*."
Like the cat which has eaten chameleons—see " *CAT*."
Like the chameleon jumping on a heap of straw—see " *CHAMELEON*."
Like the chastity of an ugly woman—see " *CHASTITY*."
Like the cobra meeting the " polonga "—see " *FIGHT*."
Like the crashing down of the temple over the worshipper's head —see " *RELIGION*."
Like the cutting down of the drumstick tree—see " *DRUMSTICK*."
Like the deer who has seen a tiger—see " *DEER*."
Like the description of curd given to a blind man—see " *CURD*."
Like the description of the elephant by four blind men—see " *ELEPHANT*."
Like the distribution of 1,000 coconuts to a 1,000 friends—see " *COCONUTS*."
Like the dog in the heap of straw—see " *DOG*."
Like the drop of quicksilver on your palm—see " *HAND*. '
Like the dumb man's dream—see " *DUMB*."

Like the dog-flea which the blind man has got hold of—see "*DOG-FLEA.*"

Like the earth from the hoe and the loin-cloth—see "*HOE.*"

Like the egg-laying of the tortoise and hen respectively—see "*EGG-LAYING.*"

Like the evidence given by the priest—see "*PRIEST.*"

Like the explanation of the coconut thief—see "*COCONUT.*"

Like the fall of the unripe fruit—see "*FRUIT.*"

Like the fate of the water-drawer and the pot-breaker—see "*MAN.*"

Like the fatherless child crying to sit and eat with his father—see "*CHILDREN.*"

Like the fool and his truss—see "*FOOL.*"

Like the fowl of the ancient capitals—see "*FOWL.*"

Like the friendship of the short-tailed dog—see "*DOG.*"

Like the frog in a well—see "*FROG.*"

Like the Gama-máyiyá's hair-cut—see "*GAMA-MÁYIYÁ.*"

Like the Gamarála, his axe and the blacksmith—see "*GAMA-RÁLA.*"

Like the Gamarála who went to Ruhuna—see "*KURAKKAN.*"

Like the Gamarála's mortar—see "*MORTAR.*"

Like the Gamarála's shot from his gun—see "*GAMARÁLA.*"

Like the gambolling of the crab till the water gets hot—see "*CRAB.*"

Like the gift of cloth to a dancer—see "*DANCER.*"

Like the herd of cattle being entrusted to the care of a tiger—see "*TIGER.*"

Like the hedge-stakes planted in the mud—see "*STAKE.*"

Like the horn and the ear—see "*EAR.*"

Like the horse not getting horns—see "*HORSE.*"

Like the jackal entrapped in the Island—see "*JACKAL.*"

Like the justice of the King of Kekilla—see "*KEKILLA.*"

Like the leaf in which putrid meat had been wrapped up—see "*FLESH.*"

Like the lid that just suits the jar—see "*JAR.*"

Like the mad woman's bag of herbs—see "*HERBS.*"

Like the man in fever asking for water—see "*FEVER.*"

Like the man of Óvitigala—see "*ÓVITIGALA.*"

Like the man who flung half a coconut at a dog carrying away the other half—see "*COCONUT.*"

Like the man who refused a little leaven—see "*LEAVEN.*"

Like the man who said: "Now, boil, for all our sorrows, my child;"—see "*SORROWS.*"

Like the man who was fed up with "kurakkan"—see "*KURAKKAN.*"

Like the man who was named the "Arrant Fool"—see "*MAN.*"

Like the man whose arrack was drunk and then beaten—see '*ARRACK.*"

Like the man with the brim round his neck—see "*MAN.*"

Like the marriage proposal of the Inaggoda people—see "*MARRIAGE.*"
Like the milk poured into a conch-shell—see "*PURITY.*"
Like the money that is not accepted—see "*MONEY.*"
Like the monkey that has eaten "Goraka"—see "*MONKEY.*"
Like the monkey's trick on an alligator—see "*TRICK.*"
Like the moon shining on a jungle—see "*MOON.*"
Like the offer of aid for the tavern-keeper's "Mal-baliya"—see "*BALI.*"
Like the outrigger that is bigger than the boat—see "*BOAT.*"
Like the Parangiya going to Kótte—see "*PORTUGUESE.*"
Like the parrot in a golden cage in the King's Palace—see "*PARROT.*"
Like the path taken by the civet-cat—see "*CAT.*"
Like the people of Maggona—see "*MAGGONA.*"
Like the people of Pasdun Kórale—see "*PASDUN KÓRALE.*"
Like the pestle made by a Paduva—see "*PADUVA.*"
Like the pigeon of the King's Palace—see "*PIGEON.*"
Like the place where the ox drank water—see "*OX.*"
Like the pot standing on its mouth—see "*POT.*"
Like the prawn's pretensions to cleanliness—see "*PRAWN.*"
Like the python which had swallowed pestles—see "*PYTHON.*"
Like the question about Lama Hámy's child—see "*DEATH.*"
Like the remark of the barren woman—see "*WOMAN.*"
Like the remark of the morrow's bride—see "*BRIDE.*"
Like the remark of the tortoise ordered to be thrown into the water—see "*TORTOISE.*"
Like the remark of the white-jaggery man—see "*JAGGERY.*"
Like the Rodiyá meeting the Kinnará—see "*FIGHT.*"
Like the saying about the construction of sheds and pavilions—see "*MARRIAGE.*"
Like the saying of the deaf man and the dumb man—see "*DEAF.*"
Like the saying of the sea becoming congee—see "*SPOON.*"
Like the saying about the three winnowing-fans—see "*WINNOWING-FAN.*"
Like the scarecrow in a paddy field—see "*PADDY.*"
Like the silversmith who thrashed his son—see "*BADÁLA.*"
Like the snake on God Saman's neck—see "*SNAKE.*"
Like the snapping of the rope when you are midway on the "atura"—see "*ATURA.*"
Like the solitary eye-fly's flight—see "*JAK.*"
Like the stone flung by the blind man—see "*BLIND MAN.*"
Like the story of Rayigamayá and Gampolayá—see "*GAMPOLAYA.*"
Like the story of the melted gold frog—see "*MELTING.*"
Like the swan sucking milk out of water—see "*SWAN.*"
Like the Tamby who sees gems—see "*MOORMAN.*"
Like the Tamby's fez—see "*MOORMAN.*"
Like the tangle in a skein of thread—see "*THREAD.*"
Like the tail running before the fowl—see "*FOWL.*"

Like the thief and master of the house combining—see "*THIEF.*"
Like the tiger jumping before the bear—see "*TIGER.*"
Like the tortoise who failed to govern his tongue—see "*TORTOISE.*"
Like the two Gama-máyiyás' praise of their husbands—see "*GAMA-MÁYIYÁ.*"
Like the Udarata man's temptation to smack the face—see "*UDARATA.*"
Like the unpluckable flower offered to Buddha—see "*FLOWER.*"
Like the untimely ripening due to hot weather—see "*WEATHER*".
Like the verses of the Ranchagoda girl—see "*VERSES.*"
Like the way a certain man took "Pansil"—see "*PANSIL.*"
Like the way a certain woman cried in anticipation—see "*WOMAN.*"
Like the way Andare ate sugar—see "*SUGAR.*"
Like the way Múchi ate "kevum"—see "*MÚCHI.*"
Like the way the Andiyás cooked congee—see "*ANDIYÁS.*"
Like the way the Gamarála went to Heaven—see "*GAMARÁLA.*"
Like the way the lady gave rice to the dhoby—see "*DHOBY.*"
Like the wild-cat which ate jungle plantains—see "*PLANTAIN.*"
Like the wisdom of Mahadenamuttá— see "*MAHADENAMUTTÁ.*"
Like the wood-apple swallowed by the elephant—see "*ELEPHANT.*"
Like throwing a stone at a cobra—see "*COBRA.*"
Like throwing in straw into a raging fire—see "*FIRE.*"
Like throwing stones at the nest of the hornet—see "*HORNET.*"
Like throwing worms into a fire—see "*FIRE.*"
Like tightening screws on a "pol-piti baliya"—see "*BALIYA.*"
Like Tokka's way of tending cattle—see "*BULL.*"
Like trying the teeth upon a file—see "*TEETH.*"
Like trying to extract oil from sand—see "*OIL.*"
Like trying to get on a tree from the top instead of from the bottom—see "*TREE.*"
Like trying to peel off the bark from a rock—see "*ROCK.*"
Like tying the "amude" with the river seven "gavvas" away—see "*AMUDE.*"
Like tying up the mortars of the village—see "*ELEPHANT.*"
Like Veddas speaking of building houses—see "*VEDDAS.*"
Like watering a "dimbul" tree to get flowers—see "*DIMBUL.*"
Like wearing a crupper to cure dysentery—see "*DYSENTERY.*"
Like what was said when the boat was upset—see "*BOAT.*"
Like writing noisy characters—see "*WRITING*"
Like yoking a bullock with a buffalo—see "*BULL.*"

LIME-CUTTING CEREMONY

Like the lime-cutting ceremony within the "labu-gediya."

ලබ්බේ දෙහි කැපුවා වගෙයි.

[In a remote village, once upon a time, when the harvesting was over, the villagers arranged for the performance of the ceremony of cutting lime (to avert the evil effects of the "evil eye" or "evil tongue"), on the day of the measuring of the paddy. When, however, the invocation of devils was in progress, a heavy shower of rain began to fall, and the chief of the exorcists asked, "How, now, friends? How can we proceed with the ceremony without a shed?" The husbandman looked around and, seeing a huge *diya-labu-gediya* (long gourd) on a creeper growing in a corner of their field, suggested they should got inside it. The exorcists agreed and entered the fruit in order to continue the ceremony interrupted by the rain. So engrossed were they inside with their incantations on the one hand, and so comfortable on the other with the warmth of their surroundings—the cold winds had no power to inconvenience them in their place—that they did not realise how exactly they were drifting. What happened was that their sheltering gourd (the *labu-gediya*), floating in a pool of water created by the heavy rains, drifted little by little to the river hard by, whence it was carried to the open sea. There, a large fish swallowed the fruit, and a little later a huge bird, gulping down the fish, rested upon a rock for a while. A man, however, then came to the scene and, shooting the bird, took it home to serve as food to a party of people who were expected to arrive shortly in connection with a marriage proposal for him. When the bird was cut open, there was seen the fish, and he exclaimed, "Two curries, not one, the Gods be praised." When the fish was cut and he saw the *labu-gediya* inside, "Three curries, my goodness, not two!" he yelled in a transport of delight. He fell back in a fainting fit, however, when he cut the neck of the fruit, for out walked the exorcists of the paddy field, still at their incantations of *Denna-dená-dedira-mande-nánú.*"]

LIME

Squeezing lime juice into the face of a leech—see "*LEECH*."

LION

However starving a lion may be, he will never eat grass.

කොපමණ සාගිනි වුණත් සිංහයා තණකොළ නොකයි.

It is unwise to rouse a sleeping lion.

නිදන සිංහයා නැගිටුවා හැරීම නුවණට නුරුනොවෙයි.

You want a golden vessel to hold the lion's grease.

සිංහ තෙල් දමන්ට රත්රන් භාජනයක් ඕනෑලු.

[This refers to the popular belief that lion's grease corrodes any vessel other than golden.]

Lion vanquished by a tortoise—see "*TORTOISE*."

LISTENERS

The duty of listeners—see "*TALK*."

LIZARD

When contact with the lizard is fatal—see "*CROCODILE*."

LOAD

Sinner who takes up a load—see "*SINNER*."

LOADING

Loading a bull with jaggery—see "*BULI*"

LOCK-STITCHES

Asking lock-stitches from a tortoise—see "*TORTOISE.*"

LOFT

Making a chair out of the loft.

අටුව කඩා පුටුව හදනවා වගෙයි.

[That is, pulling the loft down and making a chair out of the materials.]

Shrimps even in the "kemana" on the loft—see "*MARRIAGE.*"

LOGS

Placing logs of wood before mothers of children—see "*MOTHER.*"

LOIN-CLOTH

Earth in the digger's loin-cloth—see "*HOE.*"

LORD

Eat like a Lord—see "*WORK.*"

LORIS

The young of the loris is a gem to her.

උනහපුළුවාගේ දරුවා ඌට මැණිකලු.

You cannot draw tears from the eyes of the loris.

උනහපුළුවාගේ ඇසෙන් කඳුලු ගන්ට බැරිලු.

LOSERS

Losers and gainers among King's servants—see "*KING.*"

LOSING

Like losing even the mouth you had.

තිබුණු කටත් නැතිවුණා වගෙයි.

[The saying, which has been slightly altered to avoid the vulgarism of the original, has its origin in a quaint old-world story. According to Sinhalese Folklore, there was a very poor man, the cup of whose unhappiness was daily filled to the brim by a nagging wife at home. The taunts of this woman drove him one day in desperation to the forest where he began crying aloud, bewailing his fate. The God, Sakra Deviyo, taking pity on him, came thither in the guise of an old man and handed him three unhusked coconuts, saying that if he expressed any wish at the moment of breaking each one, the wish would be fulfilled. The poor man rushed home and, taking the kitchen knife, was about to break one coconut with a wish in his heart for riches, when the wife screeched out, inquiring what he was going to do. "A mouth, you fool," replied the exasperated husband as he brought down the knife on the coconut, and immediately he found himself covered with mouths from head to foot. Half demented, as it were, by this sudden and alarming development, the poor man broke the second coconut with the prayer that all these mouths be removed. And immediately the prayer was gratified fully, so fully that he found that even the mouth he had had originally was removed, The man, now at his wits' end, thereupon broke the third and last coconut, with the prayer that his original possession be restored to him, and this was fulfilled. He got back his *status quo ante.*]

Losing both branches—see "*BRANCH.*"

Losing both priesthood and "pandu-heliya"— see "*PRIEST-HOOD.*"

LOTUS

Though the lotus flower is very sweet, yet its stalk is very coarse.

මහනෙල් මල ඉතා සුවඳ නමුත් එහි දණ්ඩ කොර සැඩියි.

Frogs exist even in the lotus pond—see "*FROGS.*"
Water-drop on a lotus leaf—see "*WATER.*"

LOVE—(*See* "*AFFECTION.*")

LOVER

Serving soup to unwanted lover—see "*SOUP.*"

LUCK—(*See also* "*FORTUNE.*")

Dogs which bark at lucky people—see "*DOG.*"
Fish on a lucky day—see "*FISH.*"
On a lucky day even bulls are said to bring forth—see "*BULL.*"

"LULA"

The "lúlá" that got away is the big "lúlá."

ගිය ලූලා මහ එකාලු.

[The *lúlá* is a fresh water fish, so called. *Ophiocephalus striatus.*]

The pit which has no "lúla"—see "*PIT.*"

LUXURY

In adversity a fan is a luxury—see "*ADVERSITY.*"

MAD

Like the mad woman's bag of herbs.

පිස්සිගෙ පළා මල්ල වගෙයි.

"MAGGONA"

Like the people of Maggona who tried to carry a well on a stick.

මග්ගොන මිනිස්සු ළිඳ් තැඩලුවා වගෙයි.

[Some men of Maggona, finding a pot of sweet toddy near a certain well, thought that the liquid must be the water of the well. They, therefore, proceeded to dig out the well for the purpose of carrying it away. In order to lift it they used a slender *tampalá* (Lat. *Nothosaerua brachiata,* Tam. *Chirupilai*) plant as a lever. The story concludes that, seeing their shadows in the well, which they took to be the owners of the well, they became frightened and ran away. Thenceforward, to be a "man of Maggona" (like he of Tumpane) was to be known as a simpleton.]

"MAGUL-SAKVALA"

The light of this world is good—see "*HAND.*"

MAHA-SONA

A Maha Sóná killing—see "*DEVIL.*"

"MAHADENAMUTTA"

Like the wisdom of Mahadenamuttá.

මහදැනමුත්තාගෙ නුවණ වගෙයි.

[*Mahadenamuttá* means, literally, the great well-informed one. A certain man, whose calf had put its head into a pot, consulted Mahadenamuttá (who was proverbial for his wisdom) as to what means should be adopted in order to extricate the calf's head without any injury either to it or to the pot. The sage mounted his elephant and rode in the direction of the man's house. In order to enter the garden he had to get a wall broken down, and a house, too, to gain the inner compound where the calf was tethered. Then he ordered the calf's neck to be cut asunder, and after breaking the pot, he took the head out and gave it to the owner of the calf, saying at the same time, "How on earth will you get on when I am dead and gone."]

MALADY—(*See "SICKNESS."*)

"MAL-BALIYA"

The tavern keeper's "mal-baliya"—see "*BALI.*"

MALDIVE-FISH

The paddá-boatman's "umbalakade"—see "*UMBALAKADE.*"

"MALLA"

Rats in the "malla" even after paying for it—see "*BAG.*"

"MAMA"—(*See also "UNCLE."*)

Milk and the "Mámá's" thumb—see "*UNCLE.*"

MAMMOTY

Earth from the mammoty—see "*HOE*"

MAN

Each man in the world excels in one thing or another.

"ලොවින් එකෙක් එක දේකට වෙසි සමත."

Great men can fully understand the good qualities of (other) great men.

උත්තමයන්ගේ ගුණ උත්තමයෝ දනිත්.

Like the fellow who was named the "Arrant Fool."

ඉරව්ට මෝඩයසි නම්ලත් එකා වගෙයි.

[A certain fool, when his boat was in danger of sinking, took the pingo he had in the boat on to his shoulders, with the object of lightening the boat.]

Like the man with the brim round his neck.

ගැටිය කරේ හිටිය කථාව වගෙයි.

[A certain man, being unable any longer to suffer the ill-treatment he was subjected to by his wife, went to a distant country in search of a friend of his, with the object of acquainting him with his troubles. When the two friends were talking together, the wife of the latter came, apparently in a rage, and struck his head with a chatty, the brim of which, by a curious mischance, fell round the husband's neck. The unfortunate man, turning to his friend from Ceylon, asked him if he had witnessed similar things in his own country. "Assaults are common enough in our country, too," he replied, "but, upon my word, this is the first time I saw the brim falling round the neck."]

Like the same treatment being meted out both to the man who drew water from morning and to the man who broke the pot in the evening.

උදේ සිට දිය ඇද්ද මිනිහත්, සවස කලේ බින්ද මිනිහත්, සමසමවුණ වගෙයි.

The man who goes from tree to tree wets himself unto death.

ගහින් ගහට ගිය මිනිහා තෙමී නාහිනවාලු.

A bull butting a man fallen from a tree—see "*BULL.*"
A certain man's description of sugar-candy—see "*CANDY.*"
A dropsical man's thirst—see "*DROPSY.*"
A man who had escaped all seven gallows—see "*GALLOWS.*"
A man's best fate—see "*FATE.*"
Anger evaporates against a thousand men—see "*ANGER.*"
Blowing a chank to a deaf man—see "*DEAF.*"
Even wise men are sometimes outwitted—see "*WISDOM.*"
How a certain man took "Pansil"—see "*PANSIL.*"
Hunchback forced to walk erect—see "*HUNCH-BACK.*"
Lazy man's gift of prophecy—see "*PROPHECY.*"
Man in fever asking for water—see "*FEVER.*"
Man of patience a banner of victory—see "*PATIENCE.*"
Man who had eaten the whole earth—see "*EARTH.*"
Man who was fed up with "kurakkan"—see "*KURAKKAN.*"
Men who had eaten salt out of one bag—see "*SALT.*"
Music to a deaf man—see "*MUSIC.*"
Only man becomes unsightly by ripening—see "*RIPENING.*"
Pen of the man too lazy to write—see "*PANHINDA.*"
Poor men, too, travel on the same road as Kings—see "*KING.*"
Six months' labour of the potter—see "*POTTER.*"
The blind man and stone-throwing—see "*BLINDNESS.*"
The blind man and the gem—see "*GEM.*"
The cleverest man and his match—see "*CLEVERNESS.*"
The club for a strong man—see "*STRENGTH.*"
The deaf man and dumb man—see "*DEAF.*"
The fortunate man—see "*FORTUNATE.*"
The man beaten by a firebrand—see "*FIREFLY.*"
The man of Óvitigala—see "*ÓVITIGALA.*"
The man who can creep—see "*JUNGLE.*"
The man who flung half a coconut at a dog—see "*COCONUT.*"
The man who has no wife—see "*MARRIAGE.*"
The man who refused a little leaven—see "*LEAVEN.*"
The man who said "Now, boil" etc.—see "*SORROWS.*"
The man who spoke of coconuts in his bag—see "*COCONUT.*"
The man who swallowed a "Vihára"—see "*IMAGE*"
The man who threatened to eat his own child's flesh—see "*CANNIBAL.*"
The man who warmed himself—see "*WARMING.*"
The man whose arrack was drunk—see "*ARRACK.*"
The old man does not die—see "*OLD.*"
The over-careful man—see "*ÉDANDA.*"
The poor man, his wife, and the King—see "*POOR.*"
The road of the virtuous man and wicked man—see "*TRAVEL.*"
The shadow of a disagreeable man—see "*SHADOW.*"

The temple and the man who went to worship—see "*RELIGION.*"
The Udarata man's temptation —see "*UDARATA.*"
The white jaggery man's remark—see "*JAGGERY.*"
The white man and the Paduva— see "*PADUVA.*"
When a man with projecting teeth dies—see "*DEATH.*"
When the unlucky man shaves his head—see "*HAILSTORM.*"

"MARAPONA"

Like Kaluva's trip to Márapona—see "*KALUVA.*"

"MARAVAN"

A Kallan may become a Máravan—see "*RANK.*"

"MARAYA"

The "Mára-yuddhaya" and Buddhahood—see "*BUDDHA.*"
The "Márayá" who gives work—see "*FRIEND.*"

MARGOSA

The "karivila" round the margosa—see "*KARIVILA.*"
The worm born in a margosa tree—see "*WORM.*"

MARRIAGE

He who has no wife has one "timba" of "vi"; the "timba" gives him one "neliya" of "hál"; this "neliya" of "hál" gives him one "némbiliya" of "bat," which gives him one mouthful.

අඹු නැති මිනිහාගෙ වී තිඹට හාල් නැළියයි, හාල් නැළියට බත් නැඹිලියයි, බත් නැඹිලිය කනකොට බත් කැටයයි.

[This proverb is intended to show the domestic value of a wife to her husband—the bachelor being robbed by every one. A *timba* equals four measures, *vi* is unhusked rice; a *neliya* equals a seer (*séruva*) or one-fourth of a *timba*; *hál* being husked rice; *némbiliya* here means the quantity that will fill a *némbiliya*, which is a small chatty used in cleansing rice in water previous to being boiled, *bat* of course being boiled rice.

The Tamils, among whom (like the Sinhalese) the marriage of the daughters of the house is considered a sacred duty which must be performed as soon as possible, have the following sayings :—

(*a*) "After ten years of age a girl should be affianced, even if to a Páriah,"

(*b*) "She who has no husband is like sand in the bed of a river,"

(*c*) "She who marries will do well, whether her husband be old or poor." They regard a girl as a burden on the family until she is married, wherefore they say :

(*f*) "When a virgin is yet unmarried, may the youth, her brother, marry ?" The dowry now plays a very important part in all marriage transactions. Say the Tamils :

(*g*) "Never mind should the youth at the plough become lean; take care of the girl who has received the nuptial present." Divorce is opposed to the principles of the Hindu religion, and in the view of the Tamils :

(*h*) "Although a man may even marry a widow, he should on no account marry a divorced woman." Marriage with a deceased wife's sister is very common :

(*i*) "If my mother die, my father becomes uncle"—*i.e.*, he marries his wife's sister—is a common Tamil saying. The Tamils also say :

(*j*) "When plates are interchanged, intermarriages take place," *i.e.*, if persons can eat together they can intermarry, commensality being confined to persons of the same caste.]

For the marriage that is coming off, shrimps get entangled even in the " kemana " that is in the loft.

කරියන මඟුලට අටුවේ තිබෙන කෙමනෙත් ගංගරා වැදෙනවාලු.

[The *kemana* is a peculiar kind of basket placed in streams for catching fish. When it is not in use, it is usually placed in the loft of one's house. The point of the saying is, in effect, that " Nothing succeeds like success." Even fish proffer themselves as food to the house where everything goes off smoothly.]

Inquire when giving in marriage, but you need not when bringing in marriage.

සිරයක් දෙනකොට සොයා දෙන්ටත්, ගේනකොට නොසොයා ගේන්ටත්.

[That is, inquire well into the caste before giving a female child in marriage, but you need not be so particular about caste when taking a girl in marriage. The Tamils have a similar saying, " Know the parentage, and then give a girl in marriage."]

Like the marriage (proposal) of the Inaggoda people.

ඉනාග්ගොඩයන්ගේ මඟුල වගෙයි.

[Inaggoda is a village near Colombo. There was a young man on whose behalf certain people of this village once went to another village in connection with a marriage proposal. They were cordially received by the girl's father who, when breakfast time drew nigh, enquired of them who was their leader and spokesman, since it was customary to offer to such a person first the glass of water for washing the mouth preparatory to sitting down to the meal. Every member of the visiting party claimed to be the leader, whereupon the annoyed father drove the whole lot of them away, remarking, " I'll be damned before I give my daughter to any Inaggoda man."]

Seven thunderbolts are ordained for the match-maker.

මඟුල් කපුවාට හෙණ හතක්ලු.

[Both parties invoke curses upon his head when things go wrong, as they usually do, *after* the marriage.]

Something of the savour of marriage you will know when the children cry.

මඟුලේ රස දැනෙන්නේ ළමයින් හඬන විටලු.

The quarrel between husband and wife lasts only till the rice is boiled.

දෙන්නා දෙමහල්ලන්ගේ තරහ බත ඉදෙන කල් පමණයි.

[Conjugal quarrels are of short duration.]

The widowhood that you know is preferable to the unfamiliar marriage state.

නුපුරුදු දීගයට වඩා පුරුදු කණවැන්දුම යහෙකි.

[A single life is preferable to an unhappy marriage.]

MARRIAGE (POLYGAMOUS)

"I cook rice for all of them," says the woman.

"We earn our living in the same house," says the man.

"මම ඒ දෙදෑන්දෙනාටම බත් උයා දෙනවා" [ස්ත්‍රී].

"අපි එක ගෙයි රක්‍ෂා වෙනවා" [පුරුෂයා].

[In cases where polygamy prevails, the joint husbands do not say that they have a wife in common. The phrase employed is "*api ekageyi raksávenavá.*" Nor does the woman say "I am their wife," but "*Mama e detundenátama bat uyá denavá.*"]

Arranging a match for the crocodile—see "*CROCODILE.*"
A wife gets up before daybreak—see "*WIFE.*"
Bad to remain behind adzes and wives—see "*WOMAN.*"
Doting and widowhood—see "*DOTING.*"
Funereal fare at a marriage feast—see "*FOOD.*"
Life on boiled herbs, when married—see "*HERBS.*"
The ex-priest and his two wives—see "*BUDDHISM.*"
The poor man, his wife, and the King—see "*POOR.*"
The remark of the morrow's bride—see "*BRIDE.*"
Whomsoever anybody's mother espouses—see "*PALLIYE GURUNNANSE.*"

MASK

Masking in secret and dancing in public—see "*DANCE.*"

MASQUERADE

The dog-masquerading dancer—see "*DANCE.*"
When one masquerades like a dog—see "*DOG.*"

MASTER

For fear of the master—see "*FEAR.*"
Master of house combining with thief—see "*THIEF.*"
The master who gives employment—see "*FRIEND.*"

"MASURAN"

"*Masuran*" *in bread for the sinner*—see "*SINNER.*"

"MATARA"

Even after going to Mátara, have you learnt only to scrape coconut?

මාතර ගොස් උගත්තේ පොල් ගාන්ට විතරක්ද?

[Is that all the knowledge you have brought from such a seat of learning?]

To be educated at Mátara—see "*FATE.*"

MATCH

Arranging a match for the crocodile—see "*CROCODILE.*"
The clever man and his match—see "*CLEVERNESS.*"
The lid that just suits the jar—see "*JAR.*"

MATCH-MAKER

Seven thunderbolts for match-maker—see "*MARRIAGE.*"

"MATHE APPU"

Mathe Appu as Vedarála—see "*VEDARÁLA.*"

MATS

Spreading mats for elephants—see "*PASDUN KÓRALE.*"

MATTRESS

Will a leech remain on a mattress ?—see "*LEECH.*"

MATURITY

Premature maturity due to hot weather—see "*WEATHER.*"
Ripening before time of maturity—see "*RIPENING.*"

MEASURE

A "Láha" is a "timba," and a "timba" is a "láha."

ලහත් තිඹසි; තිඹත් ලහසි.

[Both *láha* and *timba* are terms applied to the same measure of capacity, equivalent to four *neli* (quarts) or one-eighth of a bushel.]

A "timba," a "neliya" and a "nembiliya"—see "*MARRIAGE.*"
Born unto a quarter measure—see "*FATE.*"
Measuring frogs with a "láha"—see "*FROGS.*"
Seven measures of the oil of eye-flies—see "*MEDICINE.*"
The "gavva" and the "ambalama"—see "*AMBALAMA.*"

MEAT—(*See also* "*FLESH.*")

The smell of meat and barking of dogs—see "*DOG.*"
The Vedda making meat of "Goraka"—see "*VEDDA.*"

MEDICINE

For the doctoring that will never come off, seven measures "(patta)" and a little more, of the oil of eye-flies are required.

නොකරන වෙදකමට කෝඳුරු තෙල් හත්පට්ටයකුත් ටිකක් ඕනෑලු.

Like taking medicine in anticipation of illness.

මතු පැමිණෙන ලෙඩට බෙහෙත් කන්නා වගෙයි.

Like trying to gulp down medicine without the knowledge of the throat.

උගුරට හොරා බෙහෙත් කන්නා වගෙයි.

Why use enduring medicine upon the non-enduring body ?

නොපවතිනා ශරීරයට පවතිනා බෙහෙත් මොකටද?

Doctoring for a child born to misery—see "*CHILDREN.*"
Failing Kingship, try the healing art—see "*KING.*"
Paddy and money as remedies against abuse—see "*ABUSE.*"
Tortoise shell as medicine—see "*TORTOISE.*"

MELTING

Like the gold frog that was melted.

මැකූ රත්රන් ගෙම්බියා වගෙයි.

[A certain woman had a frog made of gold which she had inherited from her ancestors. She desired to melt this frog and make some ornaments for wear out of the gold, but her distrust of goldsmiths—a thieving tribe—prevented her doing so. She, therefore, apprenticed her son to a goldsmith, and, after the young fellow had learnt the art, she handed him the gold frog with instructions to melt it and make her the required ornament. What he did, however, was what even a professional goldsmith would not have dared to do. He hid a live frog behind the small furnace near which he worked, and, when he blew into the fire, the frog hopped away, whereupon he shouted, "Mother, mother, see how the gold frog is running away."]

MERCURY—(See "*QUICKSILVER.*")

MERIT

Offering merit to a sinner—see "*SINNER.*"

"MERU"

Faults as big as Maha Meru—see "*FAULTS.*"

Hopes as high as Meru—see "*FATE.*"

"MESSA"

Like placing the "messa" in the direction in which the creeper goes.

වැල යන අතට මැස්ස දමනවා වගෙයි.

[*Messa* is a small erection or support made of sticks.]

MIDWIFE

Don't go on midwife's work if you cannot remain awake of nights.

නිදිවර ඉවසන්ට නොපිළිවන්නම් වින්නඹු කමේ නොයන්.

"MIGAMUVA"

Where can you find "nikini" in Migamuva ?

මීගමුවේ නිකිණි කොයින්ද?

[*Nikini* is a chimera, something which never existed except in the imagination. "*Migamuwa*" is the Sinhalese name for Negombo, the town 23 miles from Colombo.]

The husband at Migamuva—see "*TALK.*"

MILK

Like eating in milk and washing your hand in honey.

කිරියෙන් කාලා පැණියෙන් අත සෝදුවා වගෙයි.

Like giving milk to a venomous serpent to drink.

"පෙවූ කිරි වැන්න විස ඝොර සප්."

Like putting a little cow-dung into a pot of milk.

කිරි කළේකට ගොම ටිකක් මුහුකළා වගෙයි:
[කිරි පද්දෙ ගොම අතක් ලූවා සේ).

"Saddharmaratnāvaliya," 795[2]]

Charcoal washed in milk—see " *CHARCOAL.*"
Knocking the milky tree—see " *KNOCK.*"
Maternal uncle and breasts to give milk—see " *UNCLE.*"
Milk in the thumb of maternal uncle—see " *UNCLE.*"
Milk poured into a conch-shell—see " *PURITY.*"
Swan sucking milk out of water—see " *SWAN.*"
The mother's milk welling up when child cries—see " *MOTHER.*"
The pig and rice boiled in milk—see " *PIG.*"

MIND

One's prosperity will be proportioned to the purity of his mind.

හිතේ හැටියට කල යසි.

MISERY

Child born to misery needs no doctoring—see " *CHILDREN.*"

MISFORTUNES

Sweet cakes and misfortunes—see " *ADVERSITY.*"

MISTAKES

Even teachers trip over words—see " *TEACHER.*"

MOCKING

Like mocking (at a man) after giving him your hand.

අත දීලා දත නියවනවා වගෙසි.

MONEY—(*See also* " *PICE.*")

Five pieces of money, but ten airs.

කාසි පහට වෙස් දහයලු.

Like the money (copper) that is not accepted.

නොගන්නා සල්ලිය වගෙසි.

Seeing Money's power, Respectability went slinking to hide itself in the thicket [or Seeing the power of wealth, the (dignity of) caste crept into the jungle (i.e., *the pride of birth disappears in the presence of wealth*).]

" බලය දැක මුදලේ—කුලේ රිංගා ගියසි අකුලේ."

[Quoted from Kav-Sangaráva, 215.]

Where there is money, there lies the advantage, too.

කොතනද කාසි, එතනට වාසි.

[The Tamils have a saying : " Money spent on silver ornaments and on firewood is lost in the spending."]

Drunk on one-cent toddy—see " *TODDY.*"
Lend a friend a fanam—see " *FRIEND.*"
Money a remedy against abuse—see " *ABUSE.*"
Quarter cents among Rupees—see " *RUPEES.*"
The frog upon a silver coin—see " *FROG.*"

MONKEYS

Like the monkey that has eaten "Goraka."

ගොරක කාපු රිළවා වගෙයි

[A monkey, whose teeth has been set on edge by eating *Goraka* (which is very sour), shows his teeth. *Goraka* here is the acid fruit of the tree (Lat. *Garciniá Cambogia*, Tam. *Korakkai-puli.*)]

The monkey does not walk the ground even though three score years of age.

හැට පිරුණත් වඳුරා බිම ගමන් නැති.

The monkey that falls from a tree becomes an outcast from his tribe.

ගසෙන් වැටුණ වඳුරා රැළෙන් අත් හරිනවාලු.

What garlands for monkeys?

රිළවුන්ට මොන මල්වඩම්ද ?

[Note the similar "*What white cattle for Paduvás*" : Cf. Eng. "Pearls before swine."]

When did monkeys clear jungles ?

රිළවු කැලෑ කෙටුවෙ කවද්ද ?

When did monkeys play the "dólé" ?

රිළවු ඩෝල් ගැහුවෙ කවද්ද ?

[The *dólé* is a kind of drum.]

Why keep ladders for leaping·monkeys ?

පනින රිළවුන්ට ඉනිමං තියන්නේ මන්ද ?

[Which can climb without such aid.]

Dead body of monkey—see "*KORAVA.*"
The monkey's trick on an alligator—see "*TRICK.*"

MONTH

Vagrant who had strayed for six months—see "*STRAY.*"

MOON

Like the moon shining on a jungle.

බැද්දට පැවූ හඳ වගෙයි.

Darkness in enmity to the moon—see "*DARKNESS.*"
Dogs bark even at the moon—see "*DOG.*"
Moon unruffled by dogs barking—see "*DOG.*"

MOORMAN

Even the Tamby of the adjoining boutique will not escape.

අල්ලපු කඩේ තම්බිත් බේරෙන්නේ නැහැ.

[That is, everybody will be dragged into trouble, including even the Tamby next door, who usually minds his own business and does not meddle in the affairs and disputes of his Sinhalese neighbours. Cf. The proverb, "Like the justice of the King of Kekilla."]

It does not matter how the dying Moorman gives up the ghost, whether by too much eating or too much drinking.

නසින මරක්කලයා කාලා නැසුණත් එකයි, බීලා නැසුණත් එකයි.

Like the Tamby who sees gems.
මැණික් දැක්ක තම්බි වගෙයි.

[Tamby is a Tamil term for a Moorman. The Ceylon trade in gems is largely in the hands of the Moorman who, when he sees precious stones, is popularly supposed to keep drinking water continually to allay, as it were, the strong desire which is said to keep welling up in his heart.]

Like the Tamby's hat (fez).

තම්බිගෙ තොප්පිය වගෙයි.

[Fits nicely, whichever side of the head it is put on.]

There's no place where the Moorman and the crow cannot be found.

මරක්කලයත් කාක්කත් නැති තැනක් නැහැ.

[Both are so ubiquitous.]

Poor Moormen drink even toddy.

දුප්පත් මරක්කලයෝ රාත් බොනවාලු.

This is a great " Yon " slaughter—see " *YONAS.*"

MORROW

The morrow's bride—see " *BRIDE.*"
The morrow's elephant—see " *TODAY.*"

MORTAR

The Gama-rála's mortar—see " *GAMA-RÁLA.*"
Tying up the mortars of the village—see " *ELEPHANT.*"

MOTHER

Like placing blocks of wood before mothers (who have borne children.)

වැදූවත් ඉදිරියේ කොලොම්බු ලන්නා වගෙයි.

One's own mother and the sky are never well spoken of.

අහසටත් වැදූ මවටත් හොඳක් නැතිලු.

[Equally is this the case with the mother-in-law, of whom the Tamils have the following sayings :—
(*a*) " However cruel a mother-in-law may be, she is, nevertheless, desirable."
(*b*) " If broken by the mother-in-law it is an earthen vessel, if by the daughter-in-law it is a golden vessel."
(*c*) " It is said that six months after the death of the mother-in-law a tear came into the eye of the daughter-in-law."
(*d*) " Though a mother-in-law may be reconciled, the broken pieces of an earthen pot cannot be put together again."
(*e*) " Will my troubles never cease, will my sorrows never end, will my mother-in-law never die ? "]

What avails the father when one's mother dies ?

අම්මා නැති කාලේ අප්පා කවර පලේ.

It is when her child cries that the mother's milk wells up.

දරුවා ඇඬූකොටලු මවුට කිරි එරෙන්නේ.

A pilfering goldsmith and his mother—see "*BADÁLÁ.*"
Asking the thief's mother about the stolen goods—see "*THIEF.*"
On mother's death, father becomes uncle—see "*MARRIAGE.*"
Running away with my mother—see "*HOSPITALITY.*"
Smaller cakes even after Auntie's arrival—see "*AUNT.*"
When a maternal uncle is equal to a mother—see "*UNCLE.*"
Whomsoever anybody's mother espouses—see "*PALLIYE-GURUNNANSE.*"

MOUNTAIN

Mountain not made small by dogs barking—see "*DOG.*"
Opening up a road to a mountain—see "*ROAD.*"

MOUTH—(*See also* "*TALK.*")

Good and evil both proceed from the mouth.

හොඳත් නොහොඳත් දෙකට කටමය.

Not a saying uttered merely because the mouth itched.

කට කසනවාට කියාපු කීමක් නොවේ.

Is there a mouth above the head ?

ඉසට උඩින් කටක් ඇද්ද ?

The mouth is also a sort of sound-producer.

කටත් එක වාජ්ජමකි.

[The word *Vájjama*, used here, literally means *tom-tom.*]

Those who have the mouth have also the country for themselves.

කට ඇත්තන්ටයි රට.

A son with a mouth—see "*CHILDREN.*"
Losing even the mouth you had—see "*LOSING.*"
Like planting with the mouth—see "*TALK.*"
Mouth stinking of Kapuru Hámy—see "*KAPURUHÁMY.*"
Move the hands to move the mouth—see "*HANDS.*"
Such a mouth for such a "baliya"—see "*BALIYA.*"
The fish dies because of its mouth—see "*FISH.*"
The fox with a coconut husk in its mouth—see "*FOX.*"
The tongue and mouth for lying—see "*TONGUE.*"
Who first placed rice in my mouth ?—see "*RICE.*"

"MUCHI"

Like the way "Múchi" ate "kevum !"

මූචි කැවුම් කෑවා වගෙයි.

[Who "Múchi" is I do not know, and, though I have made diligent enquiry, I have not been able to find out the connected story. I have included the saying in this book as I am satisfied that it comes down to us from very olden times. For *kevum*, see under "AUNT."]

MUD

Hedge stake planted in mud—see " *STAKE.*"
When a tusker is stuck in the mud—see " *ELEPHANT.*"

" MUDALIYAR "

How a Kallan may become a Mudaliyar—see " *RANK.*"
Shamelessness and Maha Mudaliyarship—see " *SHAMELESSNESS.*"
Size of belly does not indicate the Mudaliyar—see " *RANK.*"

" MUKKARAYO "

Like the behaviour of the three " Mukkarayo."

මුක්කර තිදෙනාගෙ කථාව වගෙයි.

[A *Mukkaraya* is one who either has a disfigured nose, or speaks with the nose, or has no nose at all. The following story is of three brothers who spoke with the nose—a defect from birth. There was a marriage proposal for the eldest, and all three, upon invitation, had arranged one day to go for dinner to the house of the bride. Before leaving, however, their mother sternly cautioned them against speaking when in the bride's house, lest their nasal defect be discovered. At the meal one of them began behaving like a glutton, wherefore the second pinched him. " This fellow is killing me," yelled the man in pain, whereupon the second shouted to him, " Shut up, you fool." The third then intervened with the remark, " I am the only one who remained silent as mother directed." The proposed marriage was broken off.]

" MURUNGA "—*See* " *DRUM-STICK.*"

MUSIC

What music to a deaf man !

බිහිරාට ගීතිකා මොටද?

Monkeys playing the " dólé "—see " *MONKEY.*"
Playing the fiddle to a deaf elephant—see " *FIDDLE.*"
Sacred song and the tamarind fruit—see " *TAMARIND.*"

MUSTARD

Faults as small as mustard seed—see " *FAULTS.*"

" NAINAMADAMA "

Simon Gamarála's request to his wife—see " *TOBACCO.*"

NAKED

The dog goes naked—see " *DOG.*"

NAME

(Give me) your " Ge-nama " and (I will tell you) your respectability.

ගේ නමත් වැදගත්කමත්.

[The *Ge-nama* is the house name or family name. Of all the parts of a Sinhalese name, the *Ge-nama* is the most important, as it usually reveals the name, rank, occupation, residence, native place, or some particular characteristic or achievement of the original ancestor of the family bearing this *Ge-nama.*]

What does it signify to be called " Hétuhámy " if you cannot procure your daily meal ?

හේතුහාමි කිව්වාට මොකද වේල කන්ඩ නැත්නම් ?

[*Hétu-hámy* means "Mr. Fortunate." For similar Sinhalese sayings, see under *Kapuru-hámy* and "*Kosvatta.*" The Tamils have a like proverb, "Her name is *Pearl Necklace,* yet on her neck she has not a single black bead." Amongst the Tamils (according to Denham) a man who bears the same name as his grandfather would not be addressed by that name, as it would be considered a breach of etiquette and disrespectful to the elder person bearing that name. The Tamils have a saying: "If a person is present, would you call him by any other designation than that of his relationship? Why, then, when he is absent, should you use his name?"

Mouth of Kapuru Hámy—see "*KAPURU HÁMY.*"

Kosvatta, and yet no jak to eat—see "*KOSVATTA.*"

NATURE

Habit greater than nature—see "*HABIT.*"

NAVEL

Could the navel-string be cut before birth ?

උපදින්ට ඉස්සර පෙකණි වැල කපනැකැ ?

[The navel-string is, of course, the umbilical cord.]

" NAYIHAMY "

Cobra though called "Nayihámy"—see "*COBRA.*"

" NONDI PUNCHA "—*See* "*TODDY.*"

NECESSITY

In necessity, even Mathe Appu is Vedarála—see "*VEDARÁLA.*"

Necessity, and the "Hinguru" creeper—see "*HINGURU.*"

Prosperity and ebony furniture—see "*ADVERSITY.*"

[The Jamaican equivalent of *mater artium necessitas* is : "When cow can't get water to wash him pickney face, him tek him tongue."]

NECK

Snake on God Saman's neck—see "*SNAKE.*"

NECKLACE

Flesh-eater and necklace of bones—see "*BEEF.*"

Pearl Necklace, yet not one bead—see "*NAME.*"

NEEDLE

Like leading an ascetic's life on the point of a needle.

ඉදිකටු මුනේ තපස් රකින්නා වගෙයි.

What avails a needle being changed even into gold ?

ඉදි කටුවක් රත්රන් වෙලා මොටද ?

Eye blinded by a bow of eacle—see "*EYE.*"

Eye blinded by a golden needle—see "*EYE.*"

His throat is a needle—see "*AMBALAMA.*"

NEGOMBO—(*See under* "*MIGAMUVA.*")

" NELIYA "

A "neliya" of "Hál"—see "*MARRIAGE.*"

" NEMBILIYA "

A "nembiliya" of "Bat"—see "*MARRIAGE.*"

NEST

Throwing stones at hornets' nest—see "*HORNET.*"

NETTLES

The "kahambiliyá" scratches though it grows even in your own garden.

වත්තෙ කහඹිලියාත් ඇඟ කසනවාලු.

[The *kahambiliya* is a kind of nettle (Lat. *Girardinia Zeylanica*).]

NIGHT

The pit discovered at night—see "*PIT.*"

"NIKINI"

Looking for "nikini" in Migamuva—see "*MIGAMUVA.*"

NIM-SEED

Though you wash a nim-seed in water—see "*KOHOMBA.*"

NINE

Eight brinjals but nine taxes—see "*BRINJALS.*"

NOISE

Water in unfilled pot makes noise—see "*WATER.*"
Writing in noisy characters—see "*WRITING.*"

"NONDI PANCHA"—*See* "*TODDY.*"

NONSENSE

Defects exposed by talking nonsense—see "*DEFECTS.*"

OBSTINACY

It makes no difference how the wilful "Guru" goes, above or below.

කිච්චා නහන ගුරු ඉහළින් ගියත් එකයි, පහළින් ගියත් එකයි.

OCEAN—*See* "*SEA.*"

OIL

Like trying to extract oil from squeezed sand.

වැලි මිරිකා තෙල් ගැනීමට තැත්කරන්නාක් මෙනි.

"*Alu-kóbeyiyá,*" *though fried in oil*—see "*PIGEON.*"
Cake costing nothing in oil—see "*CAKE.*"
Oil of eye-flies—see "*MEDICINE.*"

"OLA"

King who tore and threw away "ola"—see "*EDUCATION.*"
Woman who can write on "ola"—see "*WOMAN.*"

OLD

The old man does not die, nor is the bed available (for others).

නාකියා මැරෙන්නෙත් නැහැ, ඇඳ කාටවත් දෙන්ටත් නැහැ.

Senile flightiness vaults even o'er the house-top.

නාකි විසේ ගෙටත් උසේ.

The devil a hermit in old age—see "*HERMIT.*"

OLD PEOPLE

Old people crawl about on their knees in the house where there are no infants.

පුංචි ළමයි නැති ගෙයි නාකී දණගානවාලු.

[The Tamils have the following saying about old people: "At fifty discrimination, at sixty moderation, after sixty no distinguishing characteristic."]

ONE

One individual can ruin a whole community.

වඝීයක් නහන්න එකෙක් ඇති.

You must say "One" before you say "Two."

දෙකට ගණන් කරන්ට ඉස්සර වෙලා එක ගණන් කරන්ට ඕනෑ.

One's own tooth-gum—see "*GUM.*"

ONION

Even the onion carpel is for the stomach.

ලූනු බිකත් බඩටයි.

ORCHARD

A single tree will not make an orchard.

තනි ගහ උයනක් වෙන්නේ නැතිලු.

[Cf. Eng. "One swallow does not make a summer."]

ORNAMENTS

A jewel worn as an ornament—see "*POVERTY.*"
The goldsmith and ornaments of fine gold—see "*DHOBY.*"

OTHERS

What you do unto others will bear fruit for yourself.

අනුන්ට කළ දේ තමුන්ට පල දේ.

OUTCAST

Monkey fallen from a tree—see "*MONKEY.*"

OVERSEAS—(*See also* "*EUROPE.*")

"*Hiramanaya*" *taken overseas*—see "*COCONUT-SCRAPER.*"

"OVITIGALA"

Like the man of "Óvitigala."

ඕවිටිගල මිනිහා වගෙයි.

[A man of Óvitigala (a village in the Kalutara District) was drawing toddy from a *kitul* tree (i.e., the Toddy Palm) when somebody from his home came running to the foot of the tree and shouted up to him that his wife had given birth to a son. Forgetting where he was, the toddy-drawer forthwith began to measure his shadow on the branch of the tree, in order to ascertain the hour of birth, for the calculation of the child's horoscope. He fell down and was killed.]

OWL

"Beauty and fortune mine, your's but a touch of these," said the owl to the yellow-bird.

"රූවට පිනට මමත්, යත්තමකට උඹත්" කියා බකමූණා කහ කුරුල්ලාට කිව්වාලු.

OX

Like the place where the ox drank water.

එළු හරකා වතුර බීපු තැන වගෙයි.

[Unlike the buffalo, the ox does not muddy the place where he drinks water. Sinhalese girls are asked by their parents to keep their homes "Like the place where the ox takes his fill."]

PADDA-BOATMAN

Maldive fish of paddá-boatman—see "*UMBALAKADA.*"

PADDY

Like rooting out "Amu" plants at the sight of Paddy plants.

වී පැළපත දුටුවාම අමු පැළපත ඉගිල්ලුවා වගෙයි.

[*Amu*—a kind of inferior paddy. See under "*AMU.*"]

Like the scarecrow in a paddy field.

කෙතට බැඳි පඹයා වගෙයි.

[The "scarecrow" here is the *pambayá, i.e.*, the figure of a man made of the *pamba*, a kind of weed.]

A "timba" of paddy—see "*MARRIAGE.*"
Dust and paddy and the illiterate man—see "*EDUCATION.*"
He who sows paddy will reap paddy—see "*AMU.*"
If fathers cultivate—see "*CULTIVATION.*"
Paddy as remedy against abuse—see "*ABUSE.*"
The Gamarála's paddy pounder—see "*GAMARÁLA.*"
Tying up village paddy-pounders—see "*ELEPHANT.*"

"PADUVAS"

Like the pestle made by a Paduvá.

පදුවා කපාපු මෝල් ගහ වගෙයි.

[Crooked and crudely done.]

The "Paduvá" gets elevated when the White Man rules the country.

සුද්දාට රටගියාම පද්දාට උඩ ගියාලු.

[The white ruler is, of course, supposed to ignore caste distinctions.]

What white cattle for "Paduvás"!

පද්දන්ට මොන සුදු හරක්ද ?

[The Paduvás—a very low caste—were in olden times forbidden the use and possession of any vehicle. The possession of white bullocks, which were highly esteemed formerly, would in their case be utterly absurd and ridiculous. They usually provided food for elephants and carried palanquins. They were also employed as scavengers, smelters of iron, and in other servile business. They represent a more progressive community today, and held in better esteem.]

PAIN

Pain of stab with a golden weapon—see " *WEAPON*."
Pain of wound no consideration to crow—see " *CROW*."
Pain of the bull and the crow—see " *BULL*."
Pains of death on top of lameness—see " *DEATH*."

PALACE

The pigeon of the King's Palace—see " *PIGEON*."

PALANQUIN

Journey afoot with talk of palanquins—see " *TRAVEL*."

" PALLIYE-GURUNNANSE "

Anybody's mother may take unto herself whomsoever she likes, but what the " Palliye-gurunnánse " wants is his five " ridis."

කාගෙ මව් කවුරු ගත්තත් පල්ලියෙ ගුරුන්නාන්සෙට ඕනෑ රිදී පහයි.

[*Palliye-gurunnánse* means, literally, " Church teacher," who in the old days was usually selected for the office of Registrar of Births, Marriages and Deaths. His fee for recording a marriage was apparently five *ridis* (75 cents to-day), a *ridi* being worth 15 cents in the local currency to-day.]

PALM

Drop of quicksilver on your palm—see " *HAND*."

PALM-LEAF—(*See " OLA*.")

" PAMBA "

Fox entangled in " pamba " thicket—see " *FOX*."

PANDIT

Hundred Pandits and a single fool—see " *FOOL*."
The " Kanaya " as Pandit—see " *PIT*."
The erudite Pandit and the " Édanda "—see " *ÉDANDA*."

PANGOLIN—(*See " ANT-EATER*.")

" PANHINDA "

The " panhinda " of the man who is too lazy to write is heavier than the " yagadáva " of King Gaja Báhu.

ලියන්ට මැලි අයගේ පන්හිඳ ගජබාහු රජුගේ යගදාවටත් වඩා බරලු.

[The *panhinda* is the iron pen or stylus used by the Sinhalese in writing or engraving their books. The *yagadáva* was a fabulous staff or iron club which King Gaja Báhu used as a walking-stick and which, according to Sinhalese folklore, " could with difficulty be raised by seven Giants." Gaja Báhu (A.D. 112-131) was a celebrated King of ancient Ceylon, renowned as the conqueror of Southern India.]

" PAN-MADUVA "

Like commencing a " Pán-maduva " in the midst of a " Gini-maduva.".

පාන් මඩු අස්සේ ගිනි මඩු පටන් ගත්තා වගෙයි.

[*Pán* " lamp," *maduva* " shed "—a temporary shed erected for the purpose of offering to and invoking demons. These sheds are so called in consequence of the devil or demon worship being performed by night, when the use of lamps is necessary. *Gini*—" fire," *maduva* " shed "—a temporary shed where offerings are made to Agni Devi, the Goddess of Fire.]

PANSIL

Like the way Abará took "Pansil."

අබරා පන්සිල් ගත්තා වගෙයි.

[By *Pansil* (*i.e.*, *Pancha*, "five," *Sila*, religious obedience or observance of law) is meant the subordinate code of moral law in Buddhism applicable to all men—(1) not to kill, (2) not to steal, (3) not to commit adultery, (4) not to lie, and (5) not to drink intoxicating liquors. A person is said to take *Pansil* when he solemnly promises in the Temple, before a Priest, to adhere to these five precepts. The origin of the above saying is in this wise : A certain woman, on returning home after taking *Pansil*, asked the husband why he, too, did not take *Pansil*. "I do not know how to do it," replied the husband. "What you have to do," said the wife, "when you go to the Temple, is to repeat, after the Priest, whatever he tells you." The husband accordingly went to the Temple. The Priest, on seeing the man, asked him. "Hallo, man ; Where are you going ?" The man, too, repeated the same words. "Are you mad ?" said the Priest, and "Are you mad ?" rejoined the man. The Priest, who had been highly offended at the way the man had spoken to him, ordered his attendants to give the man a thrashing. This order, too, was repeated by the man in the very words of the Priest. The man, however, was given a sound thrashing by the Priest's attendants. On returning home he said to his wife, "I am surprised, my dear, you look so healthy after taking *Pansil* so often, whereas I have caught a fever after taking it only once.]

There's the creature, here's the stick, I have taken "Sil."

අන්න සතා, මෙන්න පොල්ල, මම සිල් සමාදන් වෙලා.

[A man who had taken *Sil* for the day—that is, had vowed to observe the precepts, including the one ordaining "not to kill"—saw a deadly snake hard by his house. In order *literally* to follow the precept and yet have the snake destroyed, he yelled out to another near him "There's the creature, here's the stick, I have taken *Sil*."]

"PARANGIYA"

Like the "Parangiyá" going to Kótte.

පරංගියා කෝට්ටෙට ගියා වගෙයි.

[*Parangiyá* is a contemptuous term applied by the Sinhalese to the Portuguese mainly. The point of the proverb is that it was a journey accomplished by an unnecessarily long and circuitous route. The first Portuguese who landed at Colombo in 1505, desiring to go to the residence of the Sinhalese King at Kótte, then the capital of the country, engaged some Sinhalese guides to conduct them there. These guides, in order to conceal from the foreigners the proximity of the Sinhalese capital to the seaport of Colombo (the distance being only some six miles), took them through Panadure and Rayigama Kórale. Thus several days were taken for a journey which might have been accomplished in a couple of hours.]

PARASITE

Bane of the tree is the parasite— see "*BANE.*"

PARENTS

Thief's mother and the stolen goods—see "*THIEF.*"
Depraved children unlike depraved parents—see "*CHILDREN.*"
Grandfather and grandson—see "*CHAIR.*"
If fathers cultivate—see "*CULTIVATION.*"

Laziness is father of sin—see " *LAZINESS.*"
The devil as god-father—see " *HELL.*"
Parent crab and its young ones—see " *CRAB.*"

PARIAH

Affianced even to a Pariah—see " *MARRIAGE.*"
White Pariah not to be trusted—see " *BRAHMAN.*"

PARROT

Like the parrot in a golden cage in the King's Palace.

රජ මාලිගාවේ රන් කූඩුවේ සිටි ගිරවා වගෙයි.

[The parrot said that it was infinitely better for him to utter one note with his flock, than to live in a golden cage in the King's palace and enjoy delicious food.]

PARTNERSHIP

Even congee is bad in partnership.

හවුලේ කැඳත් නරකයි.

" PASDUN KORALE "

Like the people of Pasdun Kórale.

පස්දුන් කෝරලේ මිනිස්සු වගෙයි.

[The people of this Kórale, like those of Maggona and Tumpane in former times, were said to be great simpletons. On one occasion they are said to have spread mats for elephants to walk on. Pasdun Kórale is in the Kalutara district.]

PAST

Sorrows of the past are sweet—see " *SORROWS.*"

PATIENCE

Patience begets consolation.

ඉවසිල්ලෙන් සැනසිල්ල ලැබේ.

The man of patience is a banner of victory in the battle-field.

" ඉවසන දනා රැපු යුදයට ජයකොඩිය."

PATIENTS

One who has killed a thousand patients—see " *PHYSICIAN.*"

PATTING

Patting the head to gouge out the eye—see " *EYE.*"

PAVILION

Construction of sheds and pavilions—see " *BRIDE.*"

PAY

You must pay for what you do to others—see " *OTHERS.*"

PEACOCK

Crow's flesh and peacock flesh—see " *FLESH.*"
What you relish to eat is like peacock flesh—see " *EATING.*"

PEN

The pen of the lazy man—see " *PANHINDA.*"

PEOPLE

Cunning people can escape hell—see " *HELL.*"
Dogs which bark at fortunate people—see " *DOG.*"
Marriage proposal of Inaggoda people—see " *MARRIAGE.*"
Old people crawling on their knees—see " *OLD.*"
People of Maggona—see " *MAGGONA.*"
People of Pasdun Kórale—see " *PASDUN KÓRALE.*"
People with white teeth even in Gilimale—see " *GILIMALE.*"

PEPPER

How hot the pepper seed is can be found out only when you bite it.

ගම්මිරිස් ඇටේ සැර දැනෙන්නේ විකුවාමලු.

" PERAHERA "

Is there tom-toming, too, at an Ehela Perahera ?

ඇහැළ පෙළහැරට බෙරත් ඇද්ද?

[The *Ehela Perahera* is a Buddhist festival (religious procession) held in the month of *Ehela* (June-July) at which the beating of tom-toms is an absolute necessity, a *sine qua non* in fact.]

PERSONS

Story of the four deaf persons—see " *DEAF.*"

PERVERSITY

Even " Bali " cannot cure inborn perversity—see " *BALI.*"

PESTLE

Can a thorn be removed by a pestle ?—see " *THORN.*"
Milk tree and pestle—see " *KNOCK.*"
Pestle blow to a man unmoved by a wink—see " *WINK.*"
Pestle made by a Paduvá—see " *PADUVÁ.*"
Python which had swallowed pestles—see " *PYTHON.*"

PHYSICIAN

A physician will not leave until death—see " *VEDARÁLA.*"

PICE

Though the " kachchiya " goes for a " pichchiya "—see " *DOG.*"
To buy a horse for two pice—see " *HORSE.*"

PICKLES

What pickles for pigs—see " *PIG.*"

PIG

One pig will not dig for another.

ඌරෙකුට ඌරෙක් හාරා දෙන්නේ නැතිලු.

Like chopping a pig's flesh on its own back.

ඌරාගේ මස් ඌරාගේ ඇඟේ තිබා කපන්නා වගෙයි.

Like covering a pig's snout with gold.

ඌරාගේ හොස්සේ රත්රන් බැන්දක් මෙනි.

The pig fed on foeces nauseates milk-rice.

අසූචි කන ඌරාට කිරිබත් දැක්කාම ඔක්කාරෙයි.

What pickles for pigs !

ඌරන්ට මොන අච්චාරුද?

When did pigs eat saffron ?

ඌරෝ කහ කෑවේ කවදද ?

PIGEON—(*See also* " *DOVE*.")

Like the pigeon of the King's Palace.

රජ ගෙදර පරෙවියා වගෙයි.

[Free, well-fed, and a general favourite.]

An " alu-kobeyiyá " though fried in oil—see " *KOBEYIYÁ*."

PILLOW

Changing pillow to ease headache—see " *HEADACHE*."

" PIMBURA "

Like a " pimburá " hunt—see " *SNAKE*."

PINCERS

Burning your hand while having the pincers—see " *HAND*."

PINE

It's all the same whether the screw-pine is on the tree or on the ground.

වැටකෙයියා ගෙඩිය උඩ තිබුණත් බිම තිබුණත් දෙකම එකලු.

[The screw-pine is the Sinh. *Vetakeyiyá* (Lat. *Pandanus fascicularis* or *Pandanus odoratissimus*). It is also known as the *Múdukeyiyá*.]

PINGO

Can Simanchiyá know the weight of Rabanchiyá's pingo ?

සිමන්චියාගේ කදේ බර රබන්චියා දනීයැ?

[Eng. " No one knows the weight of another's burden."]

" PINKAMA "

Bear dancing at a Pinkama—see " *BEAR*."

PIT

Like emptying the pit in the nick of time.

කලදුවුදා වළ ඉහින්නා වගෙයි.

Like falling in daylight into the pit you had discovered at night.

රෑ දුටු වළේ දවල් වැටුණක්මෙනි.

The " Kanayá " is the savant of the pit (pond) which has no " Lúlá."

" ලූලා නැති වළට කනයා පණ්ඩිතයා."

[*Kanayá* is a fish found in fields and ponds. For the other, see under " LÚLÁ "]

PLANETS

It is not enough that all the nine planets are auspicious if the tenth is still unfavourable.

නවග්‍රහයෝ නව දෙනාම හොඳ වුණත්, දහවෙනි ග්‍රහයා නරක්වුණොත් බැහැ.

[By the " tenth planet " here is meant one's *wife*.]

PLANTAINS

Failing ash-plantains, even black-plantains will do.

අළු කෙහෙල් නැත්නම් කළු කෙහෙල්වත් ගත්වලු.

[According to Mr. Moon, there are over fifty species and varieties of the *kehel* (*kesel*), banana or plantain, of which the above are two.]

Like the wild cat which ate " eta-kehel."

ඇට කෙසෙල් කෑව උගුඩුවා වගෙයි.

[That is, it felt the effects only afterwards. The wild cat is the *urulévá* (Lat. *Viverra Malaccensis*). The *eta-kehel* (Sansk. *Kastha Kadali*) is a wild variety met with in the hill sides and higher elevations of Ceylon, and, according to Dr. Trimen, is the original of all the cultivated varieties. The above saying originated in Sinhalese Folklore, according to which a wild-cat, suffering from a severe disorder in the stomach by eating the *eta-kehel*, swore he would never eat them again if he got well. Soon after his cure, seeing a bunch of the *eta-kehel* on a neighbouring hill, he went up to it and handled it. The next day he went to the place and ate one. On the third day he ate to his heart's content, observing that the plantains of that hill were not unwholesome. This time, however, he was seized with a more severe complaint in the stomach than before, and he died in agony.]

The bunch of plantains jumped over the fence before the thief.

හොරාට ඉස්සර කෙසෙල්කැන වැට පැන්නාලු.

" *Kottóruvá* " *and the plantain tree*—see " *KOTTÓRUVÁ*."

PLANTING

Hedge-stake planted in the mud—see " *STAKE*."
Planter and wife when yams grow big—see " *YAMS*."

PLANTS—(*See* " *TREE*.")

PLATE

Like dirtying the plate out of which you ate.

කාපු පතේ කැත කළා වගෙයි.

Quantity of rice in the plate—see " *EAT*."

PLAY

Death to the rat and play to the cat—see " *RAT*."
Playing the fiddle to a deaf elephant—see " *FIDDLE*."
The crab's gambols in the water—see " *CRAB*."
When did monkeys play the " dólé "—see " *MONKEY*."

PLOUGHING

Plough on ploughing day, sing on singing day.

සී දාට සීය, ගී දාට ගීය.

[In other words, plough when it's time to plough, and sing when it's time to sing.]

The ploughing done by young bulls is not worth a shake of the ears of the old ones.

තරුණ ගොන් සී සානවා මහලු ගොන් කන් හලනවා වටින්නේ නැතිලු.

The bull that ploughs only half a day— see " *BULL.*"
The youth at the plough—see " *MARRIAGE.*"

PLUCKING
The hand that plucks the " labu-gediyá "—see " *HAND.*"
The fruit plucked prematurely—see " *TREE.*"

POISON
Poison in the heart—see " *HONEY.*"

" POLONGA "
Cobra meeting the " polongá "—see " *FIGHT.*"

POLONNARUVA
The fowl of the ancient capitals—see " *FOWL.*"

" POL-PITTA "
Screws on a " pol-piti baliya "—see " *BALIYA.*"

POLYGAMY
" *I cook rice for all of them*—see " *MARRIAGE.*"

POND
Frogs in lotus pond—see " *FROG.*"
The savant of the pit—see " *PIT.*"

POOR—(See *also* " *ADVERSITY* " *and* " *POVERTY.*")

Every difficulty is to the poor.

දුප්පතාටම වෙසි අමාරුව.

To whom can the poor man complain when the King takes away his wife ?

රජෙක් අඹු ගනිතම් දුගියෙක් කාට කියයිද ?

Dhoby and the poor of the village—see " *DHOBY.*"
Poor men on same road as Kings—see " *KING.*"
Poor Moorman and toddy—see " *MOORMEN.*"

PORCUPINE
Ant-eater in the porcupine's hole—see " *ANT-EATER.*"

PORTUGUESE
" *Parangiyá* " *going to Kótte*—see " *PARANGIYÁ.*"

POSSESSION
Ant-eater in the porcupine's hole—see " *ANT-EATER.*"

POT

A pot filled to the brim does not shake.

පිරුණු කළේ හෙල්ලෙන්නේ නැහැ.

Like the pot placed with its mouth downwards.

මුණින් නැවූ කළේ වගෙයි.

[That is, standing on its mouth.]

Ant in a pot of honey—see "*ANT.*"
Broken pieces of an earthen pot—see "*MOTHER-IN-LAW.*"
Mad woman's bag of pot-herbs—see "*MAD.*"
Water in a half-filled pot—see "*WATER.*"
When broken by the mother-in-law—see "*MOTHER-IN-LAW.*"
Woman and empty water-pot—see "*WOMAN.*"

POT-BREAKER

Fate of pot-breaker and water-drawer—see "*MAN.*"

POTATO

Potato leaf planting with the mouth—see "*TALK.*"

POTSHERD

Rat snake dangling a potsherd and dancing—see "*COBRA.*"

POTTER

Six months' labour of the potter is one stroke to the cudgeller.

බඩහැලයාගෙ හමාසේ වැඩ පොලු කාරයාට එක පාරලු.

[The Tamils have no good word for men of this caste. They say: "If you speak familiarly with a potter, he will not respect you, nor supply you with chatties." They also say, in connection with the change that is gradually taking place in the present day villager's cooking utensils, "When the *chembu* (brass vessel) comes in, the potter goes out."]

POURING

Milk poured into a conch-shell—see "*PURITY.*"
Pouring honey into the ear—see "*HONEY.*"

POVERTY—(*See also "POOR" and "ADVERSITY."*)

Poverty is lighter than "imbul" cotton.

දුප්පත් කම ඉඹුල් පුලුන්වලටත් වඩා හැල්ලුයි.

[Of the man who is utterly destitute, the Tamils say, "He has neither a cloth nor a knife." The lowest state of poverty for a woman they describe as "Not having a bone to pick nor an ear ornament to polish."]

Poverty of the learned—see "*EDUCATION.*"

POWER

Respectability and Money's power—see "*MONEY.*"

PRAWN

Like the prawn's pretensions to cleanliness despite the filth he carries in his head.

ඉස්සාගේ ඉසේ කුණු තිබාගෙන "මම සුදනයි" කියනවාලු.

PREACHING

"*Bana*" *preaching by Veddás*—see "*ADVICE.*"
Preaching to the wind—see "*WIND.*"

PRECAUTION

Precaution excludes wavering (*i.e.*, unsteadiness.)

සූදානමට අලෙසියාවක් නැතිලු.

PRIDE

Pride goes before destruction.

විනාශෙට පළමුවෙන් උඩඟු කමයි.

PRIEST

Like the evidence given by the priest.

හාමුදුරුවන්ගෙ සාක්කිය වගෙයි.

[For fear of being tripped up over details, he confined himself to the bare essentials of what he saw, and resolutely refused to budge from that attitude.]

PRIESTHOOD

Lost both the priesthood and the " pandu-heliya."

සාසනෙත් නෑ, පඬු හැලියත් නෑ.

[The reference is to the man who had given up or been deprived of his robes as a Priest, and thus lost not only the dignity and reverence attached to a sacred office, but also its appurtenant accessories. *Pandu-heliya* is the pot of jakwood dye in which a Priest's robes are dyed.]

Chief High Priest from Tumpane—see " *TUMPANE.*"
Devil who swallowed a Buddhist Priest—see " *DEVIL.*"
Priest who will be ruined by disclosure—see " *BUDDHISM.*"
Priests at loggerheads—see " *BUDDHISM.*"
The ex-priest's two wives—see " *BUDDHISM.*"
The Sangha's language and ex-priests—see " *BUDDHISM.*"

PRISON

Woman is the road to prison—see " *WOMAN.*"

PROPHECY

The sluggard has the gift of prophecy.

කම්මැලියාට දිවස්ලු.

PROSPERITY

When good fortune comes, it comes along a wire ; when it goes, it breaks even ropes of hemp.

එනකොට එන්නේ තන්ගුස් පට දිගේ, යනකොට ගල් කාඹත් කඩාගෙන යනවා.

[That is, in prosperity slight efforts succeed, in adversity even the highest fail.]

A female child in times of prosperity—sec " *CHILDREN.*"
When ebony furniture is a necessity—see " *ADVERSITY.*"
Prosperity and purity of mind—see " *MIND.*"

PROUD

The learned and the proud—see " *EDUCATION.*"

PROVOCATION

If you jump into a well on one provocation—see " *WELL.*"

PROW

The prow going foremost—see " *BOAT.*"

PUBLIC

Masking in secret and dancing in public—see " *DANCE.*"

" PUHUL "—(*See " PUMPKIN."*)

PUMPKIN

His shoulder gives away the ash-pumpkin thief—see " *THIEF.*"
Same hand for " labba " and " puhula "—see " *HAND.*"

PUNISHMENT

Seven thunderbolts for the match-maker—see " *MARRIAGE.*"

PUPILS

Pupils urinate standing—see " *URINATING.*"

PURGING

The iron's purging disease—see " *IRON.*"

PURITY

Like the milk poured into a conch-shell.

හක්ගෙඩියෙ වක්කල කිරි වගෙයි.

PUSHING

Like pushing down one about to fall.

වැටෙන්ට යද්දී තල්ලු කළා වගෙයි.

PYTHON

Like the python which had swallowed pestles.

මෝල්ගස් ගිලපු පිඹුරා වගෙයි.

[That is, stiff and unable to bend.]

A python hunt—see " *SNAKE.*"

QUARREL

Excessive affection precedes a quarrel—see " *AFFECTION.*"
Quarrel between husband and wife—see " *MARRIAGE.*"

QUICKSILVER

Drop of quicksilver on your palm—see " *HAND.*"

" RABANCHIYA "

Weight of Rabanchiyá's pingo—see " *PINGO.*"

RAIN

A rain shower is doubled underneath a tree.

ගහ යට වැහි දෙකලු.

One day's heavy rain is the end of many days' drought.

" සැම දා නියං එක දා වැහි වලාවයි."

The rain which fell was out of proportion to the thunder.

ගෙරවූ තරමට වැස්සේ නැතිලු.

A strong wind means rain—see ' *AFFECTION.*"
Tanks are filled by rain, not dew—see " *TANKS.*"
The " Kendettá's " thirst in spite of rain—see " *KENDETTÁ.*"
The man who goes from tree to tree—see " *MAN.*"

" RANCHAGODA "

The verses of the girl of Ranchagoda—see " *VERSE.*"

RANK

Because his belly is big he is not necessarily a Mudaliyar, and because his house is large it is not, therefore, a "Walauva."

බඩ ලොකු උණු පලියට මුදියාන්සේ නොවේය, ගේ ලොකු උණට වලව්ව නොවේය.

[Percival, writing in 1803, says: "There is no nation among whom the distinction of ranks is kept up with such scrupulous exactness as among the Sinhalese; even in the dimensions and appearance of their house they seem restricted, and a house of a certain size commonly announces its proprietor to have been born in a certain rank." Denham, who quotes the above, adds with truth that "this is far from being the case today." Any man of wealth or position, whatever his caste or origin, now calls his house a *Walauva*, a term originally used for a Mudaliyar's or other Chief Headman's house. The Tamils have a very pregnant saying: "A *Kallan* may become a *Máravan*; by respectability he may develop into an *Ayamudaiyan*, and by slow and small degrees become a *Vellála*, from which he may live to be a Mudaliyar." The *Kallan*, an inferior caste of emigrants from Tinnevelly, Madura, and the South Indian villages, are chiefly coolies in Ceylon. The *Máravan* are a class of Tamils who are emigrants from the Márava country near Ramnad. The *Ayamudaiyan*, also called *Ahambadiyan*, are those who attend to any business in the interior of Temples and palaces. The *Vellálas*, of course, are a superior caste.]

It is good to be a Headman, even in hell.

නිල ලැබීම නරකාදියේ උනත් හොඳලු.

Though the "Disáva" is friendly, still if the "dasáva" be unlucky no rank can be obtained.

දිසාව හොඳ නමුත් දසාව නරකනම් නිල ලබන්ට බැරිලු.

[*Disáva*, in the time of the Sinhalese Kings, was an official of high rank, usually the Governor of a Province—a powerful intermediary for rank or preferment. The term is now applied to a Government Agent as well, by whom recommendations are made to the executive authority for the conferment of native ranks. The *dasáva* is the period during which a person is supposed to be under the influence of any one of the planets.]

Illiterate who boast of high rank—see "*EDUCATION*."
Learned rank with highest caste—see "*EDUCATION*."

RAT

A rat, drunk on toddy, on getting down the tree, said if a cat came he would break him in two.

රා බීලා ගහෙන් බහින මීයා "බළලා ආවොත් දෙකට කඩමිසි" කීවාලු.

Death to the rat and play to the cat.

මීයාට මරලු, බළලාට සෙල්ලමලු.

So long as the cat catches a rat, it matters not that the rat is made of clay.

මැටියෙන් වුණත් මොකද බළලා මීයා අල්ලනවානම්.

Rats and "upásaka" cats—see "*CATS*."
Rats in the bag that has been paid for—see "*BAG*."

RAT-SNAKE

A young cobra cannot be made a rat-snake—see "*COBRA.*"
Rat-snake's dance when the cobra hooded—see "*COBRA.*"
Sinning by killing rat-snakes—see "*SINNING.*"
There are no charms for the rat-snake—see "*SNAKES.*"

"RAVANA"

All born in Ceylon are not Rávanás—see "*BIRTH.*"

"RAYIGAMAYA"

Story of Rayigamayá and Gampolayá—see "*GAMPOLAYÁ.*"

READING

Tambi Appu's inability to read and write—see "*VEDARÁLA.*"

REAPING

You will reap the fruit of your own action, and he of his.

උඹ කළ දේ උඹ ගෙනියසි, තෝ කළ දේ තෝ ගෙනියසි.

[This is supposed to have been said by a Buddhist Priest who, on attempting to cross a dam, was pushed off by one man, but was helped over it by another.]

He who sows "amu" will reap "amu"—see "*AMU.*"

REASON

Listeners should listen with reason—see "*TALK.*"

RED-ANT—(*See* "*ANT*")

REGISTRAR—(*See* "*PALLIYE-GURUNNÁNSE.*")

RELATIONS

What's the use of relations who do not help you when your dam is broken ?

නියර කැඩුණම උදව් නොවෙන නෑයෝ මොකටද ?

[The Tamils say : "The advantage of wealth is the maintenance of one's relatives."]

Designation of relationship—see "*NAME.*"
On mother's death, father becomes uncle—see "*MARRIAGE.*"
Daughter of one's maternal uncle—see "*UNCLE.*"

RELIGION—(*See also* "*BUDDHA*" *and* "*BUDDHISM.*")

Like the crashing down over a man's head of the "Déwála" (Temple) where he had gone to worship.

වඳින්ට ගිය දේවාලේ ඉසේ කඩා වැටුණා වගෙයි.

A shrine without fame—see "*CHILDREN.*"
Bear-dancing at a "Pinkama"—see "*TIGER.*"
How a certain man took "Pansil"—see "*PANSIL.*"
"*Labu-gediya*" *in Buddha-less era*—see "*BUDDHA.*"
Lost both priesthood and "pandu-heliya"—see "*PRIESTHOOD.*"
Preaching to the wind—see "*WIND.*"
There's the stick, I have taken "Sil"—see "*PANSIL.*"
Tiger-dancing at a "Pinkama"—see "*TIGER.*"

RESIN

Offering resin to a devil—see "*DEVIL.*"

RESISTANCE

Digging where it resists—see "*DIGGING.*"

RESPECT

A wise enemy is worthy of more respect than a foolish friend.

නුවණැති සතුරා නුනුවණ මිත්‍රයාට වඩා උතුම්ය.

No respect from the familiar potter—see "*POTTER.*"

RESPECTABILITY

"*Gé-nama*" *as test of respectability*—see "*NAME.*"
Respectability and money's power—see "*MONEY.*"

RICE

Is it you who first fed me with rice ?

මගේ කටේ බත් තැබුවේ උඹද ?

[This, like the question "*Did you name me ?,*" is a common retort amongst the Sinhalese, when it is considered that a person has presumed on an acquaintance, or claimed social equality to which he is not entitled. Amongst Sinhalese Christians they similarly ask, "*Were you my sponsor ?*" (*i.e.*, at baptism).]

"Jak" becomes bitter the day rice is seen.

බත් දුටු දා කොස් තිත්තවුණා වගෙයි.

Like having eaten the rice of the Gods.

දෙසියන්ගෙ කාල් කාලා වගෙයි.

[That is, become mad. This is said to be the punishment inflicted upon those who misuse the offerings made to Gods.]

The excellence of rice is best realised when one is starving.

බතේ අරුම දැනෙන්නේ හාමතේදිලු.

Like letting you go and then holding you by the elbow.

යන්ට ඇරලා වැලමිටෙන් අල්ලනවා වගෙයි.

The way the hand is held shows the sincerity of the invitation to eat.

අමුතු බත් දීම අත ඇල්ලීමෙන් දැනෙයි.

[The allusion here is to an obsolete custom. A man who was anxious that another should partake of his hospitality used to seize his intended guest by the wrist ; while a man whose hospitality was a mere pretence used to get hold of the elbow of his guest.]

To the "Kapurála" are the dance and the somersault, but the rice is to Tikiri-rála.

නැටුම් ගැහුම් කපුරාලටලු, බත් ටික ටිකිරි රාලටලු.

[The *Kapurála* is the officiating priest of a Devála or Kóvila. *Tikiri-rála* is the assistant who cooks the rice which the *Kapurála* offers to the Gods. At the close of the ceremony it is customary for the *Tikiri-rála* to eat the rice thus offered up.]

What gets stale is not the raw rice but the boiled remnant.

බතෙන් තිබුණොත් මිස හාලෙන් තිබුණට පිලුනු නොවෙයි.

Born unto a quarter measure—see "*FATE.*"
Cooked and uncooked rice—see "*MARRIAGE.*"
How the lady gave rice to the dhoby—see "*DHOBY.*"
"*I cook rice for all of them*"—see "*MARRIAGE.*"
If you are inclined to eat—see "*EAT.*"
"*Jak*" *also where there is rice*—see "*JAK.*"
Without eating rice-cake—see "*CAKE.*"
Rice-face overcomes elephant-face—see "*KINDNESS.*"
The pig and rice boiled in milk—see "*PIG.*"
Unhusked rice and illiterate man—see "*EDUCATION.*"
What hot rice for beggars—see "*BEGGARS.*"

RICE-POT

Quarrel till rice-pot is boiled—see "*MARRIAGE.*"

RICE-POUNDER—(*See* "*PESTLE.*")

"RIDIS"

His five "*ridis*"—see "*PALLIYE-GURUNNÁNSE.*"

RING

What's the harm in receiving a knock from a hand which wears a gold ring (in its finger)?

රන් මුද්දක් දාපු අතින් ටොක්කක් කෑවාට මොකද ?

RIPENING

Like ripening before maturity.

පැහෙන්ට ඉස්සර ඉදුණා වගෙයි.

Only man becomes unsightly by ripening.

පැහීමෙන් නරක් වෙන්නේ මනුෂ්‍යයා විතරලු.

RISING

The grandson's rising for the grandfather—see "*CHAIR.*"

RIVER

Does a man fall into the river to drink strained water?

ගඟේ වැටෙන්නේ පෙරාලා බොන්නද ?

[The point of the saying is that a man, in adverse circumstances, cannot expect to have his way or to get what he likes.]

Like not washing your body out of consideration for the river.

ගඟට ගේදමට ඇඟ නොසෝදා ඉන්නා වගෙයි.

A woman is like sand in river bed—see "*MARRIAGE.*"
"*Amude*" *and the Valave Ganga*—see "*AMUDE.*"
Coconut trees from river bottom—see "*COCONUT.*"
Cutting hedge-stakes on to a river—see "*CUTTING.*"
Jaggery and coconut in hand—see "*JAGGERY.*"
Like drinking river water, etc.—see "*WATER.*"
Man who warmed himself at river bank—see "*WARMING.*"
The crane's wait for the river to dry up—see "*CRANE.*"
Water of the celestial river—see "*CHANDÁLA.*"

ROAD—(*See also* " *HIGHWAY.*")

Like opening up a mountain road to bury an elephant.

අලියෙක් වළලන්ට කඳු පාරක් හාරනවා වගෙයි.

One vagrant asking the road from another—see " *STRAY.*"
Poor men on same road as Kings—see " *KING.*"
Road of the virtuous and wicked—see " *TRAVEL.*"
Sleeping on the road because Gods exist—see " *GOD.*"
Woman is the road to prison—see " *WOMAN.*"

ROARING

Roar of a thousand tigers—see " *TIGER.*"
Tiger roaring on the roof—see " *TIGER.*"

ROCK

A succession of blows will set even rocks in motion.

පහර පිට පහර දෙනවිට පර්වතත් ගමන් යත්ලු.

Like trying to peel off the bark from a rock.

ගලෙන් පට්ටා නගන්ට තැත්කරන්නාක් මෙනි.

A struggle on a rock—see " *FIGHTING.*"
If you dash your head against a rock—see " *HEAD.*"
Like sowing on a rock—see " *SOWING.*"
The cat which has evacuated on a rock—see " *CAT.*"
The crow on a golden rock—see " *GOLD.*"
The Gónagala rock and the waves—see " *GÓNAGALA.*"

" RODIYA "

Even a " Rodiyá " will throw a stone at you if you throw one at him.

ගහන ගලට ගල රොඩියාත් ගහනවා.

[Cf. Eng. " Even a worm will turn." A *Rodiyá* is a man of the lowest caste among the Sinhalese—a caste held at one time to be so degraded that it was said that " water over which their shadows had passed was held to be defiled till purified by sunlight."]

There is no lack of dogs in a Rodiyá's hut.

රොඩි පැලේ බල්ලෝ තොර නැත.

[The *Rodiyás* have always had the reputation of being unclean feeders, and one of the reasons for the abhorrence felt for them was probably because they devoured the flesh of cows. The bones and carcases usually found in a Rodiyá's hut account for the above saying.]

Rodiyá meeting the Kinnará—see " *FIGHT.*"

ROOF

The fowl of the ancient capitals—see " *FOWL.*"
The tiger on the roof—see " *TIGER.*"

ROOTING

Rooting out " Amu " plants—see " *PADDY.*"

ROPE

Rope snapping when on the " atura "—see " *ATURA.*"
Ropes of hemp—see " *PROSPERITY.*"

4

ROYAL

When the jungle is a Royal highway—see "*JUNGLE.*"

RUBBING

Andiyás' permission to rub ash—see "*ASH.*"

RUBBISH

All rubbish at Béruvala point—see "*BERUVALA.*"

"RUHUNA"

The man who went to Ruhuna—see "*KURAKKAN.*"

RUIN—(*See also* "*DESTRUCTION.*")

Associate of a goldsmith—see "*BADÁLÁ.*"
One man can ruin a whole community—see "*ONE.*"

RUNNING

Even the short-tailed cow runs after the runners.

දුවන්නන් පාරේ කොට එළදෙනත් දුවනවා.

Like running after runners.

දුවන්නන් පස්සේ දිව්වා වගෙයි.

[That is, without knowing why they run.]

The panting will be proportioned to the distance run.

දිව් පමණටලු හති.

Cart running before bull—see "*BULL.*"
Man unable to run has a heart of stone—see "*DOG.*"
Running away with mother—see "*HOSPITALITY.*"
Tail of the animal running away—see "*TAIL.*"
The dog always runs—see "*DOG.*"
The fox running with coconut husk—see "*FOX.*"
When pupils urinate running—see "*URINATING.*"

RUPEES

Like placing quarter-cents among the rupees.

රුපියල් අස්සේ අළුක්කාල් දමන්නා වගෙයි.

"SABAN-KUKULO"—(*See* "*HABAN-KUKULO.*")

"SABARAGAMUVA"

A deer's cry in Sabaragamuva—see "*TALK.*"

SACK—(*See also* "*BAG.*")

One's own sack is behind, others' in front.

තමන්ගේ මල්ල පිටි පස්සෙන්, අනුන්ගේ මල්ල ඉස්සරහින්.

SAFFRON

Pigs eating saffron—see "*PIG.*"

SAGO

Sago conjee for sinners—see "*SINNERS.*"

SAILING

Small boats like big ships sail on the sea—see "*SEA.*"

SALT

Like eating without salt, though living in a saltern.

ලේවායේ ඉඳගෙන කිවුලෙන් කන්නා වගෙයි.

Like men who had eaten salt out of one bag.

එක මල්ලේ ලුණු කාලා වගෙයි.

[That is, men between whom there is a strong binding attachment.]

Like going to the " Léváya " to bring salt.

ලුණු ගෙනෙන්ට ලේවා ගිය විත්තිය වගෙයි.

[*Léváya* means salt pans or salterns. A certain woman, who had seen the people of her village go to the *Léváya* to bring salt, asked her husband why he too should not do the same. " I do not know how to do it," replied the husband. " There is not much knowledge required to drive a herd of cattle and to bring salt on their backs," said the wife. The husband then set out on his journey. He kept on driving the cattle the whole day and ate the rice he had taken with him. In the evening he came to his own well and made ready to cook his evening meal. Meantime his children came out and shouted, " Father ; Father. " The man got into a rage and said : " Everywhere I go, children call me Father. Am I your mother's husband that you should call me Father ? " The wife, on being told by the children that their father was preparing to cook near the well, came and took her husband home, observing that it was high time that her husband's trip to the *Léváya* should be brought to a close.]

Hiding salt in the back of a "diya-kává"—see " *DIYA-KÁVÁ*."

SALVATION

Bear's death is the lamb's salvation—see " *DEATH*."

" SAMAN DEVIYO "

Escape from God Saman—see " *ESCAPE*."
Snake on God Saman's neck—see " *SNAKE*."

SAND

Trying to extract oil from sand—see " *OIL*."

SANDAL

The dog, though made King, bites sandals—see " *DOG*."

SANDAL-WOOD

What can be wrong with the stone if the sandal-wood is good ?

හඳුන් හොඳනම් ගලේ මොකද වැරද්ද ?

What is the good of there being so many different trees in a jungle if it has no sandal-wood tree ?

වනේ ගස් ජාති එමට තිබුණාට මොටද හඳුන් ගහක් නැතිකොට ?

Civet cats in sandal-wood forest—see " *CAT*."
Dry fish seller and price of sandal-wood—see " *FISH*."

" SANGHA "

Language used by the " Sangha "—see " *BUDDHISM*."
Toddy drinking-cup as "Sangha's" target—see "*BUDDHISM*."

SATISFACTION

Seeing is also a measure of satisfaction—see " *SEEING*."

SATURN

Saturn's fall into the beggar's bowl—see "*BEGGAR.*"

SAVANT

The "Kanayá" as savant in the pit—see "*PIT.*"

SAYING

Not a saying uttered because mouth itched—see "*MOUTH.*"

SCARECROW

The scarecrow in a paddy field—see "*PADDY.*"

SCALDING

Scalding with cold water—see "*WATER.*"

SCISSORS

Jaggery on top, scissors underneath—see "*JAGGERY.*"

SCRATCHING

Scratching begets more scratching—see "*GOSSIP.*"

SCREW

Tightening screws on a "pol-piti baliya"—see "*BALIYA.*"

SCREW-PINE—(*See "PINE."*)

SCYTHE

The scythe cuts sharply to get its neck snapped quickly ; one grows swiftly to end in death swiftly.

කැත්ත කැපෙන්නේ කරින් කැඩෙන්නයි, වහා හැදෙන්නේ වහා මැරෙන්නයි.

Like my club for your scythe—see "*CLUB.*"

SEA

Small boats, too, venture upon the sea where big ships sail.

මහ නැව් යන මුහුදේ කුඩා ඔරුත් යනවාලු.

As well look beyond the seas—see '*HAND.*"
Sea-water will not quench one's thirst—see "*WATER.*"
When the sea becomes congee—see "*SPOON.*"
Wishing long life to the sea—sec "*WATER.*"

SECRETS

Secrets are never long-lived.

රහස් හුඟක් කල් ජීවත් නොවෙයි.

Masking in secret and dancing in public—see "*DANCE.*"

SEEING

Seeing is also a measure of satisfaction.

දැකීමත් එක රැකීමක්ලු.

SELLING

Gain by selling camphor and toddy—see "*TODDY.*"
Selling back for five hundred—see "*TRADE.*"
The seller of dry-fish—see "*FISH*"

SENILE

Senile flightiness vaults o'er house-top—see "*OLD.*"

SERVANT

The servant of God Saman—see "*ESCAPE.*"

SERVING

Serving soup to unwanted lover—see "*SOUP.*"

SEVEN

Seven thunderbolts for the match-maker—see "*MARRIAGE.*"

SHADE

Your own hand the shade for your head—see "*HAND.*"

SHADOW

Even the shadow of the wife to be divorced is deformed.

අරින්ට ඉන්න දිගෙ සෙවණැල්ලත් ඇදලු.

SHAMELESSNESS

Shamelessness is greater even than the Maha Mudaliyarship.

විළි ලජ්ජා නැතිකම මහ මුදලි කමටත් වඩා ලොකුයි.

[The Maha-Mudaliyar is the Chief of the Chief Headmen of the Low-country of Ceylon, the corresponding title in the Up-country being Adigar or Maha Nilame.]

SHOWING

The goat and the lowly barber—see "*BARBER.*"
When the unlucky man shaves his head—see "*HAILSTORM.*"

SHEDS

Construction of sheds and pavilions—see "*MARRIAGE.*"

SHIP

The sea where large ships sail—see "*SEA.*"
When the axe-heads were coming by ship—see "*AXE.*"

SHIPLOAD

Dog and shipload of dung—see "*DOG.*"

SHOOTING

Like shooting from under the water.

දිය යටින් වෙඩි තිබන්නාක් මෙනි.

Like swinging about and shooting.

වනලා වෙඩි තියනවා වගෙයි.

Shot at the hare, but hit the bush.

විද්දේ හාවාටයි, වැදුණේ පඳුරටයි.

Shot at the bush, but struck the hare.

විද්දේ පඳුරටයි, වැදුණේ හාවාටයි.

Missing the elephant target—see "*ELEPHANT.*"
The eye and an eacle-bow—see "*EYE.*"

SHORTNESS

Don't go near a short man nor near a low ant-hill.

මිටි මිනිහාත් මිටි හුඹහත් ළඟින් යන්ට එපා.

[Snakes generally lie in low anthills, and short, dwarfish men (and women) are popularly held to be dangerous people. Note the Sanskrit stanza:

අති දීර්ඝෝ මහා මූර්ඛඃ An exceedingly tall man is generally foolish,
මධ්‍යමස්තු විචක්ෂණඃ A man of middle stature is sensible ;
වාසුදෙවං පුරස්කෘත්‍ය All short men are deceivers,
සර්වේ වාමනකා ශඨාඃ Of whom Vasudeva (Vishnu) is the chief.

SHOULDER

Shoulder of the ash-pumpkin thief—see "*THIEF.*"

SHRIMPS

Shrimps in the "kemana" on the loft—see "*MARRIAGE.*"

SICKNESS—(*See also* "*ILLNESS.*")

To die, there must be a malady—see "*DEATH.*"

SILVER

The frog upon a silver coin—see "*FROG.*"

SILVERSMITH

The young silversmith and his father—see "*BADÁLÁ.*"

"SIMAN GAMARALA"

Siman Gamarála's request to his wife—see "*TOBACCO.*"

"SIMAN PANCHA"

When Siman Pancha met Nondi Pancha—see "*TODDY.*"

"SIMANCHIYA"

Simanchiyá and Rabanchiyá's pingo—see "*PINGO.*"

SIN—(*See also* "*SINNER*" *and* "*SINNING.*")

Hypocrisy a threefold sin—see "*HYPOCRISY.*"
Laziness the father of sin—see "*LAZINESS.*"
The curse as a consequence of sin—see "*CURSE.*"
Sinning by killing rat-snakes—see "*SINNING.*"

SINGING

Sing when it is time to sing—see "*PLOUGH.*"
The song of the dumb man—see "*DEAF*"

SINKING

Great dhoneys sunk by one small leak—see "*DHONEY.*"

SINNER—(*See also* "*SIN*" *and* "*SINNING.*")

Even after giving "masuran" in bread, the sinner did not get them.

පාන් ගෙඩියෙ මසුරන් තබා දීලත් පව් කාරයාට නොලැබුණාලු.

[*Masuran* means gold coins. These are now not extant.]

It is not possible to offer merit to a sinner.

පව් කාරයාට පින් දෙන්න බැහැ.

On the day the sinner's head was shaved, it hailed.

පව් කාරයාගේ හිස බූ ගෑ දා ගල් වර්ෂාව වැස්සාලු.

[A variant is : "There is certain to be a hailstorm when the unlucky man gets his head shaved."]

The sinner will not take up a book, but will carry a load.

පව් කාරයා පොත නුස්සයි, තඩ ගෙනයයි.

What sago congee for sinners ?

පව් කාරයන්ට මොන සව් කැඳද ?

Wherever the sinner goes, there is hailstorm.

පව් කාරයා ගිය ගිය තැන ගල් වැසි.

SINNING

Like sinning by killing rat-snakes.

ගැරඬි මරා පව් ගන්නා වගෙයි.

" SINNO "

The " Sinno " known by his hat—see " *HAT*."

SITTING

Nothing to sit upon in carpenter's house—see " *CARPENTER*."
Sitting on the horn and feeding on the ear—see " *FEEDING*."
"Kaha-kurullá" on King-coconut—see " *KAHA-KURULLÁ*."
The learned sit proudly—see " *EDUCATION*."

SKY

A ladder to reach the sky—see " *LADDER*."
The blind tortoise peering at the sky—see " *TORTOISE*."
The sky and one's own mother—see " *MOTHER*."

SLAUGHTER

A great " Yon " slaughter—see " *YONAS*."

SLAVE

Better to be born a slave than the youngest in a family.

වාලා වෙලා උපදිනවා හොඳලු, බාලයා වෙලා උපදිනව නරකලු.

A slave woman's privilege in prosperity—see " *CHILDREN*."
The debtor is the slave of the creditor—see " *DEBTOR*."
Work like a slave—see " *WORK*."

SLEEP

There are but two, yet each wants to sleep in the middle.

ඇත්තෙත් දෙන්නයි, මැද නින්දත් ඕනැලු.

[That is, of the bed.]

Rousing a sleeping lion—see " *LION*."
Sleeping on road because Gods exist—see " *GOD*."
Uninterrupted sleep and " Bana "—see " *BUDDHISM*."

SLEEPINESS

Sleepiness is unaware of comfort.

නිදිමත සැප නොදනීලු.

Sleepiness and midwife's work—see " *MIDWIFE*."

SLUGGARD

The sluggard has the gift of prophecy—see " *PROPHECY*."

SMASHING

When wild-boars smash "Kekuna" fruits—see "*BOAR.*"

SMELL

Dung-eating dog and a little bad smell—see "*DOG.*"
Smell of meat and barking of dogs—see "*DOG.*"

SMILING

Smiling fox in death-agony—see "*FOX.*"

SMOKE

There's no smoke without fire—see "*FIRE.*"

SNAKES—(*See also* "*COBRA.*")

Like a "pimburu" hunt.

පිඹුරු දඩයම වගෙයි.

[*The pimburá* is the rock snake (*Python molurus*) which is said sometimes to grow to eighteen feet in length and twenty-seven inches in circumference. It is said that no animal can escape death once folded in its coil. According to Sinhalese folklore, the *pimburá* swallows a deer whole and then goes between the trunks of two trees growing near each other, in order to crash the bones of its prey. Its oil is said to cure any bad cut or wound.]

Like a snake that bites without discrimination.

බලා කාපු නයෙක් නොවෙයි.

Like "andu" leaves to the snake.

නයාට අඳු කොළ වගෙයි.

[Snakes are said to avoid even the shadow of the leaves of the *andu* plant which is supposed to affect them in a peculiarly distressing manner.]

Like the snake on God Saman's neck.

සමන් දෙවියන්ගේ කරේ උන් නාගයා වගෙයි.

[See under "ESCAPE" for fuller reference to God Saman.]

There are no charms for the "Garandiyá."

ගැරඬිත්ට මන්ත්‍ර නැහැ.

[The *Garandiyá* is the rat-snake (Lat. *Ptyas mucosus*). It seldom bites, but (according to popular belief) if and when it does, the wound is said to end fatally only if cowdung is trampled on.]

A young cobra cannot be made a rat-snake—see "*COBRA.*"
Giving milk to a venomous serpent—see "*MILK.*"
Impossible to make a rat-snake a cobra—see "*RAT-SNAKE.*"
Missing the blow at a cobra—see "*COBRA.*"
Python which had swallowed pestles—see "*PYTHON.*"
Sinning by killing rat-snakes—see "*SINNING.*"
The cobra's hood and the rat-snake—see "*COBRA.*"

SNAKE-CHARMERS

The gypsy tribe of Ahikuntakayás—see "*KORAVA.*"

SNIPE

Snipe also on the same path as elephants—see "*ELEPHANT.*"
Today's snipe better than to-morrow's elephant—see "*TO-DAY.*"

SOLES

Only the soles of your feet will know whensoever you tread fatal spots.

මරු ඇති තැන් දනී පය දෙපතුල්ලා.

[That is, spots where Doath awaits you.]

' SOLI "

Even in Soli tnere are starving men—see " *GILIMALE.*"

" SOLI-MANDALA "

The whole of Soli-mandala is coming.

සොළී මණ්ඩලේ පිටින් එනවා.

[This is a very ancient proverb referring to the Solian or Tamil invaders, and now used when speaking of a very large multitude.]

SOMERSAULT

A dancer's fall is a somersault—see " *DANCING.*"
Dance and somersault for the Kapurála—see " *RICE.*"

SON—(*See also* " *CHILDREN.*")

The son who does not do what his father did is a bastard.

අප්පා කළ දේ පුතා නොකළොත් ඌ නොවිච්චිගෙ පුතා.

[Cf. " Like father, like son." The Jamaicans say : " You nebber see kickin cow widout kickin' calf."]

A son with the gift of the gab—see " *CHILDREN.*"

SONG

Tamarind fruit and sacred song—see " *TAMARIND.*"

SORROWS

Like the man who said : " Now, noil, for all the sorrows we have endured, my child."

"වින්ද දුකට තම්බ පුතේ," කීවා වගෙයි.

[When the period of the South-west monsoon was over (during which they had been reduced to living on vegetables for curry) and the fishing season had again begun, the man went down to the seashore, got a bag full of fish, and, bringing it home, handed it to his young daughter with the above remark.]

Past sorrows are sweet.

පැමිණි දුක් පැණි රසලු.

Barren woman and sorrows of children—see " *CHILDREN.*"
" *Hiramane* " *and sorrows*—see " *COCONUT-SCRAPER.*"
Sorrows and the mother-in-law—see " *MOTHER-IN-LAW.*"

SOUND

The mouth is also a sort of sound-producer—see " *MOUTH.*"

SOUP

Like serving soup to the unwanted lover.

එපා වාහෙට කොදි බෙදනවා වගෙයි.

[That is, serving little in quantity, and that too in a careless style.]

Soup bubbling over does not burn a house—see " *HOUSE*."

SOWING

No crops without sowing.

නොවපුරා නොපැසෙයි.

Like sowing on a rock.

ගල පිට වපුළා වගෙයි.

Sow " amu " and you will reap " amu "—see " *AMU*."

SPEAKING

Better to act well than to speak sweetly—see " *ACT*."
Speaking familiarly with a potter—see " *POTTER*."
The boneless tongue—see " *TONGUE*."
Veddás speaking of building houses—see " *VEDDÁS*."

SPECTACLES

Spectacles and the track of the elephant—see " *ELEPHANT*."

SPICES

Even Chetties may run short of spices.

හෙට්ටින්ටත් දුරුමුට්ටු වෙනවාලු.

[The Chetties were proverbial as dealers in spices.]

SPIDER

The supply of thread in a spider's stomach will never fail.

මකුණාගේ බඩේ නූල් හිඟවෙන්නේ නැතිලු.

SPITTLE

If you look up and spit, the spittle will fall on your own face.

උඩ බලා කෙළ ගැසුවාම තමන්ගේ මුහුණේ වැටෙනවාලු.

SPOON

Like the saying, "Even if the sea becomes cong. e, the short spoon is in my hand."

"මුහුද කැඳවුණත් කෙටි හැන්ද මා අතෙයි" කීවා වගෙයි.

SPORT—(*See also " GAME and " PLAY*.")

Sport for others, worry for us.

අනුන්ට සෙල්ලම්, අපට ලෙල්ලම්.

That kind of game is good for Kótte.

ඒ කෙළි කෝට්ටේ.

[Meaning, " That won't go down with us." The person who tried on " that kind of game " and who provoked the above saying was apparently known to be a man of Kótte, for the previous reference to which see under " PARANGIYÁ."]

That (kind of) game won't do.

ඒ කෙළි නුංතෙං.

[*Nung-teng* is a Portuguese term meaning "not having" Cf. the English slang phrases, "No go" (meaning "of no use") and "That cock won't fight" (meaning "That expedient will not do"), which exactly convey the point of the Sinhalese saying.]

This is a hell of a game.

මේක හතරවරන් කෙළියකි.

[Lit. "A four-quarter game," that is, a game or deed which is bad, looked at from "all four quarters"—north, south, east and west.]

STABBING

Stab with a golden weapon—see "*WEAPON*."

STAG

No need to plant stakes for a leaping stag.

පනින මුවාට උල් හිටවන්ට කමක් නැහැ.

STAKES

Like the hedge-stake planted in the mud.

මඩේ හිටවාපු ඉත්ත වගෙයි.

Cutting hedge-stakes on to a river—see "*CUTTING*."

STARVING

A house where people starve—see "*HOUSE*."
A starving lion never eats grass—see "*LION*."
Starving dog at neighbour's wedding—see "*WEDDING*."
Starving men even in Soli—see "*GILIMALE*."
Starving though Hétuhámy by name—see "*NAME*."
When excellence of rice is best realised—see "*RICE*."

STEADINESS

No unsteadiness in precaution—see "*PRECAUTION*."

STEALING—(*See also* "*THIEF*.")

A goldsmith and gold dust of his mother—see "*BADÁLÁ*."
Not knowing to steal—see "*TOTAGAMUVA*."
Asking thief's mother about stolen goods—see "*THIEF*."
If a thief and gardener combine—see "*THIEF*."

STEEL

Teeth of steel and iron coconuts—see "*TEETH*."

STEP

Each step means the village is nearer.

අඩියෙන් අඩියවත් ගමටලු.

Stepping into the rapids—see "*WATER*."

STERN

The stern going foremost—see "*BOAT*."

STICK

Carrying a well on a stick—see "*MAGGONA.*"
The walking-stick of Gaja Báhu—see "*PEN.*"
There's the creature and the stick—see "*PANSIL.*"

STIRRING

The unstirred congee useless—see "*CHILDREN.*"

STOMACH

No use either to tree or to stomach—see "*TREE*"
Onion carpel and the stomach—see "*ONION.*"
Size of belly does not indicate Mudaliyar—see "*RANK.*"
Stomach that is an "ambalama"—see "*AMBALAMA.*"
Though eating together, stomachs are different—see "*EATING.*"
Thread supply in a spider's stomach—see "*SPIDER.*"

STONE—(*See also* "*GRINDING-STONE.*")

Charcoal and friction with a stone—see "*CHARCOAL.*"
Egg-laying between two stones—see "*EGG-LAYING.*"
Escape a stone thrown but not the evil eye—see "*EYE.*"
Heart of stone of the man unable to run—see "*HEART.*"
If ten stones are thrown—see "*TARGET.*"
Stone flung by blind man—see "*BLINDNESS.*"
Stone throwing by a Rodiyá—see "*RODIYÁ.*"
The stone and sandal-wood—see "*SANDAL-WOOD.*"
Throwing a stone at a cobra—see "*COBRA.*"
Throwing stones at hornets' nest—see "*HORNET.*"

STORY

Story of Rayigamayá and Gampolayá—see "*GAMPOLAYÁ.*"
Story of the creditor and debtor—see "*DEBTOR.*"
Story of the four deaf persons—see "*DEAF.*"
Story of the lime-cutting ceremony—see "*LIME-CUTTING.*"
Story of the man with the brim round his neck—see "*MAN.*"
Story of the melted gold frog—see "*MELTING.*"
Story of the three "Mukkarayó"—see "*MUKKARAYÓ.*"

STRAIGHTEN

Adze which straightens timber—see "*ADZE.*"
Straightening the crook in the dog's tail—see "*DOG.*"

STRAINING

Falling into river to drink strained water—see "*RIVER.*"

STRANDED

Travel without knowledge—see "*TRAVEL.*"

STRANGER

The grand-father on a wedding day—see "*GRAND-FATHER.*"

STRAW

Adding straw to a raging fire—see "*FIRE.*"
Chameleon on a heap of straw—see "*CHAMELEON.*"
The straw-covered dancer—see "*DANCER.*"
The dog in the heap of straw—see "*DOG.*"

STRAYING

Like the vagrant who had strayed about for a month, asking the road from another who had strayed for six months.

හමාසයක් මංමුළා වෙච්ච මිනිහෙකුගෙන් මාසයක් මංමුළා වෙච්ච මිනිහෙක් පාර අහනවා වගෙයි.

STRENGTH

To the strong man, what use is a club ?

හපනාට පොල්ල කමක් නැතිලු.

STRIKE

The Udarata man's temptation to strike—see "*UDARATA*."

STRUGGLE

Struggle on a rock—see "*FIGHT*."

STYLE

Pen of the man too lazy to write—see "*PANHINDA*."
Woman who can press a style—see "*WOMAN*."

SUGAR

Like the way Andaré ate sugar.

අන්දරේ සීනි කෑවා වගෙයි.

[Andaré was the most famous of the Court Jesters of the Sinhalese Kings and the last of his tribe. He enjoyed extraordinary, even unparalleled, licence in the Royal Household, and innumerable are the stories of his witticisms and drolleries, some of them vulgar and indecent. One of the stories has reference to the way in which he ate the King's sugar.

The sugar, spread on a mat, was laid out to dry in an inner courtyard of the Palace, and Andaré, passing by, pretending ignorance, asked what the stuff was. "It is a kind of sand, Andaré," said the King who happened to be close at hand, and the Jester, profusely thanking His Majesty for the information, went home. In his own house Andaré arranged a little plot with his son to be worked out the next day, and proceeded to the Palace, the following morning, for his usual duties.

At the appointed time, according to plan, Andaré contrived to lead out the King to the courtyard near the place where the sugar had again been put out to dry ; and Andaré's little son appeared on the scene almost immediately, with dishevelled hair and eyes streaming with tears.

"What's the matter, son ?" asked the jester.

"Mother has just died," replied the sobbing boy.

"*Appochchiyé*" screeched out the apparently stricken Andaré, as he fell on his knees near the mat of sugar. "This means sand in our mouth, sand in our mouth, my son," he bewailed, and he fell to ramming into his mouth, in large handfuls, the sugar which the King had described as sand, an example which Andaré's son lustily followed.("Sand in our mouth " is a Sinhalese colloquialism for "We are done for.").

When the King intervened, after recovering from his shocked surprise at the scene, there was very little sugar on the mat to save, and, making a virtue of necessity, said : "Take home what is left of the sand, Andaré. Some of it may possibly help to revive the dead woman. Place it in her mouth yourself, my man, and let me know the result to-morrow morning."]

SUGAR-CANDY—(*See "CANDY."*)

SUGAR-CANES

Sugar-canes on the day you are teethless—see "*TEETH.*"

SUN

Can a firefly shine in the sun.?—see "*FIREFLY.*"
Sun-scorched man pushed into the fire—see "*FIRE.*"

SURETY

Better to become victim than surety—see "*VICTIM.*"

SWALLOWING.

If you swallow, you will have to emit.

ගිල්ලොත් වමාරන්න ඕනෑ.

Devil who swallowed a priest—see "*DEVIL.*"
Man who swallowed a "Vihára"—see "*IMAGE.*"
The frog's threat to swallow the elephant—see "*FROG.*"
The python which had swallowed pestles—see "*PYTHON.*"

SWAN

Like the swan sucking milk out of water.

හංසයා දියෙන් කිරි උරාගන්නාක් මෙනි.

SWEET

Sorrows of the past are sweet—see "*SORROWS.*"
Sweet cakes and misfortunes—see "*ADVERSITY.*"

SWEETMEAT

Image like a sweetmeat—see "*DEVIL.*"

SWELLING

The swelling of the finger—see "*FINGER.*"

SWIMMING

Teaching the alligator's young to swim—see "*TEACHING.*"

SWING

If the swing goes forward, it will come backward again.

ඔන්චිල්ලාව ඔබ ගියොත් මොබත් එව්වු.

Swinging about and shooting—see "*SHOOTING.*"

SWORD

Are you to cut "Jak" with the sword that is not available for the day of battle ?

යුද්දෙදට නැති කඩුව කොස් කොටන්ටද ?

TACT

Tactful people will not "put their foot into it"—see "*HELL.*"

TAIL

Like catching hold of the tail (of an animal) after allowing it to run away.

දුවන්ට ඇරලා වල්ගෙ අල්ලන්නා වගෙයි.

The tail is the illness.

වල්ගෙ තමයි ලෙඩේ.

[Four cattle thieves had killed a bull in the jungle and delayed over the division of the spoil. Dawn broke before they could get through the village unnoticed. They, therefore, made a rough sort of palanquin, and, covering it up with their outer cloths and placing within their shares of the meat, bore it along on their shoulders through the village, as if they were taking a patient to the Vedarála. An early riser, squatting on his doorstep, accosted the four men. "Whither bound, friends, so early in the morning ?" he asked, and was told that they were taking a sick man to the doctor. Peering at the body of the palanquin, the inquisitive villager saw a tail protruding from the cloth, and he asked, "What is it that I see hanging up there ? Isn't that a tail, my friends ?" he inquired, and was met with the prompt reply, "Of course, it is. The tail is the illness, you fool," and the party passed safely through the danger zone.]

Catching hold of the tiger's tail—see "*TIGER.*"
Friendship of short-tailed dog—see "*DOG.*"
Tail running before the fowl—see "*FOWL.*"
The crook in the dog's tail—see "*DOG.*"
The dog without a tail—see "*DOG.*"
The order to the tail of the dog—see "*DOG.*"
The short-tailed cow and the runners—see "*RUNNING.*"

"TALAGOYA"

When returning from Dambulla—see "*DAMBULLA.*"

"*Kabaragoyá*" *and* "*talagoyá*" *eating*—see "*EAT.*"
"*Kabaragoyá*" *becoming* "*talagoyá*"—see "*NECESSITY.*"

TALK

However those who talk may talk, listeners should give ear only with reason and understanding.

කියන්නෝ කොහොම කිව්වත් අහන්නෝ සිහි බුද්ධි ඇතුව අහන්න ඕනෑ.

Like planting "batala" leaves with the mouth.

කටින් බතල කොළ හිටවනවා වගෙයි.

[Words without deeds. *Batala* is a plant, sort of bindweed, *Edulis batatas*), the root of which is the sweet potato.]

The bow is at Dunugamuva	දුන්න දුනුගමු වේ
The arrows at Kitalagamuva	ඊතල කිතලගමු වේ
The husband at Migamuva	රාළ මීගමු වේ
A deer has cried in Sabaragamuva	මුවෙක් ඇඬුවයි සපරගමු වේ

[This stanza is quoted in reference to wild and unconnected talk. Dunugamuva is a village in Kegalla District, and Kitalagamuva in Kurunegala District. Migamuva is the modern Negombo, a town twenty-five miles from Colombo, while Sabaragamuva is the Province of that name.]

Gossip begets more gossiping—see "*GOSSIP.*"
One's defects and talk of nonsense—see "*DEFECTS.*"
Talk of palanquins and journeying afoot—see "*TRAVEL.*"

TAMARIND

Will the tamarind fruit, which has resisted an iron hook, shake at a sacred song ?

යකඩ කෙක්කෙන් කඩන්ට බැරි සියඹලා ගෙඩිය ගීතිකාවෙන් සෙලවේද ?

[Denham quotes a story told of an old native Headman, whose memory went back to Dutch times and who could, therefore, well remember the coercive measures then taken for forcing Christianity upon the people. Being urged by a Missionary to adopt Christianity, the Mudaliyar, wearied of the Missionary's efforts, quoted with much animation a Tamil proverb, " Will the tamarind fruit which has resisted an iron hook (used in pulling down the fruit) shake at a sacred song ? " The tamarind is the Sinhalese *Siyambalá*, Sansk. *Tintidi*, *Amlika*, Tam. *Puli.*]

" TAMBY "—(*See* " *MOORMAN.*")

" TAMBY APPU "

Tamby Appu, the illiterate, as Vedarála—see " *VEDARÁLA.*"

TAMIL

Tamil that one knows nothing about is the ruin of his tribe.

නොදන්න දෙමළෙට ගොහින් වරිගෙ නහන්නා වගෙයි.

[In a certain village there lived the widow of a blacksmith and her only son, who was himself a blacksmith. This man's knowledge of Tamil was confined to the single expression, *Enaku teriyam*, (" I understand.") On one occasion it happened that a Tamil man brought to him a gun in order to get removed from the barrel a charge of powder and shot which it contained. The man, on handing over the gun to the blacksmith, explained to him in Tamil the object of his visit. The blacksmith looked very wise and said, " *Enaku teriyam.*" On finding out, after due examination, that the barrel contained something, he made preparations to insert in it a red-hot iron. The owner of the gun remonstrated to no purpose against such a proceeding. " *Enaku teriyam* " was the reply of the blacksmith, who immediately afterwards introduced into the barrel the red-hot iron—an act which resulted in the explosion of the powder and the death of the unfortunate blacksmith. The mother of this unlucky man ever afterwards bitterly lamented the misfortune of her son, who, by his attempts to speak in an unknown language, not only brought death on himself, but also put an end to the race of which he was sole representative.]

The tangle in a skein of thread—see " *THREAD.*"

TANKS

Tanks are filled by rain, not dew.

වැස්සෙන් මිසක් පින්නෙන් වැව් නොපිරේලු.

A breach in a tank and the widow—see " *WOMAN.*"

TARES

Tares blossom before " *amu* "—see " *AMU.*"

TARGET

If ten stones are thrown, one at least will hit the mark.

ගල් දහයක් ගැහුවොත් එකක් වදිනවාලු.

Missing the elephant—see "*ELEPHANT*."
Shot at the hare and hit the bush—see "*SHOOTING*."
Toddy drinking cup as Buddha's target—see "*TODDY*."

TASTE

Hunger knows no taste—see "*HUNGER*."
It is the eater who knows the taste—see "*EATING*."

TAVERN

The tavern-keeper's "mal-baliya"—see "*BALI*."
Truthful man finds no room in tavern—see "*TRUTH*."

TAXES

Eight brinjals but nine taxes—see "*BRINJALS*."

TEACHERS

Even teachers trip over words.

ගුරුන්ටත් අකුරු වරදිනවාලු.

[Cf. Lat. "*Aliquando bonus dormitat Homerus.*"]

When teachers urinate standing—see "*URINATING*."

TEACHING

Like teaching the alligator's young to swim.

කිඹුල් පැටවුන්ට පීනන්ට උගන්වනවා වගෙයි.

[Cf. Eng. "Teaching your grandmother to suck eggs."]

TEAK

Furniture made of teak—see "*ADVERSITY*."

TEARS

Tear for mother-in-law's death—see "*MOTHER-IN-LAW*."
Tears from the eyes of the Loris—see "*LORIS*."
When one eye is pricked—see "*EYE*."

TEETH

Can you do what is impossible, though you grind your teeth ?

"බැරි දේ පිළිවන්ද දත්මිටි කෑවාට"?

Are sugar-canes to serve (as firewood) for warming yourself on the day you are teethless ?

"දත් නැතිදා උක් දඬු ගිනි තපින්ටද"?

Like trying the teeth upon a file.

පීරට දත් ගහන්නා වගෙයි.

You can eat even iron coconuts if you have teeth of steel.

වානේ දත් ඇත්නම් යකඩ පොල් කාහැකිලු.

Eat coconuts while you have your teeth—see " *COCONUT*."
Man with projecting teeth—see " *DEATH*."
The Gamarála who has " kurahan "—see " *GAMARÁLA*."
The teeth of the dog which barks—see " *DOG*."
Tongue safe though in the midst of thirty teeth—see " *TONGUE*."
White-teethed people in Gilimalé—see " *GILIMALE*."

" TEMBILI."

A black crow on a " ran-tembili " bunch—see " *CROW*."

TEMPLE

A shrine without fame—see " *CHILDREN*."
Priests at loggerheads—see " *BUDDHISM*."
The temple crashing down—see " *RELIGION*."

TEMPTATION

The Udarata man's temptation—see " *UDARATA*."

TEN

If ten stones are thrown—see " *TARGET*."
Ten airs with five pieces of money—see " *MONEY*."

THICKET—(*See also " JUNGLE."*)

Respectability hiding in a thicket—see " *MONEY*."

THIEF

He who steals a " puhula " will be betrayed by his shoulder.

පුහුල් හොරා කරෙත් දනේ.

[For fuller reference to the *puhula* or ash-pumpkin, see under "*HAND*." The fruit has an ash coating which leaves its tell-tale mark on the shoulder, upon which, being heavy, it is usually carried by the villager, who is, of course, bare-bodied.]

Like asking the thief's mother about the stolen goods.

හොරාගෙ අම්මාගෙන් පේන ඇහුවා වගෙයි.

[The woman was a soothsayer to whom the man who lost his goods went for consultation, in ignorance of the fact that she was the mother of the thieves who were the actual culprits in the case. In the circumstances she was, of course, scarcely likely to put them on the right scent.]

Like the thief and the master of the house combining.

හොරත් ගේ ඇත්තත් එකතු වුණ වගෙයි.

[The Tamils have a saying: " If a thief and a gardener combine, one may steal till daylight." Also, "The thief is found to be the gardener."]

The thief has wisdom even greater than that of Ganadeviyo.

හොරාට ගණදෙයියන්ටත් වැඩිය නුවණ තියෙනවා.

[Ganadeviyo is Ganeṣa, the Hindu God of Good Luck and remover of difficulties and obstacles, sometimes also called the God of Wisdom.]

Explanation of the coconut thief—see " *COCONUT*."
Darkness which helps thieves—see " *DARKNESS*."
Plantain bunch jumping over the fence—see " *PLANTAIN*."

" THIMBA "—(*See " TIMBA."*)

THING

Thing for thing—see "*FRIENDSHIP.*"

THIRST

Sea-water for thirst—see "*WATER.*"
The "Kendetta" always thirsty—see "*KENDETTA.*"
The thirst of a dropsical man—see "*DROPSY.*"

THORNS

If a thorn be not removed by a thorn, can it be extracted by a pestle ?

කටුවකින් කටුවක් අරින්ට බැරිනම් මෝල්ගහකින් අරින්ට පුළුවන්ද ?

[A delicate matter requires delicate handling.]

There's no need to sharpen the thorns of a tree.

ගහේ කටු උල් කරන්ට ඕනැ නැහැ.

Clinging to a thorny branch—see "*FALL.*"
The thorns of the "Kohila"—see "*CROCODILE.*"

THOUGHTS

A woman's thoughts are afterthoughts—see "*WOMAN.*"

THOUSAND

A thousand though alive, a thousand though dead.

උන්නත් දහසි, මළත් දහසි.

[The reference is to the perquisites of the dhoby, who gets his share both when his patron is living (at marriage ceremonies, etc.) as well as when he is dead (in connection with the funeral ceremonies.)]

THRASH

The unthrashed child useless—see "*CHILDREN.*"

THREAD

Like the tangle in a skein of thread.

නූල් මලේ අවුල වගෙයි.

Thread supply in a spider's stomach—see "*SPIDER.*"

THRESHOLD

The lowliest thing in a house—see "*HOUSE.*"

THROAT

Swallowing medicine unknown to throat—see "*MEDICINE.*"
Throat a needle, stomach an "ambalama"—see "*AMBALAMA.*"
Throat-clearing in one country—see "*COUNTRY.*"

THROWING

Stone-throwing by a blind man—see "*BLINDNESS.*"
Stone-throwing by a Rodiyá—see "*RODIYÁ.*"
The man who threw half a coconut—see "*COCONUT.*"
Throw not the herbs you have plucked—see "*DEER.*"
Throwing a stone at a cobra—see "*COBRA.*"
Throwing stones at hornets' nest—see "*HORNET.*"

THUNDER

The disproportionate rain—see "*RAIN*."
The dog reared in a blacksmith's forge—see "*DOG*."

THUNDERBOLT

The thunderbolt is not a respecter even of the sweet jak-tree.

ගහන හෙණ පැණිවරකාව බලන්නෙත් නැතිලු.

Seven thunderbolts for the match-maker—see "*MARRIAGE*."

TIGER

If there's no cattle in the fold, why worry about the tiger roaring on the roof ?

වහලේ දිවියා ඇඹුවත් පට්ටියෙ ගවයො නැත්නම් බය වෙන්නේ මොටද ?

Like a tiger without claws.

නිය නැති දිවියා වගෙයි.

Like catching hold of a tiger's tail.

කොටි වල්ගෙ අල්ලාගත්තා වගෙයි.

Like going to start tiger-dancing in the midst of a "Pinkama."

පින්කම් අස්සෙ කොටි නටන්ට යනවා වගෙයි.

[This was said of a man who joined in a good and laudable matter from selfish or unworthy motives. *Pinkama* is a Buddhist religious festival. A variant is "Like going to make bears dance, etc."]

What matters even if a thousand tigers roar, if there is not even a single hair of any cattle near about ?

දිවියො දහසක් ඇඹුවාට මොකද එක ගව ලෝමයක්වත් නැත්නම් ?

Like a herd of cattle being entrusted to the care of the tiger.

කොටියාට හරක් පට්ටිය බාරදුන්නා වගෙයි.

What use to be a tiger if there be no claws ?

දිවියා උණාට මොටද නිය නැත්නම්.

The deer who has seen a tiger—see "*DEER*."

TIGHTEN

Tightening screws on "polpiti baliya"—see "*BALIYA*."

"TIKIRI-RALA"

The share of the rice for Tikiri-rála—see "*RICE*."

"TIMBA"

Wherever you strike, a "timba."

ගැසූ තැනම තිඹයි.

[That is, immediate gain or profit ensues. Cf. Eng. "Whatever his hand touches turns to gold."]

A "timba" is a "láha"—see "*MEASURE*."
A "timba" of "vi"—see "*MARRIAGE*."

TIMBER

Adze which straightens timber—see "*ADZE.*"

TIMES

The forest life in evil times—see "*LIFE.*"

" TIRIVANE "

" Tiriváne " stones in Kaliyuga age—see "*KALIYUGA.*"

" TITTAYA "

The " koká's " day as well as " tittayá's—see "*CRANE.*"

TOBACCO

Like Siman Gamarála's request to his wife for a chew of tobacco after returning from Nainamadama.

සිමන් ගමරාළ නයිනමඩමටත් ගොසින් ඇවිත් අඹුගෙන් විටකට දුම්කොළ ඉල්ලුවා වගෙයි

[Nainamadama, in Pitigal Kórale South of Chilaw District, is famous for the quality of the tobacco grown there.]

TO-DAY

If to-day is ours, to-morrow is theirs.

අද අපට නම් හෙට උන්ට.

To-day's snipe is better than to-morrow's elephant.

හෙට ලැබෙන ඇතුට වඩා අද ලැබෙන වටුවා ජාතා.

TODDY

"All this Buddha-talk and priest-talk is aimed only at my little toddy cup, is it not ? " asked the drunkard.

" බුදුන් අටවන්නෙත් සඟුන් අටවන්නෙත් මම බොන රා කැටෙටයි " කියා බේබද්දෙක් කීලු.

[The Tamils say : " It is better to gain a quarter of a fanam by selling camphor than a *kalam* by selling toddy."]

Nondi Pancha, jogging along,
Met Siman Pancha one day ;
They drank some toddy, just one cent worth,
And fought each other the whole way.

නොන්ඩි පංච යන ගම නේ
සිමන් පංච සම්බවු ණේ
සල්ලි දෙකේ රා අරග න
දෙන්න බිබී සන්ඩු උ ණේ

It is unbecoming for an " Upásakayá " to drink toddy

" උපාසක කමට නොහොබිලු රා බීම."

[An *Upásakayá* is a lay Buddhist devotee, *i.e.*, one devoted to religious exercises.]

A rat drunk on toddy—see "*RAT.*"
Poor Moormen and toddy—see "*MOORMEN.*"

" TOKKA "

Tokká's way of tending cattle—see "*CATTLE*"

TO-MORROW

To-day ours, to-morrow theirs—see " *TO-DAY*."

TOM-TOMS

Too much tom-toming means that the " tovila " is going to be spoilt.

වැඩි පද ගහන්නේ තොවිලෙ කැතවෙන්නයි.

[*Tovila* is the devil-dancing ceremony.]

Tom-toming at an " Ehela Perahera "—see " *PERAHERA*."
The mouth a sort of tom-tom—see " *MOUTH*."

TONGUE

The boneless tongue, what can it not say ?

ඇට නැති දිවට මොනවා කියන්ට බැරිද ?

The tongue does not lie, though the mouth may.

කට බොරු කියතත් දිව බොරු කියන්නේ නැහැ.

The tongue is safe though in the midst of thirty teeth.

දත් තිහට මැද දිව තියෙනවා වගෙයි.

Fencing a country but not the tongue—see " *GARRULITY*."
Honey at the root of the tongue—see " *HONEY*."
Planting with the mouth—see " *TALK*."

TORTOISE

Even the shell of the tortoise is needed for medicine.

ඉබි කබලුත් බෙහෙතට ඕනෑ වෙනවාලු.

Like asking a tortoise for lock-stitches or " feathers."

ඉබ්බාගෙන් පිස්මේන්තු [පිහාටු] ඉල්ලන්නා වගෙයි.

Like the blind tortoise peering at the sky through the chink in the oxen's yoke.

කාණකැස්බා වියසිදුරෙන් අහස බලන්නා වගෙයි.

[When does this eventuality occur ? First, a bullock-cart must break down on the road, and so heavy a shower must fall that the yoke of the cart must be washed down by a flood to the river, whence it must be carried to the sea. There, when it is floating about, tossed on the waves, a one-eyed tortoise must come along, and, keeping its single eye glued as it were to the chink in the yoke, peer at the sky. How often can this concatenation of events take place in time ? When the Greek Kalends arrive—which is the point of the Sinhalese proverb.]

Like the tortoise who cried out " Damn it," when ordered to be thrown into the water.

ඉබ්බා දියේ දමන්ටෙයි කීකල " ඇන්නෑවෙයි " කියා කෑ ගැසුවාලු.

Like the tortoise who failed to govern his tongue.

ඉබ්බාට කට රකාගෙන ඉන්ට බැරිවුණා වගෙයි.

[Two friendly cranes once met a tortoise who was in search of a pool of water. They promised to take him to a place where there was water and asked the tortoise to hold by his mouth a stick, either end of which each of them would take and fly off with him. The tortoise was strictly enjoined not to open his mouth. When he was being carried in this manner, on the way a cunning fox from below called out to the cranes and asked them why they were carrying the tortoise. The foolish tortoise, on hearing this, opened his mouth to give a reply, when he immediately fell down and was killed.]

The tortoise is said to have vanquished the lion.

ඉබ්බා සිංහයාව පරාජය කළාලු.

When did tortoises climb up trees ?

ඉබ්බෙෝ කවදා ගස් ගියෝද ?

Egg-laying of the tortoise and hen—see "*EGG-LAYING.*"

"TOTAGAMUVA"

What is the use of being born at Totagamuva if you do not know "Bana" ?

තොටගමුවේ උපන්නාට මොටද බණ බැරිනම් ?

[*Bana* means, of course, the Buddhist scriptures. Totagamuva village (on the Galle road) was the birthplace of that celebrated Sinhalese scholar and religious, Sri Ráhula Sthaviraya, the author of *Kávyasekhara*, etc. This village in recent times obtained such a bad reputation for cattle-stealing and highway robberies that the proverb was changed in the district to "What is the use of being born at Totagamuva if you do not know how to steal ?"]

TOUCH

Touch the feet to touch the head—see "*HEAD.*"

"TOVILA"

Tom-toming and the "tovila"—see "*TOM-TOMS.*"

TRADE

Like buying for a thousand and selling back for five hundred.

දහට අරන් පන්සියයට දුන්නා වගෙයි.

Herb-selling after elephant trade—see "*ELEPHANT.*"

TRAMPLE

When an elephant tramples you—see "*ELEPHANT.*"

TRAP

Animals caught in Korava's trap—see "*KORAVA.*"
Smiling fox in death-trap—see "*FOX.*"
The jackal trapped in the Island—see "*JACKAL.*"

TRAVEL

If you go knowingly, it is Kataragama ; if unknowingly, it is a case of being stranded.

දැනගෙන ගියොත් කතරගමයි, නොදැන ගියොත් අතරමගයි.

[Kataragama is the chief shrine of Skanda in Ceylon, to which many thousands of pilgrims go annually.]

Talk of palanquins and journey afoot.

කථාව දෝලාවෙන්, ගමන පයින්.

The travelled foot is worth thousands, the stay-at-home foot worse than a dog's.

ඇවිද්ද පය දහස් වටී, ගෙයි තිබු පය බලු නොවටී.

The virtuous man's road has room for many others, the wicked man's none even for himself.

සත්පුරුෂයා යන පාරේ බොහොදෙනාට ඉඩ ඇතිලු, අසත් පුරුෂයා යන පාරේ ඔහුටවත් ඉඩ මදිලු.

Conversation a ladder to the traveller—see "*CONVERSATION*."
Deer jumping from one jungle to another—see "*DEER*."
Even after going to Mátara—see "*MÁTARA*."
Hands and feet the same even in Tuticorin—see "*HAND*."
Kaluvá's trip to Márapona—see "*KALUVÁ*."
"*Parangiyá*" *going to Kótte*—see "*PORTUGUESE*."
Poor men on same road as Kings—see "*KING*."
Small boats and big ships on the sea—see "*SEA*."
Snipe on the same path as elephants—see "*ELEPHANT*."
The crab and its hole—see "*CRAB*."
The "*gavva*" *and the* "*ambalama*"—*see* "*AMBALAMA*."
The prow and the stern—see "*BOAT*."
Though a cat be taken to Europe—see "*CAT*."

TREE

It becomes difficult afterwards to cut down with an axe the tree which at first might have been nipped with your nail.

නිය පොත්තෙන් කඩන ගහ පොරොවෙන් කපන්ට අමාරු උණා වගෙයි.

Like rooting out "Ehela" trees in order to stamp out the Ehelapola race.

"අහැලපොළගේ මුල වනසමැයි" සිතා ඇහැලමුල් ඉදුරුවා වගෙයි.

[The last Sinhalese King, Sri Vikrama Rája Sinha, for a conspiracy formed against him by Ehelapola, his Prime Minister, put to death the wife and children of the latter under circumstances of the utmost barbarity. Not content with this, he ordered all the *Ehela* trees (*Cassia fistula*) in the kingdom to be rooted out in order that all traces of Ehelapola's name might be for ever destroyed.]

Like trying to get on a tree from the top instead of from the bottom.

ගහේ මුලින් නොගොස් අගින් යන්ට ගියා වගෙයි.

Made of no use, either to the tree or to the stomach.

ගහටත් නැහැ, බඩටත් නැහැ.

[Said of a raw fruit, plucked prematurely.]

The tree which will grow can be known when two leaves spring out

හැදෙන ගහ දෙපෙත්තේදී දැනෙයි.

A bull butting a fallen man—see "*BULL.*"
A drunken rat on a tree—see "*RAT.*"
A single tree will not make an orchard—see "*ORCHARD*"
Bane of the tree is the parasite—see "*BANE.*"
Coconut trees from river bottom—see "*COCONUT.*"
Every kind of bird on a fruitful tree—see "*BIRD.*"
Milky tree and pestle—see "*KNOCK.*"
Monkey fallen from a tree—see "*MONKEY.*"
No need to sharpen the thorns of a tree—see "*THORN*"
Rain doubled under a tree—see "*RAIN.*"
Showing leaves to one who knows the tree—see "*LEAF*"
The fall of the unripe fruit—see "*FRUIT.*"
The man who goes from tree to tree—see "*MAN.*"
The screw-pine on the tree—see "*PINE.*"
Trying to catch the bird on the tree—see "*BIRD.*"
When did tortoises climb up trees ?—see "*TORTOISE*"

TRIBE

Tamil that was the ruin of his tribe—see "*TAMIL.*"

TRICK

Like the trick a monkey played on an alligator.

වඳුරා කිඹුලා රවටුවා වගෙයි.

[A certain she-alligator, during the earliest stages of her pregnancy, was seized with a strong desire to eat the heart of a monkey and requested her husband to get her one. The husband, with this object in view, went up to a certain monkey and told him, "Friend, there is better food for you on the other side of the river than on this." "It may be so," replied the monkey, "but how am I to get there ?" "Sit on my back," said the alligator, "and I will take you over." The monkey accordingly got up on the alligator's back. When the alligator reached the middle of the river, he told his companion. "I am taking you to my wife, to give her your heart to eat." Quoth the monkey in return, "You fool, did you not see me hang up my heart on that tree yonder ? Take me back there that I may hand it over to you." The foolish alligator took the monkey to the bank. On reaching the bank, however, the monkey ran up a tree, leaving the alligator to rue his foolishness.]

TRICK

Be dishonest to the trickish—see "*UPRIGHTNESS*"
Gamarála's trick on the blacksmith—see "*GAMARÁLA*"
Tricks of a goldsmith and weaver—see "*DHOBY.*"

TROUBLE

The jugglery of escape from trouble—see "*JUGGLERY.*"

TRUSS

The fool and his truss—see "*FOOL.*"
The truss and the Valave-ganga—see "*AMÜDE*"

TRUST

Black Brahman and white Pariah—see "*BRAHMAN*"

TRUTH

No matter if a part of me is even eaten up if only the truth be told.

ඇත්ත කියා පැත්තක් කැවත් හොඳලු.

The truthful man finds no room even in the tavern.

ඇත්ත කියන්නාට තැබෑරුමෙත් ඉඩ නැතිලු

TRYING

If ten stones are thrown—see "*TARGET*."
Trying teeth upon a file—see "*TEETH*."
Trying to extract oil from sand—see "*OIL*."
Trying to peel off the bark from a rock—see "*ROCK*."

"TUMPANE"

Though he is the Chief High Priest, is he not from Tumpane

මහ නායක නමුත් ගම තුම්පනේ නොවේද ?

[The story is that a certain High Priest of Kandy wished to feed all the dogs of the place, and had them all collected in one pen. When the food was thrown them a free fight took place, which caused the King of Kandy to make this remark. Tumpane, in the Central Province, like Maggona, is reputed to produce simpletons.]

TUSKER—(*See* "*ELEPHANT*.")

TUTICORIN

Hands and feet the same even in Tuticorin—see "*HAND*."

TWINE

Fish caught with twine—see "*FISH*."

TWINS

Only demons are born twins of opposite sex.

ජාති දෙකින් නිඹුල්ලුව උපදින්නෝ යක්කුය.

[It is considered unlucky by the Sinhalese if the twins are of opposite sex, and it is believed that one of them sure to die, and, if both grow up, it will lead to misfortune.]

TYING

Beat the drum you have tied on—see "*DRUM*."
How the Gamarála tied his "*amude*"—see "*FOOL*."
Tying the "*amude*" *with the river still far away*—see "*AMUDE*."

"UDARATA"

Like the Udarata man saying : "I felt like smacking him."

"ලාන්ට සිතුණයි" කියා උඩරට මිනිහා කීවා වගෙයි.

[Loku Banda, a stalwart from the hill-country (*Kanda-uda-rata*), travelled down to Colombo one day on business. He came by train, got down at Maradana, took lodgings for the night at a *Bat-kade* (eating house) parading under the name of some "Hotel," and went to the Pettah next morning for the transaction of his business. At the market Loku Banda was the cynosure of every eye, particularly of some street urchins who were greatly impressed by his long flowing beard, heavily streaked with grey, which reached well below the silver *hava-*

diya (metal belt) encircling his ample waist. One brat, more mischievous than the rest, made a sudden dart at the beard, and out came three long hairs, all grey. To pull a man's beard is a gross form of insult in the Sinhalese country. Loku Bånda, however, was hurt more than in his dignity, for the three dislodged hairs had given him physical pain as well. But he said and did nothing in retaliation, never gave even a reproachful look at the culprit. Only, he moved hastily away, then went back to his "Hotel," ate a hurried meal, took the afternoon train back to Kandy, and thence proceeded on foot to his home, which was situated in distant Galagedara. His house was on the top of a little hill. He climbed up the slope briskly and then, when he had planted his foot firmly on his own verandah, and not till then, did he turn fiercely round and exclaim: "The little Pariah; he pulled my beard, didn't he? I felt like smacking him on the face, the dirty brute." The story is told to typify the man without moral backbone, who utters "brave" words and courageous sentiments from a secure place without the remotest intention of putting them into effect.]

UGLY—(*See* "*UNSIGHTLY*.")

Ugly woman's chastity—see "*CHASTITY*."

"UMBALAKADE"

Like the "umbalakade" of the paddá-boatman.

පාරු කාරයාගේ උම්බලකඩේ වගෙයි.

[That is, a thing which is constantly trotted forth and whose present value or usefulness is a doubtful quantity. There was a boatman who prepared his daily soup of Maldive fish (*umbalakade*) in this wise. Into the boiling water he lowered the piece of Maldive fish and held it there for a while for seasoning. Then he removed the Maldive fish and hung it up in a safe corner of the boat, to be brought out again and used in the same way, day after day, for each new preparation of his soup. The essence of the *umbalakade* gone after its first boiling, it was practically valueless for the subsequent preparations of the boatman's soup. The paddá-boat (*páruva*) is a flat-bottomed boat, *pára* "boat, barge" (Clough).]

UMBILICAL CORD

Cutting the cord before birth—see "*NAVEL STRING*."

UMBRELLA

Too much argument leads to brandishing umbrella-handles.

වාදෙ වැඩි වුණොත් කුඩ මිටි හරවා ගන්ට වේවි.

[From argument to fisticuffs, from words to blows. The Tamils say: "An umbrella in the hand and slippers on the feet are essentials," but conditions to-day are different and an umbrella is no longer regarded as a necessary mark of respectability. "If a low caste man obtains wealth he will carry a sunshade at midnight" is another old Tamil saying which has lost its point to-day.]

UNCLE

If one's maternal uncle has breasts to give milk, he is equal to a mother.

තනේ ඇත්නම් මාමා අම්මාලු.

[Among the Sinhalese, the greatest affection is to be looked for from one's mother's brother, who, if childless, would naturally make his nephew or niece his heir, and between whose children and their father's sister's children marriages would be arranged as a matter of course,

The prominent position taken by the maternal uncle at weddings and in all social matters is due to his special position in the family. The Tamils say, "Why enquire after the relationship of the daughter of one's maternal uncle," the point of which is that the relationship is so close, or likely to be so.]

It is said that milk wells up into the thumb of the maternal uncle.

මාමාගේ මාපටැඟිල්ලට කිරි එරෙනවාලු.

On mother's death, father becomes uncle—see "*MARRIAGE.*"

UNDERSTANDING

Listeners should listen with understanding—see "*TALK.*"

"UNDUPIYALI"

The "Undupiyali" leaf is the same in wet weather as in the dry.

උඳුපියලි කොළේ වැස්සටත් නියඟටත් දෙකටම එකාකාරයි.

[The *Undupiyali* is a medicinal plant (Lat. *Desmodium trifloris* or *heterophyllum*, Sansk. *Amalana*, Tam. *Serupillady.*]

UNLUCKY

Fishing on an unlucky day—see "*FISH.*

When the unlucky man shaves—see "*HAILSTORM.*"

UNSEASONABLE

The unseasonable fruit—see "*FRUIT.*"

UNSIGHTLY—(*See also* "*UGLY.*")

Man becomes unsightly by ripening—see "*RIPENING.*"

"UPASAKAYA"

Toddy-drinking unbecoming—see "*TODDY*"

UPRIGHTNESS

Be upright to the upright, be kind to the kind, and dishonest to the deceitful.

"*Sádhukan sádhukan chaiva*
Vaṇkaṇ vanka mivacha
Svarna támbra palan chaiva
Putro bhavati vánarah."

[The moral is illustrated by the following story: A certain man, having accidentally found a golden pumpkin, gave it to a friend for safe keeping. When the owner asked for it back, his friend gave him a brass one, and he went away apparently satisfied. Some time after, the friend entrusted the owner of the pumpkin with one of his sons; but, when the father demanded the son back, he produced a large ape. Complaint was made to the King who ordered each man to restore what each had received from the other.]

URGENT

Silversmith taking up urgent work—see "*BADÁLÁ.*"

URINATING

When the teacher urinates standing, the pupils do the same running.

ගුරුන්නාන්සේ හිටගෙන චූළිජ්ජ කරනකොට, ගෝලයෝ දුව දුව චූළිජ්ජ කරනවා.

USELESS

Unthrashed child and unstirred congee—see "*CHILDREN.*"

" UVA "

Man who went to Uva for better food—see "*KURAKKAN.*"

VAGRANT

One vagrant asking another the road—see "*STRAY.*"

" VAKKADE "

Jaggery in a " Vakkade "—see "*JAGGERY.*"

" VANGEDIYA "

The Gamarála's " vangediya "—see "*GAMARÁLA.*"

VANITY

Vanity in one's own village—see "*VILLAGE.*"

VAULT

Taking a winnowing-fan of chunam—see "*LADDER.*"

VAULTING

Senile flightiness vaults o'er house top—see "*OLD.*"

" VEDARALA "

Even Mathé Appu is Vedarála in an emergency.

ඇසිරුවට මතෙ අප්පුත් වෙදරාළලු.

[Mathe Appu—sometimes the name given is Jusey Appu—is a term of contempt for any one who has not even a smattering of medicine. Yet another variation is, "*Although Tambi Appu cannot read and write, yet he is also a Vedarála.*" Of course, there are many ignorant Vedarálas, and it is in reference to these that the Tamils say, "One who killed a thousand patients is half a physician." Another Tamil saying is, "A physician will not leave until death, an astrologer will not leave even then."]

If one cannot be a King, one should take to the healing art.

රජකම කරන්ට බැරිනම් වෙදකම කරන්ටලු.

[That is, practise medicine as a *Vedarála* or physician—in such high esteem was, and is, the medical profession held among the Sinhalese.]

VEDDAS

Like Veddás speaking of building houses.

වැද්දෝ ගෙවල් තැනීමට කථා කරන්නා වගෙයි.

[That is, something which is never likely to eventuate. When Veddás meet each other on a rainy day, they say: "Let us build a house—you had better bring one bundle of sticks, I will also bring one, etc."]

The Veddá, if he chooses, can turn "Goraka" into meat.

වැද්දා සිතුවොත් ගොරක දඩ මස් කරතැකිලු.

[*Goraka* is, of course, Gámbojo.]

"*Bana*" *preaching by Veddás*—see "*ADVICE.*"

" VELLALA "

How a Kallan may become a Vellála—see "*RANK.*"

VENOM

Milk for a venomous serpent—see "*MILK.*"

VERSES

Like the verses of the Ranchagoda girl.

රංචාගොඩ ළමයගේ කවි වගෙයි.

[There was a young married woman of Ranchagoda (a village near Mátara), who achieved some notoriety for her ability to make impromptu Sinhalese verses remarkable chiefly for their lack of rhythm and metre. Here is a sample :

මෙහෙව් රටේ රංචාගොඩ ඉපදී ලා
රුහුණු රටට මම දීලා ඉලව් වේ
දෙමට පොතු කකා කට හම් යනවා යේ
හැම දෙවියෝ අපෙ වාගේ රකෝ රකෝ

The above saying is now applied, in derision, to verses which are unmetrical, inconsequential, and inharmonious.]

" VESSANTARA "

This is not a Vessantara era.

මේක වෙස්සන්තර කාලයක් නොවෙයි.

[Vessantara was the name of the Buddha in his last birth but one, in which he gave away his treasures, his wife, and children as religious offerings. The " Vessantara Era " would, therefore, be synonymous with a very religious and charitable age."]

VESSEL

A golden vessel for Lion's grease—see " *LION*."

" VETA-KEYIYA "

The " Veta-keyiyá " on tree or ground—see " *PINE*."

VEXATION

Ambition begets vexation—see " *AMBITION*."

VICTIM

It is better to become the victim than the surety.

ඇප වෙනවාට වඩා කැප වෙනවා හොඳලු.

[Better to " foot the bill " than to be guarantor.]

VICTORY

Hurrah for the winning side !

දිනුම් පිලට හෝසියා !

Man of patience a banner of victory—see " *PATIENCE*."
Victory never for the devil-server—see " *DEVIL*."

VIGIL

Vigil in the watch-hut—see " *HOUSE*."

" VIHARA "

Man who swallowed a " Vihára "—see " *IMAGE*."
Non-disclosure will ruin the " Vihára "—see " *BUDDHISM*."
Worship at Dambulla Vihára—see " *DAMBULLA*."

VILLAGE

Like losing the village one has by going to get new ones.

අමුතු ගම් ගන්ට ගොස් තිබුණ ගමත් නැතිවුණා වගෙයි

[The Tamils have a saying "A curry made without *vendáyam* (onions) is not a curry, a village without a market is not a village." They also say : "What business has he in the village, now that he is grown up ?" and "If a crab gets fat, it will not stay in its hole."]

Vanity in one's own village and insolence in others' are both to be avoided.

තමන්ගේ ගමට බුල්ලත්, අනුන්ගේ ගමට පොල්ලත් එපාලු.

Why ask the way to the village which you are not visiting ?

නොයන ගමට කුමට මග විචාළේ?

Hired "kurakkan" workers—see "*KURAKKAN*."
The bane of the village—see "*BANE*."
The dhoby and the poor of the village—see "*DHOBY*"
The village nearer at each step—see "*STEP*."
Tying up the village pestles—see "*ELEPHANT*."
Woman's "ins" and "outs"—see "*DHOBY*."

VIOLIN—(*See* "*FIDDLE*.")

VIRTUE

The virtuous man's road—see "*TRAVEL*."

VISITING

The bat visiting another bat's house—see "*BAT*."

VOICE

I hear a voice, (the first) since Andaré's death.

අන්දරේ මැරුණාට පස්සේ කට හඬක් ඇහුණා.

[Said in derision, since Andare was a clown and buffoon.]

"WALAUWA"

Size of house does not indicate the Walauwa—see "*RANK*."

"WALAWE-GANGA"

The "amude" and the Valave-ganga—see "*AMUDE*"

WALKING

Can a hunchback be forced to walk erect—see "*HUNCHBACK*."
The monkey aged sixty—see "*MONKEY*"

WALKING-STICK

King Gaja Báhu's walking stick—see "*PANHINDA*"

WALL

A horse to jump over wall—see "*HORSE*."

WAR

"*Mára yuddhaya*" *and Buddhahood*—see "*BUDDHA*"

WARMING

Like the man who warmed himself at the river bank.

ගඟ අද්දර ඉඳ සීත තැපූ මිනිහා වගෙයි.

[Seeing a fire on the opposite bank, he sat at this bank and stretched out his hands to warm himself.]

Sugar-canes to warm yourself when teethless—see "*TEETH.*"

WASHERMAN—(*See* "*DHOBY.*")

WASHING

Not washing the body out of regard for river—see "*RIVER.*"
Giving entrails to a fox to wash—see "*FOX.*"
Washing your hand in honey—see "*MILK.*"

WASTE

It is a gain even to lick up anything that is running to waste.

ඉසිරෙන දෙය ලෙව කෑවත් ලාබලු.

WATCH-HUT

For fear of the master—see "*FEAR.*"
Vigil in the watch-hut—see "*HOUSE.*"

WATER

Drinking muddy water while gazing at clear water.

හොඳ දිය බලාගෙන බොර වෙච්ච දිය බොන්නා වගෙයි.

[Cf. Lat. *Video meliora proboque deteriora sequor.*]

Drinking river water and wishing "Long Life" to the ocean.

ගඟ දිය බීලා මුදට ආවඩනවා වගෙයි.

It is a gain to take even two handfuls of water running to waste.

බැහැ යන වතුරෙන් දෝතක් ගත්තත් ලාබලු.

Like a drop of water on a lotus leaf.

නෙළුම් කොළේ දිය බින්දුව මෙනි.

[That is; like water on a duck's back.]

Like a line drawn on water

දියේ ඇඳි ඉර වගෙයි.

Like being put in turbid water.

බොර දියේ දැම්මා වගෙයි.

Like drawing water to the wedding-house in a basket full of holes.

මගුල් ගෙදරට සිල් කූඩෙන් වතුර අදින්නා වගෙයි.

Like scalding with cold water.

ඇල් වතුරෙන් පුලුස්සනවා වගෙයි.

Like stepping into the rapids and looking for footmarks.

ඇල්ලට බැහැලා පාමං බලන්නා වගෙයි.

Sea water will not quench one's thirst.

මුහුදු වතුර බීමාට පිපාසය නොසංසිඳෙයි

Water always flows down the lowest place.

දිය මිටි තැනින් බහින්නා වගෙයි.

Water in a half-filled pot shakes.

අඩු කළේ දිය සෙල්වෙයි

Water in a filled pot does not shake

පිරුණු කළේ දිය නොසෙල්වෙයි

What matters how higher still is the rise of the water which has already risen above your nose ?

නාහෙන් ඉහළ ගැලූ වතුර කොපමණ ගැලුවත් එකලූ.

A firebrand in hot or cold water—see " *FIREBRAND*
A pot filled to the brim does not shake—see " *POT.*"
Crossing an " edanda "—see " *EDANDA.*"
Eaten the whole earth and drunk all the water—see " *EARTH.*"
Eye benefited when face is washed—see " *EYE.*"
Falling into river to drink strained water—see " *RIVER.*"
Fate of water-drawer and pot-breaker—see " *MAN.*"
Men in fever asking for water—see " *FEVER.*"
Shooting from under water—see " *SHOOTING.*"
Swan sucking milk out of water—see " *SWAN.*"
Tanks filled by rain, not dew—see " *TANKS.*"
The crab's gambols in the water—see " *CRAB.*"
The Gónagala rock and the waves—see " *GÓNAGALA.*"
The place where the ox drank water—see " *OX.*"
The tortoise ordered to be thrown into water—see " *TORTOISE.*"
The well from which water is constantly drawn—see " *WELL.*"
Washing a nim-seed with water—see " *KOHOMBA.*"
Water and a dropsical man—see " *DROPSY.*"
Water from any well, jaggery in hand—see " *JAGGERY.*"
Water not rising above frog's neck—see " *FROG.*"
Water of the celestial river—see " *CHAMELEON.*
Watering the unflowering fig—see " *DIMBUL.*"
Woman and empty water-pots—see " *WOMAN.*"

WATER-COURSE

Jaggery in a water-course—see " *JAGGERY.*"

WAVERING

No wavering in precaution—see " *PRECAUTION.*"

WEALTH

The power of wealth and the dignity of caste—see " *MONEY.*"
The advantage of wealth and relatives—see " *RELATIONS.*"
Wealth of the unlearned—see " *EDUCATION.*"
Wealth without a child—see " *CHILDREN.*"
Wealth without learning—see " *EDUCATION* "

WEAPON

The pain is the same though you stab even with a golden weapon.

රත් ආවුදෙන් ඇන්නත් රිදීම එක ලෙසමයි.

WEARING

A crupper to cure dysentery—see "*DYSENTERY.*"

WEATHER

Like the untimely ripening due to hot weather.

නියඟට පැහුණා වගෙයි.

"*Undupiyali*" *leaf in all weathers*—see "*UNDUPIYALI.*"

WEAVER

Tricks of a goldsmith and weaver—see "*DHOBY.*"

WEDDING—(*See also* "*MARRIAGE.*")

When a wedding takes place in two adjoining houses, the dog of the neighbouring house is left to starve.

අසල ගෙවල් දෙකේ මගුල් ගත්ත දාට ළඟ ගෙදර බල්ලා බඩගින්නේලු.

Drawing water to wedding-house—see "*WATER.*"
Hospitality at another's wedding—see "*HOSPITALITY.*"
The grandfather on a wedding day—see "*EATING.*"
Returning from wedding without eating rice-cake—see "*CAKE.*"

WEIGHT

Weight of Rabanchiyá's pingo—see "*PINGO.*"

WELL

If you jump into a well on one provocation, even ten provocations will not enable you to get out of it.

එක තරහකට ළිඳට පැන්නොත් දහ තරහකටවත් ගොඩ එන්ට බැහැ.

The well from which water is constantly drawn always gets fresh supplies.

ගන්නා ළිඳට දිය උනනවාලු.

Carrying a well on a stick—see "*MAGGONA.*"
The frog in a well—see "*FROG.*"
The savant of the pit (or well)—see "*PIT.*"
With jaggery in hand, water from any well—see "*JAGGERY.*"

WET

Like a wet fowl—see "*FOWL.*
Man who wets himself to death—see "*MAN.*"

WHEEL

Good as well as bad is like the cart wheel.

හොඳ නරක රත සක වගෙයි

WHITE

Friction with stone to make charcoal white—see "*CHARCOAL.*"
People with white teeth in Gilimale—see "*GILIMALE.*"
The cock's comb seen daily—see "*COMB.*"
The Paduvá and white man's rule—see "*PADUVÁ.*"
The white jaggery man's remark—see "*JAGGERY*"
White cattle for Paduvás—see "*PADUVÁ.*"
White Pariah not to be trusted—see "*BRAHMAN.*"

WICKED—(*See also* "*EVIL.*")

The road of the virtuous and wicked—see "*TRAVEL.*"

WIDOW

Marrying a widow—see "*MARRIAGE.*"
When widowhood is preferable—see "*MARRIAGE.*"
Widowhood and doting—see "*DOTING.*"

WIFE—(*See also* "*WOMAN.*")

Quarrel between husband and wife—see "*MARRIAGE.*"
Shadow of wife to be divorced—see "*SHADOW.*"
Siman Gamarála's request to his wife—see "*TOBACCO.*"
The poor man, his wife, and the King—see "*POOR.*"
When a Koravá's wife is brought to bed—see "*KORAVÁ.*"
The ex-priest and his two wives—see "*BUDDHISM.*"
The wife as tenth planet—see "*PLANET.*"

WILD CAT

Wild cat who eats jungle plantains—see "*PLANTAIN.*"

WILFULNESS

The way the wilful "Guru" goes—see "*OBSTINACY.*"

WILY

Wily people and Hell—see "*HELL.*"

WIND

Like preaching to the wind.

හුළඟට දේසනා කරන්නාක් මෙනි.

A strong wind means rain—see "*AFFECTION.*"

WINK

A blow with a pestle can make no impression on a man to whom a wink is of no effect.

ඉඟිකළාම නොදැනෙන්නාට කොල මෝලෙන් ඇන්නත් නොදැනේලු.

WINNERS—(*See* "*VICTORY.*")

WINNOWING-FAN

Like the saying, "There ought to be at least three winnowing-fans for a house like this."

"මෙහෙම ගෙදරකට කුළු තුනක්වත් ඕනෑයි" කී විත්තිය වගෙයි.

[A traveller, who stepped into a roadside house in order to take shelter from the rain, found the husband and wife under the shelter of two winnowing-fans, as the roof of the house was leaking. On seeing the stranger, the two occupants of the house exclaimed, "Sorry, we haven't another winnowing-fan for you." The traveller, on hearing this, went away in the rain, saying "There ought to be at least three winnowing-fans for a house like this."]

Carrying a winnowing-fan of chunam—see "*LADDER.*"
Women's good fortune—see "*WOMAN.*"

WIRE

Prosperity comes along a wire—see "*PROSPERITY.*"

WISDOM

Even wise men are sometimes outwitted.

දැනමුත්තොත් මෝඩ වෙනවාලු.

You cannot get even elephants to draw back the wisdom that has escaped you.

ගිය නුවණ ඇතුන්ලවාත් අද්දවන්ට බැරිලු.

You must be foolish to be wise.

මෝඩ කමක් කරලා දැනමුතු වෙන්ට ඕනැලු.

A wise enemy and a foolish friend—see "*RESPECT.*"
It is unwise to rouse a sleeping lion—see "*LION.*"
The "kanayá" as the wise one in the pit—see "*PIT.*"
Mahadenamuttá's wisdom—see "*MAHADENAMUTTÁ.*"
Thief's wisdom greater than Ganadeviyo's—see "*THIEF.*"

WOMAN

A breach in a tank and a widow in a house are alike.

වැවේ කැඩීමත් ගෙදරක ඉන්න කනවැන්දුම් ගැණීත් යන දෙදෙනාම එකයි.

Even the hen reared by a talkative woman crows.

කට බහ ඇති ගැණී ඇති කරන කිකිළිත් අඬලනවාලු.

It is bad to remain behind adzes as well as wives.

වෑ පස්සෙත් ඝිර පස්සෙත් සිටින්ට නරකලු.

[Subjection to "petticoat government" is as bad as standing behind an adze.]

It is in a corner of the winnowing-fan that a woman's good fortune lies.

ගැනුන්ගේ පින කුලුමුල්ලේ.

Like barren women getting children.

වඳුත් දරුවන්ලැබුවා වගෙයි.

Like the remark of the barren woman.

වඳ ගැණීගෙ කීම වගෙයි.

[A barren woman said to the mother of ten or twelve children: "You only bring forth once in two or three years; but, if I were you, I would by this time have brought forth twenty or thirty at the rate of one every year."]

Like the way a certain woman cried in anticipation.

එක ගෑණියක් මතු බලා ඇඬුවා වගෙයි.

[A certain woman, on the day of her husband's death, in order to work on the feelings of the bystanders, cried out, that she had a child in her womb. This child, however, was never born.]

Why take a ladder to the gallows when you can go there easily by the help of a woman ?

පෝර්කයට යන්ට ඉණිමගක් නැතිවාට ගෑණියක් ඇතිලු.

Woman is the way to prison.

සිරගෙයට මාර්ගය නම් ගෑණිලු.

[The Tamils similarly are not very complimentary to womankind. They say :

(*a*) "He who listens to the advice of a woman is a fool."

(*b*) "No matter how skilled a woman may be in numbers (figures) and letters, her judgment will be second rate."

(*c*) "The thoughts of a woman are afterthoughts."

(*d*) "Though she may wear cloth upon cloth and is able to dance like a celestial, she is not to be desired if she can press a style on a palm leaf (*i.e.*, is able to write.)"]

Women increase and the water pots become empty.

ගෑනුන් බෝවේ, කළගෙඩි වේලේ.

[It is the business of the women to draw water, and, when there are too many in a house, they are apt to neglect their duty. The Tamils say : "A wife gets up before daybreak and looks after her domestic affairs."]

A slave woman's privilege—see "*CHILDREN.*"
A woman without a husband—see "*MARRIAGE.*"
Barren women and sorrows of children—see "*CHILDREN.*"
Chastity of the ugly woman—see "*CHASTITY.*"
"*If we are of one mind*"—see "*HERBS.*"
Mad woman's bag of herbs—see "*MAD.*"
Marrying a divorced woman—see "*MARRIAGE.*"
One's own mother and the sky—see "*MOTHER.*"
Women's "ins" and "outs" and the dhoby—see "*DHOBY.*"

WOOD

Logs of wood placed before mothers—see "*MOTHER.*"

WOOD-APPLE

The wood-apple swallowed by the elephant—see "*ELEPHANT.*"

WORK

Work like a slave and eat like a Lord.

වාලා වගේ හම්බකරගන්, රාළ වගේ කාපන්.

The "Máraya" who gives work—see "*FRIEND.*"
The silversmith's urgent work—see "*BADÁLÁ.*"

WORLD

Each man in the world—see "*MAN.*"
In the world, famous—see "*FAME.*"
The light (life) of this world—see "*HAND.*"

WORM

There is no sense of sourness to the worm born on a "kohomba" tree.

කොහොඹ ගසේ උපන් පණුවාට කොහොඹ ගහ තිත්ත නැතිලු.

[See under "KOHOMBA" for fuller reference to this tree.]

Throwing worms into a fire—see "*FIRE.*"

WORRY

Sport for others. worry for me—see "*SPORT.*"

WORSHIP

Examining the "kemana"—see "*BUDDHA.*"
Temple crashing down over worshipper—see "*RELIGION.*"

WRITING

Like writing noisy characters.

ඝෝෂා අකුරු ලිවා වගෙයි.

[A son who was in a distant country was observed (by a friend) to write a letter to his mother in large characters. On being asked why he wrote such big characters, he replied : "As my mother is deaf, I write in noisy characters."]

Pen of the man too lazy to write—see "*PANHINDA.*"
Tamby Appu's inability to read and write—see "*VEDARÁLA.*"
Woman who can write—see "*WOMAN.*"

"YAGADAVA"

The walking-stick of King Gaja Báhu—see "*PANHINDA.*"

YAMS

He is patient till the yams grow, but not till they are boiled.

අල බසිනකල් උන්නැකිලු, තැම්බෙන කල් ඉන්ට බැරිලු.

If yams grow big, both the planter and his wife will benefit.

අලේ ලොකුවට බැස්සොත් ඉන්දු එකාටත් උගෙ අඹුටත් හොඳලු.

Headache commoner than jak or yams—see "*HEADACHE.*"

YAWNING

Yawning in one country—see "*COUNTRY.*"

YELLOW-BIRD

The owl's boast to the yellow-bird—see "*OWL.*"

YOKE

The blind tortoise peering through the yoke—see "*TORTOISE.*"
Yoking a bullock with a buffalo—see "*BULL.*"

YOUNGEST

Youngest in a family worse than a slave—see "*SLAVE.*"

YOUTH

When youth is old—see "*EDUCATION.*"

YONAS

This is a great "Yon" (Moorish) slaughter.

මේක මහ යොන් මැරිල්ලකි.

[*Yoná* is a term for a Moorman. The saying has its origin in the following story. A ship manned by Sinhalese and Moorish sailors was in danger of sinking at sea, and the Captain (a Sinhalese) found himself constrained to save the vessel only by sacrificing a part of his crew. Anxious to save his compatriots, the Captain assembled the crew on deck, after first secretly instructing the Sinhalese sailors so to take their position as to make a Moor occupy every ninth place, beginning from a spot he indicated. Then, when all had assembled (the Sinhalese sailors according to plan) the Captain loudly announced that every ninth man would have to go overboard, with the result that all the Moormen were sacrificed. When the last Moorman came to the "order of his going," he is said to have exclaimed, "This is a great *Yon* slaughter," as he was flung out to sea.]

ADDENDA

ELEPHANT

Like the Elephant eating the "pus-vela"

අලියා පුස් වැල කෑවා වගෙයි.

[The "pus-vela" (Lat. *Entada Scandens*), which produces what are known as the "Gilla nuts," is a thick, large climber, remarkable for its long legumes. These are sometimes seen to pass out before the elephant, which has a partiality for it, has quite done with swallowing the *vela* or creeper. The legumes contain heart-shaped seeds, the kernel of which, ground down to a paste with honey, is applied (by Sinhalese Vedaralas) to the eyes for venomous snake bites].

HEADMAN

Where can't I be within my division ?

මගේ වැසමට කොතන ඉන්ට බැරිද ?

[This was said by a Headman when he was caught in an awkward situation. He was discovered in a neighbour's house, emerging from a room where the latter's wife was reclining. The husband, unexpectedly appearing, asked what he was doing there at that time of the day. The reply was as above, and the Headman got away with it.]